TWAYNE'S WORLD AUTHORS SERIES
A Survey of the World's Literature

Sylvia E. Bowman, Indiana University
GENERAL EDITOR

FRANCE

Maxwell A. Smith, Guerry Professor of French, Emeritus
The University of Chattanooga
Former Visiting Professor in Modern Languages
The Florida State University
EDITOR

Marcel Pagnol

TWAS 391

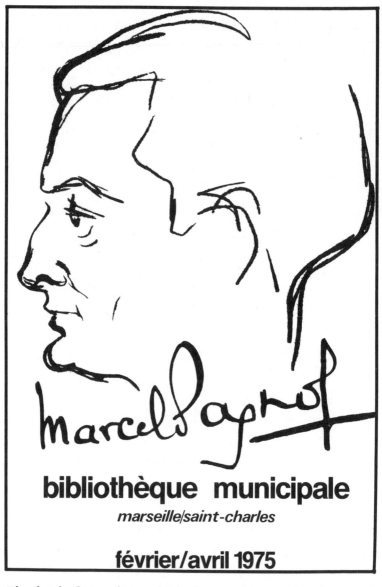

bibliothèque municipale

marseille/saint-charles

février/avril 1975

The sketch of Marcel Pagnol is by Romi and appeared in the journal *Bravo*, Nᵒ 15, March, 1930.

MARCEL PAGNOL

By C. E. J. CALDICOTT

Trent University

TWAYNE PUBLISHERS

A DIVISION OF G. K. HALL & CO., BOSTON

Library of Congress Cataloging in Publication Data

Caldicott, C E J
  Marcel Pagnol.

  (Twayne's world authors series ; TWAS 391 : France)
  Bibliography: p. 167 - 71.
  Filmography: p. 173 - 76.
  Includes index.
  1. Pagnol, Marcel, 1895-1974. 2. Authors, French —
20th century — Biography.
PQ2631.A26Z6   842'.9'12   76-45619
ISBN 0-8057-6233-7

MANUFACTURED IN THE UNITED STATES OF AMERICA

Contents

About the Author

An Englishman educated in Ireland, the author graduated as a medallist, with 1st Class Honors in French, from Dublin University (Trinity College). Awarded a French Government scholarship, he went on to the University of Aix-Marseille where he completed a *Diplôme d'Etudes Supérieures* (now known as the *Maîtrise-ès-Lettres*) in 1964. He completed his Ph.D. for the University of Dublin in 1968 while working at the University of Glasgow in Scotland, where he was French lecturer for five years, before taking up an appointment at the Trent University of Peterborough, Ontario, Canada, where he is at present as Associate Professor of French.

Dr. Caldicott's principal research interest now lies in seventeenth-century French literature and society. He has contributed several articles on diverse topics to such journals as *Revue d'Histoire du Théâtre; Modern Languages;* and *Revue de l'Université d'Ottawa.* At present engaged in research on the interplay between fiscal administration, privileges of the nobility, and patronage of the arts under the *Ancien Régime,* he is also a cinema enthusiast and hopes soon to complete a documentary film based on the iconography of seventeenth-century France.

Preface

Despite the publication of a number of biographical anecdotes about him,[1] serious appraisal of Marcel Pagnol in English and French has been confined to isolated aspects of his work.[2] The nature of Pagnol's success has undoubtedly created a certain number of difficulties, inhibiting any critical approach. A review of these difficulties will help to introduce the subject and will also demonstrate by implication the goals to be reached in this book, thus clearing the way for examination of Pagnol's work proper. The preface therefore serves as a *pre-critique* before going on to explain the method of the book itself.

I *Trends to Explore*

There is a central logic to Pagnol's career which renders his work easily accessible in its entirety: what more natural for the successful young dramatist than to turn his attention to the exciting new medium of sound movies, hailed as the ultimate form of dramatic art, which would supersede both silent movies and theater? Pagnol's attachment to his native Provence, its landscape, and its people, explains the theme of most of his films which are often adapted from the work of Jean Giono. After moving from the theater to the cinema, Pagnol progressed to the novel. But, strange to relate, the novel in Pagnol's hands is so highly charged with description and dialogue as to be indistinguishable from a screenplay. If the form changed little, the setting remained essentially the same — Provence. And yet, at first sight, the apparent variety of Pagnol's career as playwright, *cinéaste*, novelist, and impresario remains forbidding. There is much still to be documented in every phase of Pagnol's activity, as the following brief summary will show.

II *Pagnol and the Theater*

Pagnol's plays have been translated and acted all over the world; they have also been studied to some extent, if not granted the full importance they deserve. There are a number of good critical editions of his plays and there have been some valuable appraisals of his comic style, by Marcel Achard[3] and Charles Rostaing[4] in particular. Little has been published on the relationship between Pagnol's plays and the trends of French theater between the wars, although the latter have been well documented.[5] Scholarly criticism has been primarily concerned with the activity of Copeau, Gémier, and the *Cartel* of Jouvet, Dullin, Baty, and Pitoëff. Great men of the theater with admirable goals, their contribution to French theater is remarkable, yet the attention paid to their activity in particular presupposes that little else of significance was happening in the French theater of the time. Indeed, everything else is dismissed with a term of generic contempt — *boulevardier*. When such dramatists as Pagnol himself, Stève Passeur, Marcel Achard, and Sacha Guitry are frequently classified, or ignored, as *boulevardiers* it is clearly time to reassess and redefine the term.

III *Pagnol and the Cinema*

It is only Pagnol's work in the cinema that has received adequate recognition. Respected as an equal, and sometimes deferred to, by such film makers as Jean Renoir,[6] René Clair (*né* Chomette), Jacques Feyder,[7] Orson Welles,[8] and Roberto Rossellini,[9] Pagnol has also been saluted by such diverse critical creeds as those of André Bazin,[10] Pauline Kael,[11] the *Cahiers du Cinéma*,[12] Claude Gauteur of *l'Avant-Scène du Cinéma*,[13] and Claude Beylie[14] of l'Université de Paris — 1. But even here, there remain neglected areas, particularly in the matter of business transactions. Early sound cinema was a technology before it was an art form: to become an art form it required the investment of the sound reproduction industry, R.C.A., R.K.O., and Western Electric in the case of the U.S.A. Their investment in turn depended upon the prospects of commercial success. Often reviled by his contemporaries for his interest in the commercial success of his films, Pagnol was one of the few French film makers in the early days of sound to work independently of the vast German U.F.A. and American Western Electric firms. Through these two companies, associates of Tobis-Klangfilm and Paramount Studios respectively, European cinema between the wars was almost entirely in the hands of Germany and America. Pagnol, with his own studios, his own team of technicians and actors, and his own sub-contracts for sound reproduction with the Dutch company Philips, must have looked puny, even quaint, but he was free. This freedom to choose his own subject, the freedom to express himself as he alone saw fit, depended upon continuing commercial success. His originality as a film maker is an extension of his courage and wisdom in business. Without any documentation on this aspect of his activity, the dossier on Pagnol the film maker is incomplete. Recent research[15] into the technology and financial organization of early sound cinema in general, without mentioning Pagnol in particular, now makes possible a fuller understanding of Pagnol's rôle in the early days of "talkies."

IV *Pagnol and the Novel*

Pagnol as novelist has been ignored by specialized criticism, as has the Franco-Provençal literary tradition to which his prose work belongs. Enjoyed by millions the world over, his novels have been translated and well presented in good editions but they have been very rarely subjected to any sustained scrutiny.[16] Of the Provençal authors writing in French, Pagnol has the closest affinity with Jean Giono (who, thanks to Henri Peyre[17] and Maxwell Smith,[18] needs no introduction to American readers) and with Paul Arène. Born in 1843 at Sisteron, the "Canteperdrix" of his novels, Paul Arène needs an introduction both to French and to foreign readers.

Arène's three masterpieces: *Jean des Figues, La Chèvre d'Or* and *Domnine*[19] are remarkably similar in style and setting to Pagnol's novels. *Jean des Figues*, Arène's memories of childhood written in 1868, strikes a tone which Pagnol recaptures in *Souvenirs d'Enfance*, bathed in the same fragrant nostalgia. "I prefer memories to the most delightful reality" Arène once wrote to his friend Frédéric Mistral.[20] In that Pagnol's novels are widely read and translated, his fate is a happier one than that of Paul Arène, described by Anatole France as *le prince des conteurs*,[21] who is no longer read at all.

The parallels between the work of Pagnol and Arène are deep and striking; collaboration in the cinema between Giono and Pagnol was real and successful. These interrelationships with their incipient echoes of style and theme have never been studied. There are also fruitful comparisons to be made between Pagnol's treatment of childhood and that of Giraudoux (*Provinciales*), Alain-Fournier (*Le Grand Meaulnes*), and such Southern U.S.A. writers as Harper Lee.

In more general terms, autobiography as a genre deserves fuller treatment.

V The Nature of Pagnol's Success —
A Sociological Phenomenon

It is ironical that the militants of *Occitanie*, pressing for the rights and recognition of the southern *culture d'oc*, should ignore the enormous popularity of Pagnol in the Midi, that vast parish of Southern France whose southern boundary is the Mediterranean[22] and whose northern boundary runs from somewhere below Lyons (often referred to as *midi moins le quart*) to Bordeaux. A native of the Midi himself, Pagnol died at his Paris home in April, 1974, mourned by the nation, particularly in his own city of Marseilles in his native Provence. The headlines in the *Provençal* announcing *"Notre Pagnol n'est plus"* were the largest in living memory; his simple funeral at La Treille, scene of his childhood and much of his work, was attended spontaneously by thousands and the city of Marseilles organized a three-month retrospective exhibition, from February to April, 1975, about his life and work. Pagnol has achieved a phenomenal popular success in France over the last half-century with many of the characters he created now entering into folklore and his books remaining, among all age groups, best sellers of the *Livre de Poche* series.[23] The presentation of a popular legend is a sociological as much as a literary exercise and the apparent incompatibility of the two methodologies undoubtedly creates difficulties: the promotional hermeneutics of the literary critic seems either superfluous or obsequious before the accomplished fact of widespread popular success whereas the sociologist often ignores the real accident of individual talent. And so we would remain, mute, embarrassed and uninformed. . . .

VI Critical Approaches and Contemporary Issues

As Pagnol himself would have liked to boast, his popular success in France owes much to his knowledgeable use of the media. He used the cinema both as an original, creative art form and (since he owned the studios) as a means of preserving, confirming, and propagating his success. Similarly, he founded his own publishing company after the war — *Les Éditions Marcel Pagnol* which became inextricably linked with *Éditions de Provence* and *Éditions Pastorelly*. Pagnol's success may be attributed by *mauvaises langues* to a gift for marketing, but this does him an injustice and cannot alone explain the prolongation and dimensions of his popularity; other explanations have to be found for the truly remarkable acclaim universally granted, for example, to *Topaze* and *Marius* in 1928 and 1929, long before Pagnol had the means to "market" his work. Never straying publicly from a strict indifference to organized political and social life, he remained an *homme du peuple* and enjoyed this quality in others; the popular songwriter Vincent Scotto, the singers Tino Rossi and Maurice Chevalier, the ex-champion boxer Georges Carpentier, the stonemason Marius Brouquier, the actor Raimu, and the playwright Marcel Achard were among his intimate friends. They were all of the people and, specific creative and literary talent apart, shared his simplicity and good-humored gregariousness. These qualities were encouraged by the nascent theories of Populism and finally consecrated by the election of a Popular Front government at a time when Pagnol's career was taking shape. The unpretentious, often ingenuous, themes of Pagnol's work are, with a confirmed literary talent, the basis of a popular success which would subsequently be consolidated by an unusual control of the media. But, like de Gaulle governing by referendum, Pagnol unfortunately alienated many by maintaining his self-sufficiency and by mastering the media alone.

Independent, resolute, and tactless, Pagnol has contributed in other ways to the unnatural, but not uncommon, polarization between critical acclaim and popular success. He first challenged professional opinion in the enthusiastic but ill-judged *Cinématurgie de Paris* (1933 - 1934), expressing his views on the future of the cinema, and again in *Critique des Critiques* (1949). Never at his ease when handling abstract, conceptual material, Pagnol was a poor critic himself and had a pathological distrust of the profession; his work consistently demonstrates that he was a writer of instinct and verve with a joyous appetite for the concrete, physical nature of things.

While endeavoring to explain the development of Pagnol's style and subject-matter within the context of his own environment, this study also attempts to take account of present reality. The passive polarity of Pagnol's female characters is certain to excite the curiosity of readers who are interested in the progress of women's liberation; as the focus of Pagnol's pastoral values woman provides a legitimate topic for discussion in this book.

VII *The Present Study — Goals and Method*

The fact remains that, for one reason or another, the *ensemble* of Pagnol's work is inadequately documented. So much has been neglected that there is much to be included within the format of this book. It is appropriate that the initiative to publish should be American: nowhere outside France has Pagnol's work been more appreciated than in the U.S.A., either through the performing arts with, for example, the 1954 Logan, Behrman, and Rome stage adaptation of the Marseilles trilogy[24] or through translation and publication of his work. Furthermore, Pagnol has always acknowledged the value for him of his apprenticeship, albeit brief, with the European branch of the American Paramount Studios and its director Robert T. Kane; together with Korda, they produced the film of *Marius*, perhaps the most successful American production ever made in France.

The organization of the present study follows the successive phases of Pagnol's career as playwright, film maker, *académicien*, and novelist; chronological narrative is the basic vehicle for critical comment. The sequence departs from chronological order in a few specific cases since no progression in Pagnol's career was absolutely decisive. After moving on to film-making, for example, Pagnol returned to the theater with two plays, *Judas* (1955) and *Fabien* (1956). These plays will be examined with the rest of Pagnol's theatrical work before his movies. The novel *Pirouettes* (1932), one of the first completed manuscripts of Pagnol's career, is a semi-autobiographical account of school days and adolescence in Marseilles; it is thus studied as a fourth volume of the *Souvenirs d'Enfance* which were published much later. The work of Jean Giono commands such a central position in Pagnol's movies that they are studied in relation to Giono rather than in chronological order. After the sections on the theater and the films of Pagnol, there is a third section on Pagnol *académicien:* his election to the *Académie Française* seems to have put him under some constraint, creating an attitude of intellectual *noblesse oblige*. The scholarly, theoretic works written during this period were all exercises alien to Pagnol's natural talent; this section is therefore brief. It is followed by a study of Pagnol as autobiographer and novelist. In addition to these four subdivisions there are two further sections. One follows in the next chapter as a thematic introduction to the life and work of Pagnol; the second appears as a final evaluation of Pagnol's achievements. In the interests of the general reader, all major quotations from

Preface

Pagnol's work, conversations, and other *obiter dicta* have been translated into English: the original French source of the reference will always, of course, be found in the footnotes but the original French version of the quotations is not, for reasons of space, reproduced.

As is the custom, the author would like at this point to thank those who offered help and encouragement during the gestation of this book. Marcel Pagnol himself always took a kind interest in the work and willingly spoke with the author about it. The late Owen Sheehy-Skeffington, formerly Reader in French at Trinity College, Dublin, was always generous and firm in support; Raymond Jean, of the Université de Provence, Monsieur et Madame Jean Ballard of the *Cahiers du Sud* and Louis Brauquier, poet of Marseilles, introduced the author to the wealth of Franco-Provençal culture; I owe a special word of thanks to my good friends of Provence, Michel Collavizza, Alain Massabie, Michel Galy and Jean Hiriart, in whose homes I have always been made welcome. I would like, most of all, to thank my wife Elizabeth for all her wise suggestions and for her patient, practical help in typing the final manuscript.

C. E. J. CALDICOTT

Trent University, Canada.

Acknowledgments

I would like to record my gratitude to Madame Jacqueline Pagnol for her kind permission to quote from the works of her late husband. I am also beholden to the director of the Bibliothèque Municipale in Marseilles, Mr. Michel Gernet, for authorizing reproduction of Pagnol's portrait which was used as a poster for the Pagnol exhibition of 1975.

Chronology

1895 Birth of Marcel Pagnol, 16, Cours Barthélémy, Aubagne, February 28.
1897 Family moves to St. Loup.
1898 Birth of Paul Pagnol.
1900 Pagnol starts school at the Chemin des Chartreux.
1902 Birth of Germaine Pagnol.
1903 First summer spent at La Treille.
1905 Pagnol enters Lycée Thiers as *demi-pensionnaire* in October.
1910 Birth of René Pagnol. Pagnol's first poems published in *Massilia*. Death of his mother, Augustine, at the age of thirty-seven; buried at St. Pierre and subsequently reinterred at La Treille.
1912 *Lesbie*, first version of *Catulle*, a verse play in four acts.
1913 Pagnol co-founder of *Fortunio*, a literary journal which subsequently became *Cahiers du Sud*.
1914 Leaves Lycée Thiers in July; becomes *maître d'internat* at *lycée* in Digne.
1915 *Répétiteur d'anglais* at *lycée* in Tarascon, October 1915 - 1917. Degree examinations in English at University of Montpellier in November.
1916 Pagnol awarded *licence d'anglais* at University of Montpellier, February 16. Marries Simonne Collin.
1917 *Répétiteur d'anglais* at *collège* in Pamiers, October 1917 - January 1919.
1919 *Professeur-adjoint* at Lycée Mignet, Aix-en-Provence, February 1919 - September 1920. Second series, *série d'Aix*, of *Fortunio*.
1920 *Professeur-adjoint* at Lycée Thiers (*annexe de St. Charles*), October 1920 - July 1922. *Les Mémoires de Jacques Panier* (1920 - 1921), serial story in *Fortunio*. *Catulle*.

1921 *La Petite Fille aux Yeux Sombres (Fortunio,* 1921 - 1922), serial story, sequel to *Les Mémoires de Jacques Panier.*

1922 *L'Infame Truc (Fortunio,* January), a short story which was published as scenario entitled *Merlusse* in 1935. *Professeur-adjoint* at Lycée Condorcet in Paris, October. Joined staff of *Comoedia.*

1923 *Le Mariage de Peluque (Fortunio,* October 1923 - February 1924), a serial story; a revision of *Les Mémoires de Jacques Panier,* it is a first draft of *Pirouettes.*

1924 *Tonton* performed at Théâtre des Variétés, Marseilles, July 15 - 30. Final break with *Fortunio.*

1925 Performance of *Les Marchands de Gloire* at Théâtre de la Madeleine, Paris, April 15 - 27.

1926 Performance of *Un Direct au Coeur* at Théâtre de l'Alhambra, Lille, March 12 - 18. Beginning of lifelong friendship with Marcel Achard. First performance of *Jazz* at Le Grand Théâtre, Monte Carlo, December 9 and subsequently at Théâtre des Arts, Paris.

1927 Pagnol resigns from teaching post at Condorcet.

1928 First performance of *Topaze* at Théâtre des Variétés, Paris, October 9.

1929 First performance of *Marius* at Théâtre de Paris, March 9.

1931 First performance of *Fanny* at Théâtre de Paris, December 5. Completion of film version of *Marius* (directed by Korda for Paramount).

1932 Publication of *Pirouettes. Officier de la Légion d'Honneur (titre de l'Éducation Nationale).* Completion of film version of *Topaze* (directed by Gasnier for Paramount). Completion of film version of *Fanny* (directed by Marc Allégret for Pagnol). Giono signs agreement permitting Pagnol to make movie adaptations of his work. Death of Paul Pagnol.

1933 Completion of film versions of *Un Direct au Coeur* (directed by Boulay for Pagnol); *L'Agonie des Aigles* (by Richebé for Richebé and Pagnol); *Léopold le Bien Aimé* (by Arno - Brun from the play by Jean Sarment). Creation of film production company, *Les Auteurs Associés.* Creation of cinema journal *Les Cahiers du Film. La Cinématurgie de Paris,* in first issues of *Les Cahiers du Film,* December 1933 - March 1934.

1934 Completion of following films, all directed by Pagnol: *Le Gendre de Monsieur Poirier* (from Augier and Sandeau); *Jofroi* (Giono); *L'Article 330* (Courteline); *Angèle* (Giono).

Pagnol also produced *Tartarin de Tarascon, Toni,* and *Marseille,* directed by Raymond Bernard, Jean Renoir, and Monti and Marguerite respectively.

1935 Pagnol directed and completed the films *Merlusse* and *Cigalon.*

1936 He directed and completed his own film versions of *Topaze* and *César.*

1937 Directed and completed the film version of Giono's novel *Regain.*

1938 Completion of *Le Schpountz* and *La Femme du Boulanger* (from Giono).

1939 Pagnol produces *Monsieur Brotonneau* (from the play by Flers and Caillavet) and *Le Président Haudecoeur* (Ferdinand and Dréville).

1940 Completion of *La Fille du Puisatier.* Pagnol elected President of *La Société des Auteurs et Compositeurs Dramatiques.*

1941 Pagnol abandons the film *La Prière aux Etoiles* and resigns from the Vichy *Comité d'Organisation de l'Industrie Cinématographique.* Legal action by Giono against Pagnol, October 14, Marseilles. Charges dismissed.

1945 Pagnol completes *Naïs,* the film version of Zola's short story. Marries Jacqueline Bouvier, his second wife, at the *mairie* of Malakoff; Pagnol's childless first marriage had broken up when he left Marseilles for Paris in 1922.

1946 *Le Premier Amour,* unperformed scenario. Elected to the *Académie Française,* April 4. Death of Raimu, September 26.

1947 Officially received at the *Académie Française,* March 27. Translation of *Hamlet.* Publication of *Notes sur le Rire.*

1948 Completion of a film version of life of Franz Schubert, *La Belle Meunière.* Birth of son, Frédéric.

1949 Publication of *La Critique des Critiques.*

1950 Directs his second film version of *Topaze* and produces *Le Rosier de Madame Husson* (from Maupassant).

1951 Death of Joseph Pagnol. Buried at La Treille, November 11.

1952 Completion of film version of *Manon des Sources.*

1953 Produces *Carnaval* (made by Henri Verneuil).

1954 Sometime consul of Portugal in Principality of Monaco, abandons residence and post in Monte Carlo after death of daughter Estelle. Completion of film version of *Les Lettres de Mon Moulin.*

1955 First performance of *Judas* at Théâtre de Paris, October 6.

1956 First performance of *Fabien* at Théâtre des Bouffes Parisiens, September 28. *Rapport sur les Prix de Vertu, Académie Française*, December 20.

1957 *Souvenirs d'Enfance;* Volume 1: *La Gloire de Mon Père*, Volume 2: *Le Château de Ma Mère*.

1958 Verse translation of Virgil's *Bucolics*.

1959 Official address of welcome to Marcel Achard at the *Académie Française*, December 3.

1960 *Souvenirs d'Enfance*, Volume 3: *Le Temps des Secrets*.

1962 Official opening of Lycée Marcel Pagnol, St. Loup, Marseilles, October 6. Adaptation for French television of Dumas' *La Dame aux Camélias*.

1963 Publication of *L'Eau des Collines* in two volumes: i) *Jean de Florette*, ii) *Manon des Sources*.

1964 Publication of *Le Masque de Fer; Gloires de la France* (articles by the forty *académiciens;* Pagnol wrote on Michel de Montaigne).

1965 *Merlusse* adapted for French television.

1967 *Le Curé de Cucugnan* made by Pagnol for French television.

1970 Official opening of Collège Joseph Pagnol, Saint Laurent - du - Var, November 28.

1971 Translation of *A Midsummer Night's Dream. Grand-officier de la Légion d'Honneur*.

1974 Death of Marcel Pagnol in Paris, April 18.

1975 Official opening of Bibliothèque Municipale Marcel Pagnol, Aubagne, April 19.

CHAPTER 1

A Bio-thematic Introduction

PAGNOL arrived in Paris in 1922 at the age of twenty-seven, having spent all his life in Marseilles and its immediate surroundings. He arrived like Rastignac — penniless and unconnected, feeling he had outgrown his native province and determined to forge a career in the capital. Unlike Rastignac, however, Pagnol had completed his studies, had his qualifications (in English), and had a job waiting for him in Paris. There are several indications, which will be mentioned later, that Pagnol had no intention of remaining an English teacher for the rest of his life, even though appointed as *répétiteur*, auxiliary master, at the Lycée Condorcet. The energy, ambition, and idealism which animated him were probably already focussed on literary success; unknown outside the literary salons of Marseilles, he had come to Paris to make his name without so much as an editor's verbal promise to encourage him. This simple, naive boldness was characteristic; within four years it led to a success that Pagnol himself had probably never anticipated.

An examination of the first twenty-seven years in Marseilles and of the priorities observed by Pagnol in that time will substantiate this thumbnail portrait and provide a basis for understanding his subsequent work, all written after his definitive move to Paris. The texts of his plays, films, and novels will provide their own simultaneous commentary but many of their themes can be anticipated by an examination of Pagnol's early life. It is always dangerous for the reader to assume a causal link between the observable life of a writer and the themes of his subsequent work. It is only after contact with the texts that an author's themes are recognized: they cannot be predicted from a study of biographical details. It is thus not possible for the reader to reverse from the texts to early life and, confusing *a priori* with *a posteriori*, to return from there to the text brandishing a sheaf of causal explanations. Reasons of space dictate a compromise,

however, between a fully comprehensive view of Pagnol's early life
and those themes of which the reader has prior knowledge via the
text. It is therefore in this spirit of compromise that a selection of
potentially significant incidents in Pagnol's early life will be
presented under the rubrics of family situation and education,
cultural heritage and recreational activity.

I *Family Situation and Education*

The Shandean circumstances of Pagnol's birth in 1895 are
described in *La Gloire de Mon Père* — first volume of *Souvenirs
d'Enfance:* the same happy, poverty-stricken chaos was to mark all
the activities of the young, vulnerable Pagnol family. Claude Beylie,
in his otherwise sound work, timorously imitates Roland Barthes in
stating that Marcel Pagnol was born under the sign of Pisces and, advancing from cause to effect, he says that water became a dominant
theme in Pagnol's work.[1] There is no need to take this theory any
more seriously than Beylie himself does, although one can confirm,
on the basis of empirical observation, that water is a frequent theme
in Pagnol's work. The *questionnaire Marcel Proust* is a more reliable
basis than astrological hypothesis for the investigation of latent
forces. Pagnol completed such a questionnaire in 1964[2] but it is best
left *sans commentaire*.

Marcel was the eldest of the four children of Joseph and
Augustine Pagnol. The next child, Paul, was handicapped and sub-
sequently found work as a shepherd, dying in 1932 aged thirty-four.
Marcel wrote a touching epitaph to his younger brother, "the last
shepherd of Virgil," in his beautiful translation of Virgil's *Bucolics*.[3]
The third child was Pagnol's sister Germaine, now Madame
Gombert, and the fourth child was the other brother, René, who
became an associate of the *Société des Films Marcel Pagnol*.
Pagnol's mother, Augustine Lansot, was of Norman stock,[4] young,
pretty, but always in delicate health. Joseph Pagnol, a humbler version of Atticus Finch in *To Kill a Mocking-bird* and like him treated
to Christian-name terms by his children, was in the lower echelons
of the liberal professions. Fifth son of a stonemason, with therefore
no private means, he accomplished what was, in the circumstances,
the prodigious feat of passing the entrance requirement of the *École
Normale*, the teachers' training college, and graduated as an
elementary schoolteacher. Such a position under the Third Republic
held a status and a significance which will be examined shortly. The
autodidact was also an enthusiastic hunter but, above all, a solicitous

husband: in the summer of 1903,[5] out of concern for Augustine's health, he rented a villa in the hills outside Marseilles, between La Treille and Les Bellons. Sharing the costs with his brother-in-law, Joseph rented the villa for many more consecutive summers.

With the exception of Augustine, the family was fit and energetic; unlike Giraudoux or Proust, Pagnol enjoyed robust health in his childhood. The life he led in the summer months, hunting with Joseph or running free in the hills, is evoked both accurately and graphically in *Souvenirs d'Enfance*. In 1905 Marcel graduated from the elementary school of the Chemin des Chartreux to the high school at the Lycée Thiers in Marseilles. The school records show Pagnol at the end of his first year (1905 - 1906) in Grade 6A, Section 1 (the grades in French schools are in reverse of the American system, the senior students being in Grade 1), and winning a prize for arithemetic. By 1909 he was publishing poetry in a Marseilles social and literary fortnightly, *Massilia*.[6] The young poet's work is strongly marked by the pastoral poetry of the classical Latin syllabus; the following extract also reveals a personal experience of the affinity that exists between the Provençal and Virgilian landscapes:

Nuits d'été

Les grands pins, les tilleuls les chênes, les érables,
Balançant doucement leurs têtes vénérables,
Pleurent en frémissant au vent des nuits d'été.

Et ja rêve, en songeant aux dieux du doux Virgile,
Là bas, je vois passer une Dryade agile.
Et lorsque les rameaux s'agitent, au lointain
Dans le vent à la tiède et légère caresse,
Moi, je crois voir passer la blonde chasseresse
Portant son arc d'argent dans sa petite main.[7]

Summer Nights

The tall pines, the linden trees, the oak and the sycamore
Gently rocking their sage old heads
Sigh with shivering leaves in the breeze of a summer's eve.

While musing upon the dieties of the kindly Virgil
I see flitting past a sure-footed nymph.
And when the branches stir in the soft caressing breeze,
I can see the blonde huntress passing by
bearing a silver bow in her diminutive hand.

This was Pagnol's first published work and might have been published earlier, judging by the editor's reply to Pagnol's first communication: "This is fine, but write only on one side; use a bigger sheet of paper, send it all back and we'll use it."[8] The joys of proofreading were not the only adult responsibility to which Pagnol was introduced at an early age.

Augustine Pagnol died in 1910 following the birth of her fourth child, René, when Marcel was fifteen, a sensitive adolescent for whom this would have been a particularly traumatic experience. All the same, bereaved in his fortieth year and having to work to support his family, Joseph must have leaned heavily on his eldest son in order to cope with the baby, his daughter Germaine aged seven, and the handicapped Paul aged twelve. A well-stocked family photo album shows what a happy, united family life Marcel had known until then.[9] With the death of his mother, the memory of whose funeral was blocked out of his mind "as if at fifteen I had refused to admit the force of a grief which could have killed me,"[10] the parameters of Pagnol's childhood were immutably fixed. His recollections of those times must have been all the more precious for the nature of his loss but his childhood would already have seemed a remote, completed phase of his life at an age when his schoolmates were scarcely adolescent. Self-sufficiency and companionship with his father came early in life.

As an *instituteur* under the Third Republic in France, Joseph Pagnol represented a generation and a type whose memory is still respected. Pagnol's revered father, in particular, reached such fame through Marcel's work that, like his son, he finally had a school in Provence named after him. The Collège Joseph Pagnol was opened at St. Laurent-du-Var on November 28, 1970. Joseph's honor, unlike Marcel's, was bestowed posthumously: over and above the man himself, whom few would have known personally, the honor recognized the exemplary qualities of that generation of schoolteachers whom Joseph Pagnol represented, the earliest products of the educational system of the Third Republic.

In the opening pages of *La Gloire de Mon Père*, Pagnol speaks of his father's colleagues: "The most extraordinary part of it all was that these anti-clericals had a missionary devotion. All the better to thwart the local clergymen (whose virtue was considered a sham), they lived like saints themselves and their morality was as austere as that of the first Puritan. The school inspector was their bishop, the supervisor of the school board was their archbishop, and the

Minister of Education was their Pope."[11] Pagnol's father was one of these men and his sense of mission, while never seeming to affect his gentle humanity, led him to set exacting moral standards and to contest the rôle of the clergy. Marcel Pagnol eventually became a schoolteacher himself, doubtless encouraged by his father's trust in the value of a good education, without ever being dominated by his father's example. Joseph gave his son unlimited freedom to choose his career and, as will be seen, the strongly patriarchal nature of Pagnol's world, from *César* to *Jean de Florette*, probably owes as much to the example of Latin pastoral verse and to the forceful personality of Raimu, as to Joseph's strong convictions. Pagnol never followed his father's example to the same anti-clerical extremes.

The portrait of the *curé* recurs so frequently in Pagnol's work and is so authentic that an anthology of Pagnol's sermons has been compiled by the Vicar-General of the order of *Prémontrés*, the White Fathers of the abbey of St. Michel-de-Frigolet, where Daudet set one of the *Lettres de Mon Moulin*, later filmed by Pagnol. The *Sermons de Marcel Pagnol*[12] contains extracts from *La Femme du Boulanger, Manon des Sources, L'Elixir du Père Gaucher, Les Trois Messes Basses,* and *Le Curé de Cucugnan* (an adaptation of Daudet's tale for TV); Father Norbert Calmels, who compiled the anthology, could also have included Father Elzéar of *César* who administered the last rites to Panisse. As pointed out by Michel Delahaye in a thorough analysis of the themes of Pagnol's films,[13] the *curé* and the *instituteur* play parallel rôles: both men of learning, they are often referred to as a last tribunal. As with the *Don Camillo* stories, their rivalry is constant with neither gaining the upper hand; the climax of their relations is undoubtedly in *La Femme du Boulanger* when the *curé* has to accept a ride on the *instituteur's* back in order to cross the marshes to the island where the baker's errant wife is in hiding.

Although Pagnol included schoolteachers in his work right up to *Manon des Sources*, his last work of substance, their rôle *qua* schoolteachers is reduced after *Topaze*. The schoolroom played a preponderant rôle in Pagnol's early work with the sequence of *Merlusse, Pirouettes* (both adapted from contributions to the journal *Fortunio* in 1922 and 1924 respectively), *Jazz* (1926), and *Topaze* (1928). Marcel's own direct experiences as a teacher undoubtedly count for a lot in this cycle culminating in *Topaze* with the vision of a schoolmaster corrupted — a veritable apocalypse, coinciding with a significant change in Pagnol's own career. This coincidence helps to demonstrate that the classroom in Pagnol's work is a microcosm of society.

It was only in 1927, after the success of *Jazz*, that Pagnol abandoned the haven of his teaching career to devote himself entirely to his writing. Until then, his career as a teacher had progressed normally and the principal details can be found in the Chronology of this book. Pagnol left school in July, 1914, after an erratic year in *Première Supérieure B*, a *khâgne* class which prepares students for the highly competitive entrance examination to the École Normale Supérieure. The level of attainment in this class is traditionally very high (entrance to the class was itself competitive) so it comes as no surprise to see Pagnol sitting and passing the English degree exams at Montpellier University sixteen months later in November, 1915. He received his degree in February, 1916. The true goal of the students in *khâgne* is the *agrégation*, a postgraduate degree which is normally the climax of their studies at the École Normale Supérieure. By opting out of the entrance examinations for "Normale Sup." and taking his degree, Pagnol had gone only halfway toward his anticipated goals. For as long as he remained in *l'enseignement national* it would be normally assumed that, while teaching, he would study and prepare in his own time for the *agrégation*. As will be seen, Pagnol found other things to do with his spare time. He had, for example, already founded in 1913 a literary journal entitled *Fortunio*. In an early editorial describing the goals of the journal, Pagnol wrote: "It is the expression of an important section of today's youth. The majority of the editorial team are still doing translations and problems. . . ."[14] Such diversions from the official school program affected Pagnol's studies at the Lycée Thiers, as the report on his last year's work testifies: "could have been excellent in all departments, but has not worked seriously enough. I hope he won't regret it."[15]

It thus becomes increasingly evident that the teaching profession was for Pagnol a provisional base from which to launch a more hazardous career as a writer. The records of the Lycée Thiers indicate that in 1919 Pagnol quite simply failed to attend an all-important "viva voce" examination which was part of his teaching qualification. He even looked the part of the creative artist: a student of Pagnol in the twenties at the annexe St. Charles in Marseilles, Lucien Grimaud, recollects: "in winter, he wore a voluminous black cape much like Bruant with a black, broad-rimmed hat. We called him 'Judex.' "[16] It is reasonable to suppose that Pagnol opted out of a permanent teaching career as early as 1913, but his school days were undoubtedly a happy time of fulfillment: his friends at school subsequently followed him in his career (some even worked for him) and he remembers his teachers with affection.

II *The Cultural Heritage*

Apart from the republican values of his father, Pagnol was exposed at an early age to the classical humanism of his Latin teachers at the Lycée Thiers, Emile Ripert and Pierre Poux. He pays homage to them both in the preface to his translation of Virgil's *Bucolics:* "Emile Ripert was a true poet who was absorbed by his teaching. One morning, the daily papers of Marseilles announced on the front page that he had published an anthology of poems entitled *La Terre des Lauriers* and that it had won the *Grand Prix de Poésie de l'Académie Française.* I was his pupil in 3A, section 1. From then on we spoke only with condescension to the underprivileged students of section 2 and not at all to the philistines of the 'B' sections. Our teacher was a poet like Virgil, Ronsard, and Victor Hugo and we also shared his laurels."[17] Pagnol's memory misleads him since *La Terre des Lauriers* was published by Grasset in 1912 when he would have been in *philo'*, in his last years at school. Ripert had, however, published other collections of poetry prior to this: *Le Golfe d'Amour* (1908) and *Le Chemin Blanc* (1904).

It was probably Ripert's example that inspired the young Pagnol to write and publish his own poetry in *Massilia;* it might even be supposed that Ripert helped his pupil to polish and revise his poems before having them published. Pagnol's poetry has the same classical style and themes as *La Terre des Lauriers* which is nothing less than a history of Provence in verse from the commentaries of Strabo and Tacitus, Virgilian pastiche, to contemporary times. The real value of Ripert's example went beyond improvisations from the Latin primer, however; by transposing the landscape of Latin pastoral verse into Provence, Ripert endowed the familiar surroundings of Pagnol's summer holidays with a new dignity. The natural beauty of Provence thus enhanced by its cultural setting is a constant theme of the authors of the Provençal literary revival, Frédéric Mistral and the *Félibrige* of which Ripert was a member: the links between classical scholarship and the modern, nineteenth-century Provençal cultural revival will be discussed in the following section.

Pagnol's other Latin teacher at school, Pierre Poux, seems to have been more of a grammarian, "a great Latin scholar who would not tolerate a shadow of ambiguity in translation."[18] Beneath the disguise of Pierre Pons, the master of *rhétorique* described by Pagnol in the opening pages of *Pirouettes,* can be discerned the traits of Pierre Poux: "he insisted in French upon a strict plan with numbered sequences, parentheses and solid links to join paragraphs. It was most important to mask these links with a transitional veneer and we could not always manage to do that. Then Monsieur Pons, full of scorn, would dictate some of his own, prepared examples. His literary work, if he ever publishes any, will be like that young woman whose particular beauty was in the dimple of her elbow, the fold of her armpit and in the satin hollow behind her knee."[19]

In the course of time, Pagnol was able to say of Poux, as well as of Ripert: "They were men of a past age: they were learned and wise: thank you Emile and Pierre."[20] Of the two, Ripert exerted the most influence. Pagnol maintained his relationship with Ripert after leaving school and they even became colleagues when Ripert contributed to *Fortunio,* the literary journal founded by Pagnol. The vein of pastoral classicism remained evident in Pagnol's work until publication, through the auspices of *Fortunio,* of *Catulle* in 1922. The first version of the play, originally called *Lesbie,* is a handwritten text in a school exercise-book dating from 1912.[21] A four-act play in verse, *Catulle* will be examined more fully together with Pagnol's other contributions to *Fortunio.* The span of Ripert's measurable influence falls appropriately between 1912 and 1922, dates of the first and final versions of *Catulle.* A number of Pagnol's poems published in *Fortunio* during that time imitate the style of Ripert and in March, 1920, Pagnol wrote an editorial for *Fortunio* entitled "La Renaissance Provençale" which was a homage to Ripert on the occasion of his election to the provincial academy of Marseilles.[22]

A   *Classical — Virgil*

The most valuable lesson learned in that decade which preceded Pagnol's departure for Paris in 1922 was an appreciation of the cultural setting of Provence. Rural Provence changes so slowly and it so closely resembles the countryside of ancient Rome (of which it was part, Provincia/Provence) that Pagnol, like Paul Arène in *Jean des Figues,* might have written: "ever since then, Horace and Virgil and early impressions of my schooldays, memories of my native province, are all intermingled and part of each other."[23] As the landscape of Southeast Gaul must have seemed familiar to the early

Roman settlers, so that of ancient Italy seems familiar to the educated Provençal. The cypress and the ilex trees offer the same welcoming shelter from wind and sun alike; the fruits of the almond, olive, and wild grape ripen under the same Mediterranean sun; the bare, stony peaks of the hills are similarly softened by the cistus, myrtle, and laurel shrubs while the familiar fragrance from the tufted rosemary and thyme also lingers in the air. The Romans brought not only their straight roads but also their language. As every student of French knows, the Romance languages are simply a phonetic development of the language spoken by the Roman conquerors. Provençal is a linguistic variant which remains syntactically and phonetically halfway between Latin and modern French. The nineteenth century revival of Provençal culture inspired by Frédéric Mistral and his followers guaranteed the survival of the language which has its own dictionary (*Lou Trésor dou Félibrige* compiled by Mistral) and its own organization for protecting the language, *Le Félibrige*. Although never a *félibre* himself, Pagnol spoke Provençal fluently and was profoundly imbued with a sense of the dignity and tradition of the simple scenes of Provençal life.

In this perspective, his translation of Virgil's *Bucolics* (1958) is a most important work. It is striking evidence of the way in which Pagnol, as a Provençal, felt himself to be part of a continuing, age-old pattern of life. The translation itself is highly regarded by Latin scholars and ranks with those of Saint-Denis and Paul Valéry; its particular quality is its intuitive, sensitive rendering of the mood of Virgil's original. Professor Talladoire, *professeur titulaire* in Latin at the University of Aix-en-Provence reviewed the translation thus: "he takes consciously to the man of Mantua with all the affection of a Provençal who was brother of a shepherd, brother himself of Tityrus and Menalcas and who has gathered the same herbs as Virgil. . . . Pagnol enables us to appreciate much better a number of verses, an appreciation which is due more to the mood than to the precision of the translation."[24] Pagnol's feeling for Virgil moved him, it should be added, to undertake a translation in verse and with *rimes riches;* he was thus obliged to translate freely, and this enabled him to inject his own lyric experience into the work. In his delightful preface to the translation Pagnol seeks to demonstrate the affinity between Roman and Provençal cultures as a continuing, living experience — an experience which he himself had lived. And so the most banal gesture of the humblest Provençal peasant is enhanced by his ancient origins. As Pagnol pointed out in a conversation with the author, the Provençal greeting *Que nove!* is a virtually unchanged form of the Latin *Quid novis (Quoi de neuf,* freely translated as "What's new?"). Even in a casual greeting, the Provençal becomes an actor in a time-honored tradition: a rich significance and a weightier sense of reality are attached to the behavior of the Provençal countryman as seen through the eyes of a classical student like Pagnol.

The aesthetic consequences of such an attitude are enormous. Not for Pagnol the anguish of a Sartrean hero doubting his own existence, or the self-deception of a Leiris for whom writing should seem as dangerous as bullfighting to have the impact of authenticity.[25] In the interminable debate about the aesthetics of cinema, the concepts of Art, Truth, and Reality are nervously shuffled by uncertain souls (or gleefully juggled by the malicious): Pagnol's art lies in asserting that the *monde visible existe;* the external world is made even more tangible by the third dimension of his learning. As a countryman by adoption, Pagnol is peculiarly sensitive to man's place in the scheme of things: the cycle of the seasons may sometimes seem harsh but it is metaphysically reassuring. The emergency, drought, frost, or blight, with which the peasant has to cope, demands a swift, decisive response; the rotation of fixed tasks to be accomplished during the year is dictated by the massive confidence that rain nourishes, sunshine ripens, and the seasons follow each other; the distribution of responsibilities between men and women is dictated by their natural aptitudes and the need to survive. Like the old Roman culture of pastoral Provence, these things do not change; for the child born under Garlaban, where the soldiers of Marius lit fires to celebrate victory over the Gauls of Teutobochus,[26] the world was full of certainties.

It was his confidence in the real substance and certitudes of things that enabled Pagnol to present with such epic simplicity his fundamental, pagan theme of the therapy of nature. All things have their season and youth is a time for love; as a consequence to the natural love practiced in Pagnol's work, the theme of the unmarried mother recurs persistently. The *fille-mère* (or *mère célibataire,* as some prefer) is normally an outcast from society, but society is a notable absentee from the close, sensuous, tactile world of Pagnol's small communities, often living in contact with a familiar nature. The freedom of youth and the related force of nature, both human and external, maintain an uneasy compromise with the respect due to the patriarch who, in turn, has difficulty in distinguishing between destructive license and constructive love. The modes of society are to be found, either directly or via the microcosm of the classroom, in Pagnol's satirical work. After *Topaze*, he abandoned his scornful contemplation of society, doubtless as pessimistic about its future as his hairdresser ("You know, sir, if society does not change it will end up destroying the good"[27]), to return to the well-tried values of the close-knit community, like Montesquieu in the *Lettres Persanes* retreating from the spectacle of contemporary society to the community of the *Troglodytes*.

B Modern — Dickens

Given the bent of his school career with occasional prizes, and an expressed interest, in Latin, it comes as a surprise to see Pagnol opting for a degree in English; it represents a decisive option for "moderns." The reasons which dictated this choice remain unknown, as do Pagnol's relations with his English teachers and the curriculum both at school and university. Pagnol informed the author in conversation that he had had to study Dickens and that of all Dickens's novels his favorite was *Dombey and Son*.[28] Pagnol's gallery of pedagogues[29] certainly calls up the ghosts of Dickens's formidable teachers; *Merlusse*, a story of Christmas in the school dormitory, also invites comparison with *A Christmas Carol*. But Dickens, the English degree, and Pagnol's first cycle of plays culminating in *Topaze* appear in many ways to be an interlude preceding Pagnol's return to the sources of his art.

C Mistral and the Félibrige

Emile Ripert, as a *félibre*, may also have introduced Pagnol to modern Provençal literature; for Frédéric Mistral (1830 - 1914) and his followers, the *Félibrige*, Provence was more than an echo-chamber for the voices of classical antiquity. In their concern for the survival of the present they frequently evoked the past: the proud origins of Provençal culture were an effective weapon in their struggle for the revival and survival of the local language and customs. Charles Maurras, in his book on Mistral, mentions how the great Provençal sage liked to demonstrate that "in the Provençal language the vocabulary of the farming community was Virgilian while the fisher-folk had a vocabulary which derived from the ancient Greeks."[30] But the past was evoked as a means to an end: the qualities of the language and the dignity of contemporary Provençal values emerge as the leitmotiv of Mistral's great works from *Mireille* and *Calendal* onwards. Believing that the survival of the language was the basis for any future revival of Provencal culture, Mistral devised a formal organization called *Félibrige* (individual elected members were called *félibres* with successive ranks of *capoulié* and *majoral*), which still exists, to protect the Provençal language; in the light of Mistral's beliefs, it could be argued that his most valuable achievement was the compilation of the Provençal dictionary, *Lou Trésor dou Félibrige*, which was completed in 1878.

Mistral died in the year Pagnol left school: although there is no explicit evidence in Pagnol's work of his opinion of Mistral (as a teacher and son of a teacher he was an agent of centralization, to which Mistral was opposed), there are several Mistralian themes in his work. The pastoral setting is, of course, common to Mistral, as is the condemnation of the protocol of society: the refusal of Ramon, proud patriarch of the *mas des Micocoules*, to allow his daughter Mireille to marry Vincent the humble basket-weaver of Valbrègues results in tragedy. The promise of renewal is implicit in the capacity of youth to pardon and to love. The hope that accompanies this unstoppable force of youth is also a constant theme of Pagnol's work: the converse is also true, i.e., tragedy results from an uncompromising contradiction of the legitimate, equally uncompromising claims of youth. Tragedy is the defeat of youth and Comedy its success. Calendal, the young fisherman of Cassis, falls in love with the beautiful Esterelle, last princess of Les Baux and alienated wife of Count Séveran. Without realizing her rank and status, Calendal pays court to Esterelle in her retreat on Mount Gibal: the inequality of social rank once more symbolizes the strength of youth and the fragility of formal etiquette. The strength of Calendal's love overcomes the indifference of Esterelle and the redoubtable hostility of Count Séveran: so a ruined woman is redeemed and the future is rebuilt as in Pagnol's *Angèle, Regain, La Femme du Boulanger, La Fille du Puisatier, Naïs*, and *Manon des Sources*. Where such an issue is blocked by existing hierarchies and institutions, the result is the social satire or black comedy of *Les Marchands de Gloire, Jazz*, and *Topaze*. Pagnol does not necessarily and consciously borrow his themes from anyone, least of all Mistral himself. It is more likely that the cultural climate of his youth, dominated by the apotheosis of Mistral (Nobel Prize for Literature in 1904), sensitized him to some recurrent, popular echoes of the *Félibrige*, especially when they coincided with the early lessons of Ripert and other classical scholars.

D. *Emile Sicard and* le Feu

The convergence of classical scholarship and modern, Mistralian themes and settings revitalized a hitherto stiff, scholastic convention; interested in the one, Pagnol was certain to have met the other. In the unlikely event of Pagnol never having read Mistral, he would have become familiar with the predominant themes of the *Félibrige* through the bi-monthly literary journal *Le Feu*, published in Aix-en-Provence from 1906 to 1914 and in a second series from 1917. Aix is only twenty-five miles from Marseilles and the literary life of the two cities was correspondingly close: Ripert contributed to *Le Feu* and gave lectures on Provençal literature at the university in Aix. Pagnol was posted to the Lycée Mignet in Aix in 1919 when the editorial team and *collaborateurs* of the journal would certainly have become personally acquainted with him; they had much in common since Pagnol was founder of a literary journal in Marseilles and was still its titular director, although the publication of *Fortunio* from 1913 to 1920 was anything but regular. Given these circumstances, it is most improbable that Pagnol had no contact with *Le Feu* and its director, Émile Sicard, before the transfer to Aix in 1919.

The personality of Sicard explains the character of the journal which Pagnol, as director of a literary journal himself, must have read frequently. In a collection of poems entitled *Le Laurier Noir* (1917), an elegy to Mistral and to the dead of the First World War, Sicard recognizes the importance of the *Félibrige* movement but he does not linger in hagiographic nostalgia. He reveals himself as a classical scholar in another collection of poems in praise of Aix (*Le Jardin du Silence et La Ville du Roy*, 1913) where, almost inevitably, he doffs his hat to Virgil: Sicard no more accepts a straitjacket of classical pastiche, however, than excessive sentiment on the occasion of Mistral's death. At all times his work shows a greater freedom of inspiration than the verse of Ripert, Pagnol's first master, who was so dominated by a sense of the past that he finally turned to writing guidebooks (*Au Pays de l'Aude*, 1929, and *Avec Mistral sur les Routes de Provence*, 1931, etc.). In short, Sicard was a modern, assertive Provençal, conscious of his roots and therefore all the more sure of himself in the defense of contemporary Provençal issues. The editorial line of *Le Feu* was aggressive and politicized, reflecting the temperament of Sicard who lived resolutely in the present. Pagnol's contemporary, Louis Brauquier, the poet of Marseilles and its colorful, bustling dock-life, wrote for *Le Feu* but prior to that he also had founded a journal in Marseilles; entitled *La Coupo*, it published Mistralian pastiche in Provençal. Through contact with Sicard, Brauquier found an undeniably modern idiom and a mode of expression more appropriate to his nature: he has frequently acknowledged his gratitude to Sicard for this emancipation. Pagnol's own progress as a creative writer, from scholastic imitation to a contemporary idiom, follows a similar pattern to Brauquier's and his debt to Sicard may be just as great. The plot of Sicard's *La Fille de la Terre*, (*Le Feu*, April 15, 1920) for example, announces that of *Angèle*.

E   Paul Arène

Whether an influence or simply an early example of a theme which was also to interest Giono or Pagnol, *La Fille de La Terre* is only one of several manifestations of Provençal culture that Pagnol could have seen in *Le Feu*. It was probably at this stage, after contact with the relative militancy of Sicard and his team, that Pagnol became aware of the significance of Paul Arène (1843 - 1896). There are frequent allusions in *Le Feu* to Arène's work. A contemporary of Mistral, Arène wrote verse in Provençal and prose in French; still largely unknown in France, his three major novels, *Jean des Figues* (1870), *La Chèvre d'Or* (1889), and *Domnine* (1894) are masterpieces whose anti-Naturalist lightness and grace were imitated by Pagnol in his *Souvenirs d'Enfance*. Less heavy and brutal than Sicard's work, the novels of Arène are permeated with the gentle charm of Mistral but flavored with Arène's own unique, whimsical irony. *Jean des Figues*, a semi-autobiographical story of childhood, holds such a significant position in the passage from the social realism of Pagnol's movies to the poetic realism of his prose that there is insufficient space to deal with it here. Pagnol would most certainly have encountered the work of Arène at a later date, outside the scope of this chapter, when *La Gueuse Parfumée* (a collection of stories including *La Mort de Pan* and *Jean des Figues*) was re-edited in 1929 by Fasquelle. By then, Pagnol had become the resident, official Provençal of Paris with all his own work in the hands of his good friend Eugène Fasquelle.[31] Alphonse Daudet, author of *Lettres de Mon Moulin*, was another contemporary of Mistral to write prose in French but, even if Pagnol did base a movie on *Lettres de Mon Moulin*, Arène is a more important figure. Many *félibres* now go so far as to suggest, like Charles Maurras, that much of *Lettres de Mon Moulin* was written by Arène.[32]

F Marseilles

Pagnol undoubtedly learned much during his short stay in Aix-en-Provence; Marseilles was a cultural suburb of the elegant *ville d'eau*. The contrast between Aix, traditionally intellectual capital of Provence, and Marseilles, the commercial capital, is symbolized by the organization of the University of Aix-Marseille which has its arts and humanities departments in Aix and its science departments in Marseilles. This contrast, emphasized by the close proximity of the two cities, was particularly striking between the wars, when Marseilles was the boom-town of the French Empire, enjoying an unprecedented prosperity. A busy, materialistic city, insensitive to such social issues of the present as anti-Arab racism or the narcotics traffic, Marseilles owed its prosperity to its thriving seaport which, after completion of the Suez Canal, became the hub of the Second French Empire with its colonies in Africa, Madagascar, and Indo-China. The Colonial Exhibition of Paris 1931 marks the high point of French colonial power; this period also coincided with the fabulous growth of Marseilles and the fairy-tale success of Pagnol's Marseilles trilogy. Louis Brauquier, himself a Marseillais working for a French steamship company, evoked the bustling clamor of those times in a collection of poems entitled *Et l'Au-Delà de Suez* (1923). Pagnol later claimed that Brauquier with his yearning for distant, exotic climes, was the model for Marius,[33] also lured away from home and his loved ones by his wanderlust.

Pagnol was anxious to return to Marseilles from Aix;[34] eighteen months after his arrival in Aix, he packed his bags to take up a post in September, 1920, at the *annexe St. Charles* of his old school, the Lycée Thiers in Marseilles. It is not known precisely why Pagnol wished to return to Marseilles; the active cultural life of the city is understandably hard to trace in the raucous din of the docks and the carousing of the free-spending sailors. The most accessible, legitimate forms of entertainment appear to have been the movies and the music hall, vaudeville. *Le Feu* often comments scathingly on the poor artistic facilities of Marseilles: of the equipment of the Grand Théâtre de Marseille, the Marseilles correspondent writes that "a country fair would not envy such a collection of bric-à-brac."[35] Marseilles, however, commands a fierce loyalty. Its citizens have a reputation for their civic pride; loyal to their city and proud of its past, they are also aware of their shortcomings (of which they seem just as proud). But woe betide the outsider who presumes to criticize those faults that the Marseillais himself is ready enough to admit. The image of the Marseillais is so unique and distinctive in French popular mythology that something should be said about it.

It is as difficult for a Frenchman to remain serious when talking about the Marseillais as it is for an Anglo-Saxon when speaking of Irishmen; the caricatural myth becomes confused with reality in both cases. The legendary characteristics of the Marseillais and the Irish even resemble each other: volatile, prone to exaggeration, and naive, they are given to erupting in quaint accents and colorful expressions. Instead of "Top o' the morning," "Begorrah," and "Bejabers," the Marseillais goes through life muttering "Bagasse," "Tron de l'air," and "Peuchère." Although the great actors Barry Fitzgerald and Raimu (who was from Toulon) have corrected these aberrations, portraying authentic Irishmen and Marseillais to audiences all over the world, the myth persists and there are still as many jokes about Irishmen as there are *histoires marseillaises* about Marius and Olive, two simple citizens of Marseilles.

An early example of this Marseillais emulation of the myth is the book of Joseph Méry: *Marseille et les Marseillais* (1860). The book is written as a protest against the continuing misrepresentation of Marseilles by northerners "who make us all appear quaint and stupid. We all say '*bagasse*' and '*troun de l'er*' and we all say: 'If there was a Canebière [the main street of Marseilles] in Paris it would be a little Marseilles!'"[36] Rejecting such a caricature, he goes on to describe authentic scenes of life in Marseilles such as the *partie de boules:* ". . . a game of bowls should be played heatedly. Running, fidgetting, gesticulating, quarreling and measuring, the players hop in idignation in a temperature of 40° Réaumur. . . ."[37] Warming to his subject, Méry describes the would-be hunters of Marseilles: ". . . in the month of October, an enterprising thrush can sometimes be seen in the vicinity of Marseilles and fifty thousand marksmen arise as one to take aim and miss it."[38]

The myth plays leapfrog with reality in Marseilles. Like Méry, Pagnol stands as a champion of Marseilles against the outsider but in reality is simply claiming the privilege to tell the story himself; his Marseilles trilogy, *Marius* (1931), *Fanny* (1932), and *César* (1936), seems unreal from afar, but is it? Transported on a magic carpet to Marseilles and still rubbing one's eyes, one finds that Marius is a common name in the city and that there are even bars called Chez Marius; there is a ferryboat called *César* which crosses the Vieux Port where there is a Bar de la Marine. Fanny is the name of the little statuette offered as a booby prize to the loser at bowls. The whole clientele of the Bar de la Marine is reproduced in effigy as *santons*, the terra-cotta Nativity figures which have been traditionally made in Marseilles for centuries. As with the characters of the *commedia dell'arte*, one asks oneself if they are real. Did they really exist? They do now and are even larger than life. Such transformations are only possible in a city such as Marseilles where the natural ebullience and imagination of the population are sovereign. Nowhere else in France do *estrambord* and *galéjade* traditionally reign so freely on such a massive, popular scale. Even if the cultural life of Aix were superior to that of Marseilles, it was a duller place to be. Besides, Marseilles was home; Pagnol's family was there and he had acquired a wife.

Although subdued, a cultural life did exist in Marseilles. Pagnol's literary journal, *Fortunio*, appeared regularly and without interruption after his return and it became the greatest literary journal of the Midi under the title *Cahiers du Sud*. Jean Ballard, Pagnol's early colleague and subsequently director of the journal, suggested in a conversation with the author[39] that it was in order to ensure the success of *Fortunio* that Pagnol had been anxious to leave Aix; the presence in Aix of *Le Feu* precluded the possibility of *Fortunio* moving there. Always independent and dominant, Pagnol was a natural leader and his desire to become his own master impelled him to return to his home town and his long-standing circle of friends. The early numbers of *Fortunio*, *Massilia*, and the fiftieth anniversary issue of *Cahiers du Sud* (1963) shed light on the ensuing years of energetic, creative activity. *Fortunio*, produced with the help of a tightly-knit group of friends, absorbed all Pagnol's literary output until 1924; his *dada* and his brain-child with all expenses paid out of pocket, *Fortunio* was Pagnol's principal recreation in the years preceding his departure for Paris.

III   *Recreational Activity*

A Fortunio

Although founded in 1913, the publication of *Fortunio* remained sporadic until 1920, after the so-called *série d'Aix*. The third and final series began with Pagnol's return to Marseilles in 1920 and continued uninterrupted until 1967, surviving his departure for Paris in 1922 and his total rupture with the journal in 1924. The climax of Pagnol's own involvement in the journal was thus sandwiched between the *reprise* in Aix and the departure for Paris in 1922; although he continued contributing until 1924, the material was

largely revision of manuscripts written in Marseilles. The period
1920 - 1922 was one of great productivity for Pagnol, with his work
filling the pages of the journal: editorials, poems, and plays followed
each other in bewildering succession. He even invented a new
literary genre: *le roman bouche-trou*. This was, in fact, the usual
standby of the magazine editor short of copy but more often known
as the serial story. The editorial policy, if there was one, was certainly less firm and clear than that of *Le Feu;* the editorial team of
1920 was composed of Charles Arno-Brun, Pagnol, Jean Ballard,
Marcel Gras, Jean Cayol, Julien Coutelen, Gaston Mouren, and Yves
Bourde who were, for the most part, former classmates. Their
solidarity was that of long acquaintance from childhood rather than
that of shared intellectual goals. The journal represented for them all
their first artistic adventure and the first rash enthusiasm of youth
was abundantly expressed in *Fortunio*. The title came from the
name of Musset's hero in *Le Chandelier* and, like Musset, the
youthful editorial team were all in a hurry to live and to go they were
not sure where. There was no manifesto or any other statement of
their creed until 1923, after Pagnol had left Marseilles. In their first
flush of enthusiasm, united by their existing friendship, the founders
worked spontaneously together with no conscious thought of a goal;
it was as if the journal itself were an expression of their high spirits
and friendship, setting itself no targets beyond that. The manifesto
published in 1923 (identified by Ballard as Pagnol's composition)
marks the abatement of the early, vaguely directed idealism; when
their enthusiasm was spent they paused to take stock of what they
were doing. Pagnol's manifesto, then, is probably more of a summary of their past mood than a genuine aspiration for the future. He
had, after all, left Marseilles for Paris and was soon to sever all contact with the journal. The manifesto represents the inchoate goals of
Fortunio under Pagnol's leadership; energy and enthusiasm abound
but there is no clear sense of direction.

Ballard likes to relate how, swaggering down the Boulevard
Longchamp, Pagnol would turn to him and say: "You know, my
friend, *Fortunio* will be the *Mercure* [a distinguished French jour-
nal] of the twentieth century." When the only subscriptions to the
journal were those taken out by the editors themselves for uncles,
brothers, sisters, cousins, mothers, and fathers, Pagnol's great-
hearted optimism must have been an inspiration to his colleagues.
Even more valuable were his innumerable contributions to the journal. Only two works dating from this period (*Merlusse* and *Pirou-*

ettes) have been retained by Pagnol in the successive editions of his *Oeuvres Complètes;* with the four-act verse play *Catulle* and some random poems, they represent the sum total of Pagnol's original, creative work for *Fortunio.* Pagnol's editorials and theater criticism occupied a lot of space in *Fortunio* but they need not occupy more than a paragraph of the present study.

It can safely be said that Pagnol's critical reviews (and that included editorials) for *Fortunio* clearly demonstrate that his temperament was not congenial to this kind of work: accuracy is always sacrificed to the *bon mot.* In the period 1920 - 1924 Pagnol wrote approximately twenty editorials (since they are often literary reviews, it is difficult to distinguish them at times from criticism proper). They range over diverse topics in a search for novelty which is always rewarded: Bacon as Shakespeare, Rider Haggard as H. G. Wells, Rostand as the greatest dramatist in the world (and a Marseillais at that), the stagnation of the *Académie Française,* and scandal in the academic world are but a few of Pagnol's spine-tingling topics. He was always scrupulous in making a clear distinction between critical and creative writing; the editorials and reviews were signed "J. Roche" and he put his own name only to his creative work. Such a distinction is, of course, quite Romantic and, in Pagnol's case, highly salutary. The critical reviews became more frequent after the move to Paris and, in the January, 1923, number, a new series, *Les Premières à Paris,* was unaugurated by "J. Roche." Here again, Romantic idealism, true to the spirit of Musset, is evident in the further distinction made between *Théâtre* and *Commerce.* In making the distinction between the expression of a pure, unsullied art, to be reviewed under the rubric *Théâtre,* and the productions of the commercial theater industry, which would be summarized under the rubric *Commerce,* "J. Roche" added that there was no pejorative interpretation to be attached to the second category.

Such a distinction, as observed in practice, is both naive and dangerous: insofar as it represents in itself a preclassification, it encourages the worst vices of a critic, i.e., prejudgment and a respect for reputations. In effect, the plays which fell into the *Commerce* category were generally lashed by *Fortunio's* Parisian theater critic: of *Ponche* by René Peters and Henri Falk, playing at the Potinière, he wrote: "A bit more funny than a funeral invitation and a bit more moving than a prospectus."[40] Conversely, nothing classified under *Théâtre* met with adverse criticism. Pagnol's favorite dramatists of the time, to judge by the comments of "J. Roche," were Marcel

Achard (*Voulez-vous jouer avec Moâ* — "that's theater, real theater and modern theater"),[41] Sacha Guitry (*Un Sujet de Roman* — "a beautiful play which might have been a masterpiece but which will only be the best play of the year"),[42] and Georges de Porto-Riche (*Le Vieil Homme* — "our prolonged applause rendered something that can never be offered at the box office").[43] With Pagnol himself, these three dramatists were among the most professional craftsmen of the theater between the wars. How they would have laughed had they known that they were assumed, as "artists," to have no interest in the box office. A combination of idealism and misjudgment marks the criticism of "J. Roche" but it should be added that, with "M. Pagnol," he regularly provided most of the copy for successive issues of *Fortunio*.

The work to which Pagnol put his own name and to which, manifestly, he attached most importance was his original, creative material. Apart from a few poems in the Ripert mold, this consisted of *Catulle* (1922), *L'Infâme Truc* (1922 — it reappeared as *Merlusse* in 1935), and *Les Mémoires de Jacques Panier* (1920 - 1921 — afterwards revised and republished as *Le Mariage de Peluque* in 1924, which in turn reappeared as *Pirouettes* in 1932). *Catulle* is Pagnol's last original work in verse; it is also the last work in the old, scholastic style and it really dates from long before 1922, having been started in 1912. *L'Infâme Truc*, for which, as *Merlusse*, Pagnol will express much affection, is a turning point: it is Pagnol's first piece of work in a contemporary mode of expression. As Pagnol would prove later with *Topaze* (1928) and as Vigo would confirm with *Zéro de Conduite* (1933), the schoolroom is an appropriate idiom through which to analyze the society in which we move. *Les Mémoires de Jacques Panier* represents a remarkable solo performance — it was Pagnol's famous *roman bouche-trou*, the interminable serial story which finally became *Pirouettes*. After the superfluous padding is removed, one is left with a light, amusing tale of adolescence; the classroom remains present in the background and, above all, Pagnol is himself, emancipated from Neoclassic scholasticism. The substance of the last two works and the transformations of the text are to be found in Chapters 3 and 5 respectively, where *Merlusse* and *Pirouettes* are discussed at length.

B   Catulle

Catulle is the story, in verse, of the Roman poet: the classical setting is charged with the Romantic mood of "better to have loved and lost. . . ." Catullus, aged twenty-eight, has had his career damaged by his involvement with a courtesan named Clodia; what is worse, he loves her and is heartbroken by her alleged association with Cicero. The action of the play begins with Catullus holding a banquet in honor of his friends, where he tries to shrug off the memory of Clodia and thus reassert his former personality. His most trusted friend, Licinus Calvus, is present at the banquet; believing in the greatness of Catullus but imagining it to be threatened by the influence of Clodia, Calvus is determined to destroy the memory of the latter. And so the guests arrive, from Demetrius the cynic to Cornificius the dandy. In Act 2, Catullus (Musset in a toga) is profoundly disturbed by the arrival of Clodia. For him, it is a question of not loving honor so much, loved he not Clodia more. Learning that Calvus's henchman, Sporus, has killed himself after admitting to the false libel (or white lie, depending on the narrator) of Clodia's infidelity, the languishing Catullus yields to Clodia's charms. Act 3 shows the justification of Calvus's misgivings since Clodia confesses to her handmaid, Melita, that she is bored with Catullus but that she will remain faithful to him for as long as his present illness endures. Clodia's boredom is temporarily allayed by Catullus suggesting a sojourn in the country. The idea charms Clodia who has a naive, city-dweller's impression of the country; after Catullus's departure, Coelius arrives to mock Clodia's idyllic misconceptions about well-combed sheep and courteous shepherds. With a well-feigned feminine horror Clodia throws herself into the arms of Coelius, presumably to forget the odor of manure and molasses. Calvus, who has overheard all, emerges to plead with Clodia to remain faithful to Catullus, if only to save his life. Too late: Catullus had also overheard all and he appears to dismiss Clodia. There are six scenes in Act 1, seven in Acts 2 and 3, but only two in Act 4, which is a long death-bed scene. It takes Catullus a long time to die, repeatedly reviving from his coma only to subside again. For sixteen pages the reader (there were never any spectators) thinks that each speech of Catullus is his last. The hero finally dies sighing "A kiss is better than immortality."

As will be divined from the synopsis, the historical reconstruction is impressive but the play is too literary to work on stage, the death-bed scene being much too long. The play is, in a sense, completion of a contract: Pagnol had been living with it for a long time and wanted it out of his system. The concept of the play is good if a little too heroic for present tastes: Pagnol's knowledge of classical history and his sympathy for Musset enable him to establish an interesting balance between the self-sacrifice demanded of Catullus to attain future greatness and the voluptuousness of Clodia's present charms. It is perhaps Pagnol's very erudition that stifles this play. Set in ancient Rome and written in verse, it is far removed from what proved to be Pagnol's particular talent — observation of the world about him.

Never subjected to the test of a stage performance and never revived by Pagnol (normally so attached to all his old manuscripts) in any of the increasing number of editions of his complete works, the play has interesting, lighter passages. Coelius, the cynical philanderer, has some good lines: "Me drink an inheritor's wine! Not so foolish."[44] Some of Catullus's lines describing his family living in their country retreat provoke a comparison with Pagnol's own situation.

The autobiographical element is also noticeable in the long death-bed scene when Demetrius, trying to revive Catullus's will to live, speaks of the mirror of the past: "And then, with an increasing tenderness, you will see the mirror become misty as if under the breath of a kiss and slowly, oh, so slowly, will emerge the beloved countenance of your departed mother."[45]

It is a trait of Pagnol's that, like Oscar Wilde, he cannot let a good line escape by stealth. A successful *boutade* or conceit is often carried over from one work to another. A characteristically Marseillais image taken from *Catulle* is used again in *Fanny*. Ridiculing the empty-headedness of Cornifucius, Demetrius says to him: "When you walk, I can hear distinctly the noise of your brain rattling inside like a dried pea."[46] Panisse uses the same image in *Fanny* (Act 1, scene 2) to describe a particularly pathetic case he knows. The *dénouement* prefigures the theme of Pagnol's subsequent plays. The disillusion of the noble-minded, the futility of self-sacrifice become a leitmotiv in the plays which criticize society for thus humiliating the individual. This note of increasing scepticism recalls the work of Henri Becque and Octave Mirbeau whom Pagnol later adopted as his models.

C *Departure, 1922*

Catulle was published under the auspices of *Fortunio* in the year Pagnol left for Paris, but his departure did not mark the end of his association with *Fortunio*. His contributions even increased; in 1923, he began his *Premières à Paris* theater reviews, wrote the *Fortunio* manifesto, and started *Le Mariage de Peluque,* a polished and revised version of the serial story prevously published under the title *Les Mémoires de Jacques Panier.* With the tenacity that marked his completion of *Catulle,* Pagnol saw *Le Mariage de Peluque* through to the final episode (February 15, 1924) before ceasing to contribute to *Fortunio.* One can take it that the rupture was complete the following year when *Fortunio* changed its name to *Cahiers du Sud.*

By the time he arrived in Paris, Pagnol had displayed many qualities and reviewed several options. He had shown determination, a capacity for work, and the gregarious temperament of an extrovert. His decision to be a writer and to work at it is implicit in the time and energy devoted to *Fortunio.* It was only a question of when and how he would succeed as a writer; he had already taken a decisive first step in shaking off the Neoclassical scholasticism inherited from a successful school career. It was presumably because the activity of the *Félibrige* was too closely associated in his mind with this scholasticism that he did not seek to work more closely with them, although everything in his background showed this to be a natural outlet for his talent. The somewhat surprising decision to take a degree in English can be seen as an early, impatient desire for material and intellectual independence. *L'Infâme Truc,* which had appeared in *Fortunio* in January, 1922, was an expression of that independence, showing the desire to find a different, new idiom. But Pagnol doubtless felt the need to talk to his peers about the development of his new approach. He had known his companions in *Fortunio* since school days and familiarity had dulled their capacity to challenge and test each other's ideas. The fresh opinions and the new faces of Paris offered the possibility of that informed, uncommitted advice for which he was looking.

CHAPTER 2

Perfection of a Formula
for the Theater

THE ostensible reason for Pagnol's arrival in the capital was his appointment to the Lycée Condorcet, one of the most famous schools in Paris, where Mallarmé before him had taught English. Until this point Pagnol's teaching career had served as a platform for a hazardous existence as a writer. In the abundant memoirs later written by Pagnol about this period of his life, more evidence emerges to prove that his first priority was a theatrical career;[1] this required that he stay in Paris. *Fortunio*, with which he remained associated for a further two years, was a readily available outlet for all but his theatrical work, but at a time when theatrical life in the provinces was insignificant in comparison with the Parisian productions, Pagnol's permanent move to Paris certainly suggests that he had made a deliberate decision to write for the theater.

Almost immediately after his arrival in Paris, Pagnol was introduced to the alert, stimulating atmosphere of *Comoedia*, a distinguished theatrical and literary review of the time. It was through the *Comoedia* theater critic Paul Nivoix, with whom Pagnol had been acquainted in the days when Nivoix had attempted to found a journal named *Spectator* in Marseilles, that Pagnol gained his first entrée into the *tout-Paris* of the theater world; after being introduced to Gabriel Boissy, editor of *Comoedia*, Pagnol was given part-time work with the journal. Shortly afterwards the *Premières à Paris* column began to appear in *Fortunio*. André Levinson, Fréjaville, André Lang, and J-P. Liausu were among the able, well-informed critics who were now Pagnol's colleagues in his other life outside school. One connection led to another; Pagnol met some of the most successful dramatists of the time and soon began to work on his own play. Written in collaboration with Nivoix, as the following two plays would be, this first joint venture caused Pagnol so much embarrassment that he wanted nothing further to do with it. Since

Nivoix had registered the play at the *Société des Auteurs,* had had it performed, and insisted on his co-author receiving royalties, Pagnol eventually agreed to acknowledge authorship, but he bashfully signed himself "Castro." Pagnol never thought highly enough of the play, entitled *Tonton,* to revive it. So little is known of it that it cannot even be established whether segments of the text were used in later work but it must have encouraged Pagnol, despite his reticence, to see it run for two weeks at the Théâtre des Variétés in Marseilles (July 15 - 30, 1924), with Hippolyte Gerny in the lead. The play has never been published but Pagnol saw his own work performed for the first time and became a professional dramatist with the seven hundred francs he earned in royalties. The twenty performances of *Tonton* are thus a landmark signalling the start of Pagnol's career as a dramatist; only four years later, after *Les Marchands de Gloire, Un Direct au Coeur,* and *Jazz,* it would be crowned with the famous *doublé,* the *coup du roi* of *Topaze* and *Marius.*

Small wonder, then, that Pagnol loved to reminisce about this period in his life: his talent seems to have resolved itself as a dramatic one and the incredible gamble of his move to Paris was to be handsomely rewarded. The advice and company of his Parisian associates played an important part in shaping the theatrical style that led to Pagnol's success. An examination of his social circle and of the circumstances in which he wrote his plays will serve as an introduction to the plays themselves.

I *A Way of Life*

The early recollections of Pagnol and his comrades reveal a sociable but purposeful young man sacrificing most of his leisure time to his writing; his apartment in the boulevard Murat was modest but, excited by the relative success of *Tonton,* he was too absorbed in his next play to pay much attention to his physical surroundings. All his friends were people of the theater and his one distraction, a curious amateur's interest in mechanical physics, seems a natural complement to his work as an architect of well-made plays. As described by Marcel Achard, Pagnol's apartment in these years was dominated by a mass of dirty washing and by a complicated piece of machinery constructed by Pagnol in his search for perpetual motion; Archard recalls how he and Stève Passeur would round off a Sunday afternoon at the football match in the Parc des Princes with a social call on Pagnol:

Every Sunday, before and after the match, we would ask him:
— Well, have you found it?
— What?
— Perpetual motion.
— I got it the day before yesterday but I lost it again yesterday evening.[2]

Pagnol's companions frequently tried to take him along to the football match with them but, as Achard continues, "he preferred to work and when we returned he would shame us by reading the two or three pages he had written."[3]

Always an extrovert, Pagnol was able, as in Marseilles, to cultivate a large circle of friends with similar interests. He did not always shun the conviviality of Stève Passeur and Marcel Achard for the sake of his work and he also enjoyed the company of Jacques Théry and Alfred Savoir. If these were his intimates, several other rising dramatic talents were close acquaintances. As he recollects, "the gang included Léopold Marchand, Henri Jeanson, Roger Ferdinand, Jacques Natanson, Jean Sarment, Paul Vialar. And from time to time Armand Salacrou, Paul Nivoix, or Jacques Deval joined us: they were a good crowd."[4] This list of names includes many of the most promising young dramatists of the Parisian stage in 1924. Pagnol's commitment to the theater increased with two more plays written in collaboration with Nivoix: Les Marchands de Gloire (1925) and Un Direct au Coeur (1926). The commitment became total in 1927, when he resigned from Condorcet and from teaching forever after the successful performances of Jazz, which he had written alone.

From their purely spontaneous, sociable origins, the frequent gatherings of Pagnol's circle of friends gradually assumed a professional complexion, almost in time with Pagnol's own developing involvement with the theater. They finally organized themselves into a group called Les Moins de Trente Ans (The Under-Thirties). Since they remained essentially united through their friendship, Les Moins de Trente Ans had little need to encumber themselves with statutes or, worse still, an archive of any kind. The information currently available about their activity and their goals is consequently scarce. Given the potential significance of their contribution to Parisian theater life in general, and to Pagnol's career in particular, they deserve further research: Marcel Achard, André Antoine (son of the founder of the Théâtre Libre), and Pagnol himself[5] have left a nucleus of information with which to reconstruct, in general terms, the life of Les Moins de Trente Ans.

II   Les Moins de Trente Ans

In about 1926 a former actor named Hauterive became the owner of *La Fleur de Lys*, a restaurant in the Square Louvois near the Bibliothèque Nationale in Paris. He was indulgent toward hard-up literary people to the point of not presenting them with a bill: "the news of this amiable idiosyncracy, spreading by word of mouth through the ranks of the young dramatists of the inter-war period, led to the congregation around this latter-day Ragueneau [a seventeenth-century *restaurateur* friend of actors] of the brilliant but impoverished flower of the rising theatrical generation."[6] Among Hauterive's clients were Henri Jeanson, Marcel Archard, Jean Sarment, Stève Passeur, Georges Lannes, and his brother Pol Rab, the cartoonist. It was the latter who had the idea of arranging a banquet at regular intervals for their own particular circle: the banquets were arranged as planned and held on a monthly basis at *La Belle Aurore* near the Marché St. Honoré. Out of these monthly banquets grew *Les Moins de Trente Ans* which, in André Antoine's words: "did not so much represent a well-defined theatrical or literary movement, each of its members being very different, as a shared desire for renewal of literary forms and an anxious protest against the lamentable situation of the theater in Paris between the wars."[7] Naturally preferring the company of those who shared his interest in the theater, full of the reforming zeal of *Fortunio* and with a well-tried aptitude for the irreverent chaff and banter of the literary group, Pagnol penetrated almost unconsciously into a theatrical élite. And *Les Moins de Trente Ans* provided a perfect induction in Paris for the raw provincial from Marseilles.

Despite the informal, almost frivolous, style of their meetings, the members of the group were all motivated by the same intense interest in the theater; they were demanding, constructive critics of each other's work. Achard describes a characteristic session: "We would sometimes talk till dawn about our future dramatic works and anyone who had just completed an act would read it to his companions who, for the most part, were seated on the floor around him with a glass of whisky handy. We were quite the opposite of a mutual admiration society."[8] Badinage and serious criticism were mixed judiciously.

Membership of such a community was undoubtedly fun but it also imposed exacting standards. An arbitrary list of plays which benefitted from such generous and rigorous communal revision includes:

Jean de la Lune and *Marlborough s'en va-t-en Guerre* (Achard);
L'Acheteuse and *Les Tricheurs* (Passeur); *Topaze* and *Marius*
(Pagnol); *Le Fruit Vert* (Jacques Théry); *Durand Bijoutier*
(dedicated to Pagnol) and *Nous ne Sommes plus des Enfants*
(Léopold Marchand); *Léopold le Bien Aimé* (Jean Sarment); *Eve
toute Nue* (Paul Nivoix); *Le Greluchon Delicat* (Jacques Natanson);
Toi que j'ai Tant Aimée and the scenarii for *Pépé le Moko, Carnet
de Bal,* and *Hôtel du Nord* (Henri Jeanson). There are a number of
masterpieces in this list which, as Antoine suggested, is not at first
sight homogeneous; all these plays share, however, an attention to
detail and the craftsman's care for the finished product. In short,
they are all well-made plays and it is this quality that explains both
the unity of the output of *Les Moins de Trente Ans* and the neglect
into which their work has consequently fallen. Robert de Beauplan
pointed out that much of their work is marked by "a crushing contempt for sensitivity . . . and a lack of gallantry in their portrayal of
sexual relations."[9] These attributes are shared, it is true, by Passeur
and Pagnol (an admirer of Becque, a great exponent of the *comédie
rosse,* as black comedy is called), but Beauplan's analysis is not universally applicable and does not explain enough. With very few exceptions (Passeur and Achard notably), the members of *Les Moins
de Trente Ans* did not have their work performed by the *avant-garde*
directors of the time, Copeau and the *Cartel* of Jouvet, Dullin, Baty,
and Pitoëff, yet the *comédie rosse* figured frequently in the program
of *avant-garde* theaters.

    The reasons for this lack of understanding are complex and only
the broadest of analyses can be offered at this point. The *comédie
rosse* of Becque as staged by Antoine in the Théâtre Libre, had been
Naturalist; it was also well made. The tight composition of Becque's
plays and their penetrating *mots d'auteur* are frequently found in
the plays of *Les Moins de Trente Ans.* Although they would not have
gone as far as Antoine in his search for authentic realism in the days
of the Théâtre Libre (1887), *Les Moins de Trente Ans* were undoubtedly flattered by the interest which the grand old man of
French theater, nearly eighty years old and still influential, took in
their work. Antoine (1858 - 1943) was a patron of *Les Moins de
Trente Ans: Topaze* is dedicated to him and his son has written the
most important article yet about the group. The well-made,
Naturalist play was displeasing to the *Cartel* on two counts. The
authorial strength implicit in the well-made play frequently proved
incompatible with the directorial strength of such people as Baty

who abandoned human actors for more biddable puppets. On the second count, it was difficult for the innovative dynamism of the *Cartel* to settle for what, rightly or wrongly, seemed like routine reproduction of reality in Naturalist stage design. Dorothy Knowles recalls the famous exchange between Antoine, Pagnol's mentor, and Pitoëff. Thoroughly dismayed by a modern stage design, Antoine cried:

— Where do you ever see bedrooms without ceilings?
— In the theater, Mr. Antoine, replied Pitoëff.[10]

III   *The Boulevard Theater*

The most constant, pressing problem for the authors of *Les Moins de Trente Ans* was the question of an outlet for their work, the availability of a theater, and the cooperation of its director. The Vieux-Colombier had closed and the remaining *avant-garde* theaters (La Comédie des Champs-Elysées, l'Atelier, and Les Mathurins) were, as a general rule, closed to them. The alternatives seemed equally bleak for young dramatists concerned with ideas and the nature of theater; most of the remaining theaters of Paris seemed to be dominated by the *style Capucines* [name of a theater], "a star in six costume changes and three acts caught in compromising situations."[11] It was difficult to find a director and an audience for a play which did not comply with this formula of the *boulevard*. Even more successful than drawing-room comedy was the music hall and operetta. *Phi-Phi*, with lyrics by Willemetz, had finished a three-year run (1918 - 1921) at the time of Pagnol's arrival in Paris. The Dolly sisters, Josephine Baker, Mistinguett, and Maurice Chevalier regularly performed to packed houses at the Casino de Paris. A handful of tycoon-impresarii had control of the *boulevard* theaters and music hall alike: Quinson (La Michodière); Volterra (l'Olympia, L'Apollo, Le Casino de Paris, and Le Théâtre Marigny); the Isola brothers (La Gaieté Lyrique and Le Théâtre Mogador); and Victor Silvestre (Le Vaudeville) ruled the popular theater life of Paris. Sandwiched between the extremes of the *avant-garde* and the hackneyed formulae for commercial success, Pagnol and his comrades felt understandably frustrated, as the *Fortunio* manifesto of 1923 demonstrates.

There existed other possibilities made available by disinterested lovers of theater and there were a number of independent theaters, but *Les Moins de Trente Ans* had to place their plays where they could. Without necessarily compromising their own standards, they sometimes had to adapt their style to the popular *boulevard* formula in order to find a theater. Some of them were highly successful in adapting to more popular taste. For this, they have been dismissed by many a latter-day Lysidas as *boulevardiers;* such a judgment is a collective injustice unless the precise meaning of *boulevardier* is amplified. A welcome change in this stereotyped approach is announced by Paul Surer's indignant outburst: "Why persist in trying to please a chapel of snobs interested only in hermetic difficulties? When a work gives pleasure, is it not foolish to resist and to seek reasons for not enjoying it?"[12] *Les Moins de Trente Ans* represented a *troisième force* in the Parisian theater of the late 1920's, an independent alternative to the cultural fortress of the *N.R.F.* associations on the one hand and the empire of popular entertainment on the other. The individual merit of Pagnol as a dramatist remains to be established through a closer examination of his plays. They will be studied in chronological order; *Judas* and *Fabien*, written more than twenty years after Pagnol's first cycle of plays, will be included in the examination.

IV   Les Marchands de Gloire

This play was the second, after *Tonton*, to be written by Pagnol in collaboration with Paul Nivoix. Originally consisting of a prologue and four acts,[13] the play was given a minor face-lift by Pagnol for republication in 1964[14] and now simply consists of five acts. The text itself remains unchanged from the original version in which it is impossible to distinguish the individual contributions of Pagnol and Nivoix; Pagnol later wrote[15] that Nivoix was largely responsible for the female rôles. Although completed in 1925, just before it could benefit from a reading to the full, formal sessions of *Les Moins de Trente Ans*, the play has all the hallmarks of the "school." Pagnol's early associates, Achard and Passeur, probably played an advisory rôle but it was Nivoix's colleague on the *Comoedia* staff, J-P. Liausu, who was principal counselor. Liausu encouraged Pagnol and Nivoix to go out and seek an explosive contemporary issue, urged them to put more venom in their dialogue, and, most important, made the production of the play possible.[16] Liausu put the young co-authors in touch with *Les Escholiers*, a wealthy association of *mécènes* whose aim was to discover and launch new theatrical talent. At a number of regular intervals in the year *Les Escholiers* selected a play they considered deserving of support and then made, and paid for, the arrangements necessary for its production. After a reading by René Simon, *Les Marchands de Gloire* was retained by *Les Escholiers* and the directors of the Théâtre de la Madeleine (André Brulé and Robert Trébor) accepted a commission to stage the play in April, 1925. The play opened at the Théâtre de la Madeleine on April 15, 1925, and ran for thirteen performances to much critical acclaim but little popular interest.

A combination of Balzac's *Le Colonel Chabert* and Bertolt Brecht's *Drums in the Night*, *Les Marchands de Gloire* is an adaptation of the Enoch Arden theme to the issues of the French Third Republic: a French soldier given up for dead in the First World War returns to find not only that his return is embarrassing but that his death is a source of revenue and power to his father, now living off the war-hero cult. Whether or not Pagnol and Nivoix were familiar with Brecht's play, which opened in Munich in 1922, the plot bears a remarkable resemblance to *Drums in the Night*, written before Brecht's conversion to Marxism. In Brecht's original, pre-Marxist version, the war veteran Kragler returns from the dead to find that his wife Anna and the sinister Murk are considerably put out by his survival. In *Les Marchands de Gloire*, Henri Bachelet returns to find his wife Germaine remarried and Berlureau, the conniving *entrepreneur*, profiting from his presumed death. The systems which, in Brecht's play, demand yet another sacrifice of the returning veteran and, in *Les Marchands de Gloire*, conspire toward the hero's re-disappearance are exposed as equally savage. The theme has lost little of its original topicality which was appreciated in the U.S.A. as early as 1926 when the Theater Guild of New York bought the rights of reproduction in English. The parallels between Brecht and Pagnol will be taken up later in this chapter in a general appraisal of Pagnol's theatrical career.

Les Marchands de Gloire opens with a prologue[17] set in the provinces in 1915, in the Bachelet household. The set shows a modest interior which includes a dresser surmounted by a small photograph of Henri Bachelet, currently serving at the front as a sergeant in the French army. Henri's mother, his wife Germaine, and his cousin Yvonne are preparing a food parcel for him while awaiting the return of his father from work. The father is a free-thinking republican with the austere virtue of a Cato; he is a senior clerk at the prefecture where he is responsible for the estimates submitted for contracts with the department. His position exposes him to the propositions of an influential arms manufacturer named

Berlureau who is hoping to secure a contract for meat supplies with the department. If Bachelet agrees to inform Berlureau of the competitors' estimates, Berlureau will use his influence to secure the return of Henri Bachelet from the trenches to work in a munitions factory. Bachelet treats Berlureau's offer with scorn but at the end of the prologue he learns of the heroic death of his son.

The next act opens with a distinctly richer décor in the same house but nine years later, in 1924. The small photograph of Henri has now become a gold-framed portrait on the wall; on a nearby dresser are displayed the *Croix de Guerre, la Médaille Militaire,* and *la Légion d'Honneur* which were posthumously awarded to Sergeant Henri Bachelet. Bachelet *aîné,* it is understood, has recovered from the grief of his bereavement to become president of *La Société des Parents des Héros:* in a desire to represent his cause at a national level, he responds to Berlureau's advances and throws in his lot with the latter's recently formed Radical Nationalist political party. The contrast with the Bachelet-Berlureau relations of the prologue symbolizes the gradual falling away of Bachelet's integrity. And so the plot develops with the growing cult of the dead hero represented by the size of his portrait swelling in time with the political corruption which benefits from his vicarious sponsorship. Bachelet's increasing venality and self-importance are further exposed in this act by the contrast with the quiet, inner grief of Grandel, a former friend and colleague who also lost his son in the war. When Bachelet encourages him to reconcile himself to his loss and to take a war pension, Grandel retorts: "They took him, they killed him, but they cannot pay me for him!"[18]

Act 2 opens on the same set but Sergeant Bachelet's portrait is now even larger; it soon becomes apparent that there are family divisions arising out of Bachelet's infatuation with the privileges that accompany his son's military honor. Bachelet's adoptive niece Yvonne and Madame Bachelet grieve silently; the pomp and trappings have little meaning for them. In scene 4 Yvonne exclaims against the inhuman cult into which her uncle is sinking and assails the monstrous portrait: "I hate that portrait; it's killed our memories. You imagine an infantry sergeant fighting off an enemy battalion and you think that's your son! No, that's just a picture, that's not Henri: he was a footstep on the stairs, a faded straw hat in the hall, a woollen glove on the table, the smell of his tobacco . . . and you revere the medals and decorations which he never even saw!"[19] The humanity of this sweet woman is not generally heeded.

Henri's wife Germaine has remarried; Bachelet is preoccupied with
an election campaign which is destined to carry him to the *Assemblée Nationale* as representative of the *radicaux-nationalistes*. In
the concluding scene 6 of this act, Sergeant Henri Bachelet returns.
It is now 1924; reported missing in 1915, he had been suffering from
amnesia in a hospital where nobody knew him.

Acts 3 and 4 show the attempts of the long-lost hero to adapt
himself to a way of life that has for its basis his own death and
absence. His father is so heavily committed to his political life and
election campaign that he cannot withdraw from it. His son cannot
even regain his identity: it would cost his father the thirty thousand
francs Berlureau has spent on his publicity campaign. In view of the
embarrassed reticence that greets his return, Henri Bachelet has to
find out some of the unsavory changes for himself. His father dares
not explain his commitment to a political cause and the necessity for
his son's incognito. The Royalist section of the electoral district
adheres at the last minute to the father's party. As Bachelet's election to the *Assemblée* is now virtually assured, so his ambition in-
creases. Scene 12 of Act 3 is supremely ironical. Henri sees his father
marching away at the head of a procession and questions Yvonne:

Henri: What is it? An accident?
Yvonne: No, it's politics.
Henri: Ah! *(going to the window)* My father is in the lead. Where are
              they going?
Yvonne: To your grave.

In Act 4 the corruption of Bachelet *aîné* is completed and the
portrait is almost life-size. The scene is now a parliamentary office in
Paris. Always promising to restore his son's identity and thus destroy
his political platform, Bachelet fails to rise to this parental sacrifice
now that he is an elected *député* and has the Ministry of Pensions in
his grasp. The exasperated Henri cannot understand his father's continuing ambition. In a lapidary moral, typical of the later Pagnol
style, the war hero says: "It is useless for you to climb higher if you
are only going to fall further." Since he wishes to marry Yvonne, he
needs his name and personal identification papers. What he does not
realize is that his father is too weak to renounce his prospects of
political advancement, even if his career is based on a lie. Henri
Bachelet understands his father's moral disintegration only after
Berlureau has produced the papers of a fictitious contemporary

named Henri Denis. By marrying Yvonne, Henri will be partially restored to his birthright in becoming Henri Denis-Bachelet. In scene 7 he realizes with disappointed bitterness that he must run with the tide. Yvonne pleads with him to leave his father's office but the transformed Henri snarls: "Leave! I'm not so stupid. This is where we divide the spoils and I want my share. I'll exploit the family capital too!"

The crowning irony of the play is in the symbolic last scene. Leaving his father's office, Henri is told by the Comte de Lieuville (one of his father's supporters) to salute the new portrait of the hero, Sergeant Henri Bachelet, which he has just presented to the proud parent, now the Minister of Pensions. The large portrait, now life-size, dominates the office of Bachelet *aîné* — to just the same extent as the lie on which he has based his career. In saluting his own portrait, even the war hero renounces his former values to acquiesce to a rotten way of life. Thus decay reaches purity itself, since the moral qualities of Bachelet and his courage were allied. He represented a way of life. In saluting his own portrait, Bachelet is "Valiant-for-truth" no more, and he bids adieu to everything he stood for:

Lieuville to Henri (sharply): Take your hat off to a hero.
Take your hat off.
Henri (after hesitating): I'm sorry, sir . . . it's the emotion.
(bowing profoundly to the portrait): I knew him well.

Curtain

The savage irony of the play is apparent in the most summary synopsis. Pagnol's republican forebears would have been proud of him but there was much specific comment of a topical nature that would have made the thesis of the play hard to stomach for many of the *Ligues d'Anciens Combattants* who were claiming parliamentary representation. The detailed social comment of the play is a reflection of Antoine's influence but it results in a top-heavy effect. However interesting or amusing it may be to learn, for example, that *eau de Cologne* was rebaptized *eau de Louvain* during the First World War, too many such observations slow the development. From Acts 3 to 4 the *dénouement* becomes ponderous, but the incredulity of Henri, slow to understand his father's pusillanimity, is full of pathos.

The play was directed by Gabriel Signoret, a former actor, and had a distinguished cast including Pierre Renoir as Sergeant Bachelet, Constant Rémy as his father, Suzy Prim as his wife, and Berley as Berlureau. Photographs of the set[20] reveal an orthodox, picture-frame authenticity. Piscator, or even Pitoëff, would have done something very different with it. The swelling portrait of the heroic sergeant was a brilliant idea and more could have been made of the caricature with lighting effects and less clutter elsewhere. By tightening and trimming the set, which expressed the central idea of the play, the director would have provoked changes in the text without necessarily sacrificing the better parts of the dialogue. The play lends itself to a more figurative, Brechtian set and certainly deserves a revival with this in mind.

The critical acclaim that greeted the play must have been a very satisfactory compensation for its poor box-office record. "This important work is among the most interesting of the season and reveals two dramatists of whom we can expect much" (Antoine, *L'Information*);[21] "a remarkable play" (Gabriel Boissy, *Comoedia*); "they have begun their theatrical career in a masterly fashion and I would be most surprised if one or both of the young authors did not become a great dramatist" (André Rivoire, *Le Temps*); "their play is dramatically well constructed, it's skillful, packed with action and with well-engineered climaxes" (Etienne Rey, *L'Opinion*); "this gigantic, ferocious irony nourishes an ample comedy" (Lucien Dubech, *Candide*); "in their first attempt the authors have pulled off something like a masterpiece" (Robert de Flers, *Le Figaro*). The most satisfying compliment paid to the co-authors must have been the typewritten, pirated version of the play which had a successful run at the Korsch Theater in Moscow. The most touching compliment was undoubtedly the one published in *Cahiers du Sud*, signed Charles Arno-Brun: "the warmest affection could not find any praise higher than that pronounced the day after the *première* by the professional Parisian press."[22] Pagnol's Parisian début could hardly have been more auspicious; all the play now required was an audience. Signoret, the director, could not understand the play's lack of popular success and included it in a two-week tour of Belgium. *Les Marchands de Gloire* was chosen to open the tour with a gala performance in Brussels where King Leopold personally congratulated the two authors. On his return to Paris, Signoret left the play in the hands of Fernand Rivers at the Folies Dramatiques where it was performed four times before sinking into an oblivion it did not deserve.

V   Un Direct au Coeur

For the last play on which they collaborated, Pagnol and Nivoix turned to corruption in the world of boxing. They once more chose a topical subject for their play, which was written shortly after the U.S.A. tour of Georges Carpentier, the champion French boxer. Little can be said of the structure of the play since it has never been published and the synopsis is derived from the movie version made in 1932 by Roger Lion.

Kid Marc, a successful boxer, owes his string of victories to the bribery and dishonest dealing of his manager Cassebois; he remains unaware of his manager's nefarious activity until his cousin Clairette lovingly tells all. The self-doubt and anguish that accompany the realization of the truth echo the sentiments of Henri Bachelet in *Les Marchands de Gloire* and anticipate the famous *volte-face* of Mr. Topaze. The discovery of a developing pattern in Pagnol's plays constitutes the principal interest of *Un Direct au Coeur*, which was only a modest non-failure. It was first performed in Lille at the Alhambra on March 12, 1926; it ran for a week to a polite reception. Not even Nivoix's own paper, *Comoedia*, could raise much enthusiasm, calling the play "a pleasant satire of the sporting world."[23] The anodine reviews of the play, which are providentially preserved in the *Dossier Rondel* at the Bibliothèque de l'Arsenal, record an almost negative impact, despite the participation of Pierre Bertin of the Comédie Française and André Berley who had played Berlureau in *Les Marchands de Gloire*. Charles le Marchand directed the play.

VI   Jazz

Pagnol's solo début in Paris was marked by the popular success which had eluded his joint ventures with Nivoix. The play was originally entitled *Phaëton* and written in five acts, but its title was changed to *Jazz* and the number of acts reduced to four during negotiations for its performance. The play opened in its revised form at the Grand Théâtre of Monte Carlo on December 9, 1926, before beginning its successful Parisian run at the Théâtre des Arts on December 22, becoming Pagnol's first play to pass the *centième*, the one hundredth performance. It was Antoine who first read *Jazz* and put Pagnol in touch with Rudolphe Darzens, a former associate at the Théâtre Libre, who had become director of the Théâtre des Arts;[24] Darzens had also founded *La Coopérative des Jeunes Auteurs*, an organization with the same goals as *Les Escholiers*. After discussion with Darzens and Harry Baur, who was to play the lead, arrangements were made for the performance of the play subject to some modifications in the text.

From *Ligues d'Anciens Combattants* and corruption in the boxing world, Pagnol turned for his setting to the milieu of the university. The eminence of Jean Blaise, professor of Greek at the University of Aix, is based entirely on his discovery and interpretation of an ancient Greek manuscript in Egypt which he attributed to Plato. His numerous, learned publications on the subject have made him an international authority; it is understood at the start of the play that he is shortly to receive the final accolade, a chair at the Sorbonne. The cost of such academic distinction is a solitary, celibate life with few companions. It transpires that Blaise is the dupe of his own ideas; on the eve of his nomination to the Sorbonne, he learns of the discoveries of an English researcher, Colson, which serve to refute his interpretation of the Greek manuscript. Far from being an important text of Plato, the manuscript is the work of a minor Alexandrian poet named Phaëton. His career and life's work in ruins, Blaise realizes the cost of all his now-invalidated hypotheses: he had sacrificed his youth and the pleasures of companionship to a futile task. It is at this point in the play that the incarnation of the professor's other self appears, a Freudo-Mussettist embodiment of the sensual appetite of youth, encouraging him to abandon the way of life he had previously led. This ghostly young man is reminiscent of the spectral premonitions which assailed Scrooge in Dickens's *A Christmas Carol*. Instead of replying "Humbug," the professor responds eagerly to the voice of his suppressed *alter ego junior*, going so far as to resign his position at the University of Aix. In an attempt to savor the freedom and the pleasures he had hitherto shunned, Blaise even proposes marriage to one of his students, Cécile Boissier. The student accepts Blaise's proposal but in the ensuing few days the vacillating professor fails to consummate both his union and his conversion to the doctrine of life and love. Mlle Boissier abandons him and the desperate ghost of the younger Blaise taunts the professor for his failure, finally driving him to suicide.

The development of the play is nicely judged. In the first act, the complacent professor fails to heed the advice of his friend Barricant who points out the dangers of excessive isolation; the animosity of the Dean toward Blaise also serves as a hint of impending disaster. Sure enough, the end of the act brings the shattering news of the Englishman's discoveries. In the second act, Blaise continues mechanically with his job. Finally, in the course of a lecture, he declares his conversion by renouncing teaching and scholarship, exhorting his class to enjoy their lives, unlike him. Where the conversion of Henri Bachelet was delayed for the sake of a final *coup de théâtre*, the conversion of Blaise occurs in the middle of the play. This turning point is marked by a long speech in the form of a lecture in which Blaise deploys all his eloquence and erudition; in order to maintain the flood of inspired rhetoric Pagnol borrows passages from *Le Mariage de Peluque*, the serial story written for *Fortunio* in 1924, later to be published as the novel *Pirouettes*.[25] As Pagnol's self-borrowing suggests, much of Blaise's tendentious speech is better suited to the novel but when delivered as a lecture it becomes theatrically justifiable. The turning point in the play thus arrives in Act 2, after the destruction of the dikes which had artificially protected Blaise's pseudo-scholarship and isolation. The balance of the play, the remaining two acts, maintains the links between wasted scholarship and the resentment caused by suppressed pleasures. The last two acts show Blaise's failure to adapt to intellectual then sensual disappointment. He does too little, too late, to redeem his situation. He resigns his position in Act 2 and his marriage proposal is accepted in Act 3 but he hesitates: not sure whether he has already gone too far or not been decisive enough, he finally loses his bride-to-be to her classmate Stepanovitch in Act 4. The double disappointment is now complete and irrevocable. Having lost his intellectual platform in life, he had sought consolation in the pleasures of youth which he had never yet tasted; Blaise's indecision before the urgent pressing of his younger self immediately suggests, however, that his search for sensual consolation is doomed to failure. The intervention of the younger self merely postpones the inevitable recognition of total failure. Rather than face reality, Blaise grasps at the illusory possibility of reliving the past. When finally confronted with the reality of failure, he takes his own life.

The moral of the story is far from original and is, at times, ponderous, but the development of Pagnol's technique is evident. The plot shows control and organization; the formula is in constant progression from *Les Marchands de Gloire* to *Topaze*. The *scène à faire*, the *coup de théâtre* of the hero's conversion, has now shifted from the conclusion to the middle of the play. On this fulcrum depends the *dénouement*. Blaise's conversion was halfhearted and artificially induced by the ghost of the younger self; it took two acts for

the inspired poet-orator of Act 2 to shrink in stature to nothing, losing his reputation, his position, and finally the girl who represented
the success of his conversion. The contrasts and parallels with
Topaze will prove to be remarkable. Pagnol's particular talent for
the punch line, the *formule à l'emporte-pièce*, is also confirmed in
Jazz. When spoken by as redoubtable an actor as Raimu, the effect is
devastating, but the Dean's remark to the janitor could hardly be
more cutting: "My poor Bazin, if stupidity were painful you would
never stop howling."[26] Sometimes tinged with the crudeness of a
street-corner *apache*, the *formule* can also be touched with cynicism,
as with the worldly Stepanovitch's "Most of the women you've
never had are the ones you've never asked for."[27] Inevitably, the
sententia can lapse into trite cliché: "When you've missed the train
there's no point in running after it."[28] In this particular case, Pagnol
uses a *formule* that lacks originality in order to match the un-
imaginative traditionalism of the speaker, Melanie, Blaise's maid. In
the course of his plays and scenarii, Pagnol shows an increasing
mastery of this device which has been so often dismissed as a distinctive stigma of the *boulevard;* this criticism has been too often applied too mechanically to be reasoned with here. Admittedly, the
formule can be dangerous if used indiscriminately, without due
regard for shades of character. The increased use of the heavy punch
line in Pagnol's subsequent work is simply evidence of the impact of
Raimu whose explosive style of acting it so admirably suited and for
whom Pagnol so often created a leading part.

The cast for the 1926 Théâtre des Arts production was perhaps the
best that Pagnol had had until then: Harry Baur took the lead, Pierre
Renoir played the part of the professor's younger self, and Orane
Demazis played the part of Cécile Boissier. Pagnol's association with
Orane Demazis was to last, professionally at least, until 1938 with *Le
Schpountz:* in the meantime, she bore Pagnol a son, whom they
named Jean-Pierre. *Jazz* was directed at the Théâtre des Arts by
Rodolphe Darzens to whom it is dedicated. The play was revived at
the Gymnase in 1940 but it could hardly have consoled Parisians
during their first Christmas under German occupation to be ex-
horted to make hay while the sun shines. *Jazz* lacks the verve and
satiric edge of *Les Marchands de Gloire* but, although weighed
down by the mediocrity of the dull professor Blaise, it impresses as a
better-organized play. It is *Horace* after *Le Cid* and the same
impression of anticlimax prevails.

VII Topaze

Justifiably famous, *Topaze* is such a milestone in Pagnol's career that he has often written about the circumstances of its composition and the events of the memorable first night.[29] Marcel Achard issues a salutary word of warning about his close friend Pagnol's overexuberant memory: "On the days when Marcel is well disposed toward humanity, as is usually the case, six directors accepted the play simultaneously and with raving enthusiasm . . . on the days when he is not well disposed toward humanity, then everybody refused it and Max Maurey only accepted it after an aggressive intervention by Antoine."[30] Pagnol's definitive version of the story is a compromise: five directors, Gémier (l'Odéon), Max Dearly (Théâtre de Paris), Quinson (La Michodière), Jouvet (Comédie des Champs-Elysées), and Darzens (Théâtre des Arts), accepted the play but Antoine obliged Max Maurey (Théâtre des Variétés) to stage it.[31] Antoine's goodwill and cooperation is a constant: *Topaze* is dedicated to him. Everything augured the play's success, from the final reading to *Les Moins de Trente Ans*, which it triumphantly negotiated,[32] to the all-important patronage of Antoine. Success this time mattered more to Pagnol than for any of his previous plays; he had resigned from his teaching post to write it. His confidence was amply rewarded by a continuous run of nearly three years for over six hundred performances; so long, in fact, that the children's rôles had to be recast. As Achard wrote: "Marcel, who lived an impoverished existence before the play, suddenly found fame, fame of a kind that is just impossible to convey to people nowadays."[33] The play opened at the Théâtre des Variétés on October 9, 1928, and a wonder-struck Achard could only suppose that this must have been like the first night of Rostand's *Cyrano*.

Pagnol, of course, had left a school to write about one. Topaze is a humble teacher in the *pension Muche*, a private boarding school run by the pompous, Dickensian bully Muche. Ensconced in his dingy classroom, dedicated to his unruly pupils, and infatuated with the sly Ernestine (a colleague and the director's daughter), the naive and gullible Topaze fails to see how he is being exploited; he is even content to be awarded *moralement* the *palmes académiques* (a routine recognition of teaching services which consists of a purple rosette worn in the buttonhole). When the Baroness Pitart-Vergniolles visits the school to ask why her son's academic record is so poor, Topaze fails to understand that such an influential person (with three children at the school) should and could be placated by an immediate upgrading of the son's marks; on being asked why Pitart-Vergniolles is bottom of the class, Topaze gives the stunningly honest answer: "Because he got zero."

Incensed by his employee's tactlessness, Muche finally learns that Topaze, completely deceived by Ernestine who had flirted with him only to wheedle him into marking her scripts for her, has presumed to raise his eyes to the director's own daughter and to propose marriage. Although Topaze was indignantly rebuffed by Ernestine, Muche seizes the proposal as an opportunity to rid himself of such an embarrassing element on his staff. Act 1 closes with the dismissal of Topaze. Fortunately for Topaze, he is acquainted with Madame Suzy Courtois, whose son is having private lessons with him. In Act 2 the unemployed teacher turns for help to Suzy. At the beginning of the act she is seen in her boudoir in conversation with Castel-Bénac; their dialogue is unexpectedly tough and racy, coming as a surprise after one's earlier impressions of Suzy in Act 1, seen through the respectful eyes of Topaze. It soon transpires that Suzy is no more nor less than the mistress of Castel-Bénac, who is a crooked local politician. As a town councillor and contractor at the same time, Castel-Bénac conducts a lucrative business by selling to the city the equipment or property which he had previously incited them to buy. He takes two basic precautions. The first consists of maintaining a dossier of incriminating evidence on all potential enemies. His main defense, however, is in the creation of artificially independent companies headed by a front man, an *homme de paille*, who is in Castel-Bénac's pocket. The main qualifications for the *homme de paille* are ignorance, obedience, and silence. The dismissal of Topaze from the *pension Muche* comes at an opportune moment for Suzy and Castel-Bénac since their previous *homme de paille*, Roger de Berville, was beginning to show too much initiative, asking for too much money for his signature. Topaze is offered the job in terms which flatter his integrity and at a salary, derisory for Castel-Bénac, which seems fabulous to the ex-schoolteacher. A brief crisis is encountered when Topaze's predecessor, de Berville, returns to take his revenge for his expropriation by explaining the crooked machinery of Castel-Bénac's business to the horrified Topaze. The experience and guile of Suzy save the day: she responds to the moral outrage of Topaze by playing the part of a defenseless damsel, victim of the machinations of the unscrupulous Castel-Bénac. She sows the seeds of real hope in the fast-beating heart of innocent Topaze by suggesting that he provisionally comply with Castel-Bénac's demands, insinuating himself into the ogre's confidence: "Thus, bit by bit, you can study him, find out where he is vulnerable and then, when you think the moment is ripe, you can strike him down and save me."[34] And so the knight-errant Topaze enters Act 3 and the offices of Castel-Bénac's shady business.

Act 3 shows the torments and revelations of Topaze's new life: plagued by his conscience and would-be blackmailers (who are quickly nullified by Castel-Bénac's dossier of incriminating information), Topaze loses his nerve to a point where Suzy and Castel-Bénac, fearing he will give the game away, start to look for another *prête-nom*. In the meantime, however, impressed by the tangible signs of Topaze's new status, Muche arrives unsolicited at the office to give him his daughter's hand in marriage; then Castel-Bénac arrives with the *palmes académiques*. These prizes, which once seemed so remote on the most distant horizons of Topaze's ambitions, now fall unwanted into his lap. Although he has learned of Suzy's duplicity toward him, Topaze has also learned that she does not really love Castel-Bénac; in the hope of conquering Suzy and with the evidence of his new prestige that Muche has just presented, Topaze resolves to assert the authority, hitherto nominal, which is legally his. He accepts the *palmes académiques*, refuses Ernestine, and asks Castel-Bénac for one more chance to prove himself.

In Act 4, some time later, the new Topaze appears. In an amazing transformation from the previous act, Topaze is now crisp, decisive, and authoritarian. Wielding the power that was always legally his as head of the firm, *l'homme de paille* becomes *l'homme de fer* and fires Castel-Bénac, discreetly inviting Suzy to remain; as Nero pointed out to Britannicus's fiancée, she goes with the job. Contrary to all expectations, Topaze has executed the plan proposed as a bluff by Suzy in Act 2. The play closes with a visit from Tamise, Topaze's former colleague at the *pension Muche*, to whom Topaze offers a job and a summary of the new philosophy before withdrawing to Suzy's next-door boudoir.

The play has the verve of *Les Marchands de Gloire* and the control of *Jazz:* the dialogue, *jeux de scène*, and *dénouement* are impeccable. Rarely have Pagnol's stage directions been so well conceived and purposeful, complementing to maximum effect the innumerable crackling exchanges in the play. A few examples will suffice:

The Baroness (ominously):	And why is my son bottom?
Muche (turning to Topaze):	Why bottom?
Topaze:	Because he got zero.
Muche (nervously to the Baroness):	Because he got zero.
The Baroness:	And why did he get zero?
Muche (sternly to Topaze):	Why did he get zero?
Topaze:	Because he did not understand the question.
Muche (ingratiating to Baroness):	Did not understand the problem.[35]

Suzy's antics in the last scene of Act 2 (her bogus love scene with Topaze) are so clearly defined by Pagnol as to border on Feydeau-esque farce. Later on, the anguish of Topaze, caused by his pangs of conscience, is succinctly conveyed at a number of points in Act 3; the most concise is:

Castel-Bénac:	Ring me with the results at Maxim's at about eight o'clock. [*To Suzy*] Come on, dear. . . .
Suzy:	Yes, the state attorney must be waiting.
Topaze (terrified):	The state attorney? What for?
Castel-Bénac:	To eat, of course!"[36]

Some of Pagnol's better turns of phrase occur in the dialogue of *Topaze*. There is the deathless pragmatism of Panicault talking of discipline at school ("You don't look for the culprits, you choose 'em.") and the outraged dignity of the dismissed Roger de Berville ("Sir, in your family people may 'scram' but in mine they take their leave."). The plot is tight with good links: at the end of Act 1, after his dismissal from the *pension Muche*, Topaze writes on the blackboard a simple message for his class which also serves as a symbolic announcement of what is to follow: "The class on morals is postponed." The following act opens in Suzy's boudoir. Topaze in love enters Act 3 and Castel-Bénac's business in the belief he is helping Suzy. He learns in Act 3 that Suzy has deceived him but, at least reassured that she never loved Castel-Bénac, he can still live with hope and an adaptation of the plan originally proposed by Suzy in Act 2. The transformation in his life is marked by the contrast between his classroom in Act 1 and the office he nominally controls in Act 3; where the former is adorned with such slogans as: "Money does not bring happiness," the latter contains such reminders for its

occupant as "Time is money." There is a further echo of the classroom in Act 4 when the map of Morocco is hung on the wall to il-
lustrate Topaze's interests there.

In Act 4 Topaze takes over. His transformation is motivated by
love, just as Henri Bachelet's conversion in *Les Marchands de Gloire*
is provoked by his desire to marry Yvonne, but the composition of
Topaze is tighter than anything that preceded it. The play virtually
bowls along of its own volition with the actors simply executing the
instructions left in place by Pagnol; his control is so absolute that it
creates some of the elements of farce, in the most elevated meaning
of the word: unidimensional characters resembling types and bold,
rapid dialogue. The plot, as a vehicle of social criticism and the
author's will, reigns supreme.

The moral of the play has sometimes caused confusion. Since he
had himself been a schoolmaster like Topaze, Pagnol seems to be admitting corruption and advocating abandonment of disinterested
public service. The play is, of course, ironical from beginning to end.
Irony implies a choice between real and improbable alternatives;
Topaze is an allegory which presents the contemptible alternative to
the obvious remedy for the ills of society. So contemptible is this
alternative that it provokes a return to probity and plain dealing.
The irony of the allegorical alternative contained in the play may, in
one sense, be taken at face value: if everyone were to turn to graft,
then the present profiteers are warned that they will soon be ousted.
Pagnol is genuinely concerned at the state of society, as the words of
the hairdresser *en epigraphe* to the play remind us: "You know sir, if
society does not change, it will end up destroying the good." Pagnol
has written that the personality of his father Joseph is not entirely
alien to the character of Topaze,[37] but there is also a suspicion that
Marcel Pagnol himself finds expression in *Topaze*. Satire often aims
to provoke reform; the fact that this is Pagnol's last satirical play
might therefore suggest that he here abandons hope of further
reform. Certainly the extensive irony of the play is in itself a startling
supposition of wholesale corruption in a society where the simple
schoolmaster is the last to receive tangible benefits. As Topaze sar-
castically explains to Tamise at the end of the play: "The wealthy
have always been very good to us intellectuals, granting us the joy of
studying, the honour of working, and the sacred pleasure of duty
done: for themselves they only keep second-rate pleasures like
caviar, partridge *salmis*, the Rolls Royce, champagne and central
heating. . . ." Pagnol had always intended to be a writer but the tim-

ing of his resignation from Condorcet coincides curiously with the theme of *Topaze*.

The play is a classic indictment of corruption in Third Republic politics. It is perhaps *the* satiric masterpiece of this period; with *Knock* (Romains) and *Voulez-Vous Jouer avec Moâ* (Achard), it is one of the most successful plays of the time. Achard's play saved Dullin from bankruptcy and Romains's play saved Jouvet many times. On fourteen occasions, over a period of twenty-five years, Jouvet avoided financial disaster by turning to a *reprise* of *Knock*, "*pièce clé, pièce phénix, pièce st-bernard, pièce providence, protective et tutélaire.*"[38] Pagnol himself admired the play: when he changed the title of *Monsieur Topaze* to *Topaze* it was in order to emulate the staccato enigma of *Knock*.[39] *Knock* and *Topaze* have subsequently been compared many times; both plays were revived in 1966 and Poirot-Delpech wrote in *Le Monde:* "The doctor-promoter of Jules Romains and the teacher-businessman of Marcel Pagnol are of the same family. Each in his own way more or less resigned, they both symbolize the panic of a generation of university graduates, still naive and utopian, before the rampant immorality of capitalist *mores.* . . . Like Jules Romains, Marcel Pagnol demonstrates the enduring theatrical qualities of bold, deft strokes."[40]

It would perhaps have been better for Pagnol's reputation, and for French theater, if *Topaze* had been performed, like *Knock* and *Voulez-Vous Jouer avec Moâ,* at the Atelier or the Champs-Elysées instead of at the Variétés; better use might have been made of his capacity to create lively, well-defined comic characters. Such a rendezvous, so full of promise, was not to be and *Topaze* was presented on a heavy, naturalistic set. Pagnol was not himself unhappy with Maurey's production and he was delighted with his cast: André Lefaur as Topaze, Pauley as Castel-Bénac, a talented newcomer Pierre Larquey as Tamise, and Jeanne Provost, of the Comédie Française, as Suzy Courtois. The impact of the play was such that it has been performed many times since and has been adapted for the movies on three occasions: in 1932 by Louis Gasnier, starring Louis Jouvet as Topaze, in 1936 by Pagnol himself, with Arnaudy in the lead, and in 1950 by Pagnol again but this time with Fernandel in the lead. The limitations of the initial theatrical production are perpetuated in the film versions of the play: the inherent realism of the cinema was no more suited to the allegory of *Topaze* than the naturalistic set which had traditionally weighed it down in the theater. The influence of Antoine was not always beneficial

although, according to some, *Topaze* would never have been performed without his intervention.[41]

VIII   *The Formula*

Topaze is the superb culmination of a cycle of development in
Pagnol's theater; all the previous plays were steps toward the perfection of *Topaze* with its sparkling dialogue, tightly controlled structure, and cutting irony. It is evident that Pagnol concentrated on the
conversion/*coup de théâtre* structure in his plays up to this point.
Sergeant Bachelet, Kid Marc, and Professor Blaise were all, in a
sense, *hommes de paille* before a painful revelation transformed
them; the revelation corresponds to conversion and climax. Pagnol
tried his formula with the climax at different points. Only at the end
of the play do Sergeant Bachelet and Kid Marc, nonparticipants in
their respective frauds but indispensable front men, discover how
they have been used. The conversion provoked by bitter disillusion
will lead to deeds which can only be guessed at. In the case of Blaise,
a dupe of his own spurious scholarship and misplaced values, the
revelation and climax arrive in the middle of the play during his lecture in Act 2; the last two acts show his failure to sustain his bold
new resolution. The conversion of Topaze is invisible; somewhere
between Acts 3 and 4 he steeled himself to his task, with love as the
spur. Only the consequences of the conversion are observed, and the
effect derived from the contrast between "before" and "after," with
the intervening conversion suppressed, is extraordinary. Compared
with Blaise's conversion, Topaze's is all the more decisive for not being seen; where Blaise's resolve took two acts to peter out, Topaze
moved swiftly in the last act to acquire a position, prestige, and the
woman who symbolized his success. Where Blaise lost Cécile Boissier, Topaze won Suzy Courtois.

These variations on the same structural theme reveal Pagnol's
patient, methodical search for a formula: all the elements of the
equation fell neatly into place with *Topaze*. Like the man who has
discovered perpetual motion, Pagnol could go no further along these
lines. *Topaze* is the last of the structured protest plays; all dominated
by a thesis, they sacrifice character to plot, humor to satire. In a
volte-face as amazing as that of Topaze himself, Pagnol turned to
the comedy of character where the plot is never more than a simple
pretext for the presentation of full, rich, and enduring portraits.
Where Sergeant Bachelet, Professor Blaise, and Topaze are puppets
manipulated to demonstrate an idea, Marius, Fanny, and César have

an immutable authenticity which at times seems almost independent of the author. There will be no more conversions, revelations,
and *coups de théâtre;* the characters are warmly presented as they
are.

IX   Marius

Although the two plays are so different, *Topaze* and *Marius* were
written concurrently. As a brilliantly constructed satire, *Topaze*
called for arduous concentration — "and when my inspiration
flagged," writes Pagnol, "I typed the manuscript of *Marius* and so
finished both plays at the same time."[42] Where the allegory of
Topaze verges on caricature, the free-wheeling dialogue of *Marius* is
an authentic echo of the colorful *vieux-port* in Marseilles; joyous,
spontaneous, and free from polemics, *Marius* might almost have
been written as a relaxation. Where universal corruption is depicted
in *Topaze,* all the characters in *Marius* are likable. Like *Topaze,* the
play contains some oblique references to Pagnol's own life. In a state
of technical unemployment, he may sometimes have recalled with
nostalgia the apparent security of his life in Marseilles; he had, after
all, experienced the same pangs of departure as Marius. According
to Pagnol, the play would never have been performed in Paris
without the disinterested advice of Esposito, director of the Alcazar
and Variétés in Marseilles; it was he who convinced Pagnol that the
play was of more than mere regional interest but who encouraged
him, at the same time, to look for a cast of authentic Marseillais to
interpret it. The first actor on Pagnol's list was Raimu, who accepted
the offer and thus entered into a partnership that became legendary.
Of a temperament and a build that the French call *une force de la
nature,* Raimu had strongly held opinions about most matters;
whatever the text of *Marius* may originally have been, it underwent
a number of modifications as a result of Raimu's intervention.
Indeed, Raimu's contribution to Pagnol's career is so important that
he should be properly introduced.

X   *Raimu*

An actor of proportions as epic as his name, Jules-Auguste-César
Muraire was born in Toulon on December 18, 1883.[43] He was a
prompter at the Alhambra in Marseilles before becoming an actor
there with the stage name of "Rallum"; after long experience in
Marseilles music hall, he subsequently moved to the Concert Mayol
in Paris where he changed his stage name to "Raimu," a pun on his

family name. He was employed at the Théâtre Marigny when Pagnol approached him with the part of Panisse in *Marius*. His performance (as César) in the stage and screen versions of *Marius* catapulted him into celebrity relatively late in his career. Apart from his work with Pagnol, Raimu's most notable subsequent performances were to be in *Gribouille* (Marc Allégret, 1937), *Les Inconnus dans la Maison* (Clouzot/Decoin, 1942), and *Le Bourgeois Gentilhomme* at the Comédie Française in 1943. He died on September 20, 1946, deeply mourned by Marcel Pagnol with whom he had developed a remarkable understanding: "It is not possible to make a speech over the grave of a father, a brother, or a son and you were all three for me: I shall not speak at your grave. Besides, I never knew how to speak, it was Raimu who spoke for me. Your great, eloquent voice is silent and my grief silences me. . . ."[44] The effective, working association of Pagnol and Raimu spanned a decade from 1929 with *Marius* to 1940 with *La Fille du Puisatier*. Much of Pagnol's work in that time was built around the extraordinary character of the bear-like Raimu.

Raimu was one of the few people to whom Pagnol consistently deferred; in practical matters of stage interpretation the judgment of Jules, as his friends called him, was law. With his intuitive flair, Raimu sensed that it was the part of César (*patron* of the Bar de la Marine) that he should play in *Marius*, even though Pagnol had come to him with the part of Panisse. The scene with Pagnol in which Raimu refused the part of Panisse, insisting on the amplified rôle of César for himself, demonstrates, in Pagnol's words, "the intuition of genius but an absurd irrationality."[45] After Pagnol had remonstrated with Raimu, pointing out the importance of the rôle of Panisse (as originally conceived), Raimu exploded: "I want to be the owner of the bar and I want the play to happen on my premises! Your Charpin [the actor who was to play César but who eventually became famous as Panisse] is less well known than me and I, Raimu, should not have to put myself out to visit him. Charpin should come to my place. . . . If you are not sensitive enough to understand that, there's no point in continuing the coversation."[46]

Dogmatic, explosive, petulant, irascible, touchy, and vain, Raimu displayed all his faults with the candor of a child; it was his fundamental naiveté which made him so suspicious and yet so lovable. He had serious misgivings about Pagnol's inviting Pierre Fresnay to play the part of César's son Marius: "he only laughs once a month. And what's more, what's more, this PROTESTANT is from Alsace!

And what's more, he's a tragic actor in the Comédie Française. . . .
It's very difficult to maintain a Marseilles accent in a part as long as
Marius, but for that protestant Alsatian from the Comédie Française, it's impossible!"[47] With the sure instinct of a father, Pagnol
guessed that these objections were only pretexts, that Raimu's
hostility was based on suspicion:

Raimu:	Have you seen his contract?
Pagnol:	I drafted it. Besides, you know very well that you top the bill. . . .
Raimu (after some thought):	Well, it's worth a try. We can give him lessons on the accent. . . . You should call him and invite him to dinner tonight.

This was precisely the character that Raimu portrayed in *Marius:* he
was given the rôle of César (which was revised and expanded for
him) but his part required essentially the projection of his own in-
imitable personality. Raimu may have had some limitations as an actor but he was peerless as himself. Breathing confidentially, like a
sage old patriarch to his son: "*Marius, l'honneur c'est comme les al-
lumettes: ça ne sert qu'une fois,*"[48] or opening his lungs with a fierce
bark: "*Quand on fera danser les couillons, tu ne seras pas à
l'orchestre,*"[49] Raimu found the perfect expression of himself in the
lines that Pagnol composed for him. With his stage life overlapping
his real life, Raimu became the *grand patron* not only of the Bar de
la Marine but of the rehearsals and production of *Marius;* he took
charge of all stage preparations for the production of the play.

XI   *The Play before the Trilogy*

With Raimu as the sheet-anchor of *Marius*, a certain number of
decisions were taken entirely out of Pagnol's hands; former associates from the Marseilles music halls (Alida Rouffe as Honorine;
Dullac as Escartefigue; Maupi as the chauffeur) were accom-
modated with parts and it was, of course, Raimu's idea to revamp
the rôle of César and to offer the rôle of Panisse to Fernand Charpin.
Pagnol's judgment prevailed in the selection of Pierre Fresnay as
Marius; like the great professional actor he was, Fresnay prepared
himself for the part by working for two weeks in a bar on the *vieux-
port.* The rôle of César's son Marius, a prey to sea fever and the call
of distant lands, runs parallel to Pagnol's own situation insofar as it

entailed departure from Marseilles. Pagnol has often claimed that his contemporary, Louis Brauquier, a sea-faring poet from Marseilles, was the original model for the rôle.[50] Brauquier has just as often repudiated the claim but many of the poems in an early anthology entitled *Et l'au delà de Suez*[51] (1923) are indisputable reminders of the lure of strange-sounding countries. Like Raimu, Orane Demazis as Fanny also had a tailor-made part: both Demazis and Fanny came from Oran in Algeria and both had fair complexions.[52] The sequel to *Marius* is entitled *Fanny* and is dedicated to Orane Demazis "who was Fanny herself, to a point where we could not imagine her differently."[53]

With all these components to bear in mind, the shape of Pagnol's play was virtually dictated to him. With parts written for Raimu, Fernand Charpin, Orane Demazis, and a fourth part based on a mixture of Pagnol's own experience and a syndrome which was common in Marseilles, *Marius* could be nothing other than a romance in which a young man abandons his betrothed and his aging father for the sea. The play is, in short, the result of a corporate effort. This first experience of work with a team, where everybody attended all rehearsals whether required or not, made a profound impression upon Pagnol and his work. Not only was the experience extremely enjoyable to all concerned but the work, written by a Marseillais, set in Marseilles, developed and modified by a team of experienced southerners (with Fresnay as the talented exception), was able to catch and hold the elusive note of genuine authenticity. It is to Pagnol's eternal credit that he recognized the value of a corporate contribution and admitted it; it was to become his particular style and the team of *Marius* would be the nucleus for most future enterprizes. The pleasure and the theoretic logic of the experiment were confirmed by the stunning success of the play. Only a few months after the *première* of *Topaze*, currently running at the Variétés, *Marius* opened on March 9, 1929, at the Théâtre de Paris; it ran for three years continuously (including a summer reprise) with over one thousand performances, breaking all box-office records of the time; like *Topaze*, it has never been included in the repertoire of the Comédie Française. When it completed its run, Pagnol followed up immediately with a sequel entitled *Fanny*.

Despite the later creation of two sequels to *Marius* with *Fanny* (1931) and *César* (1936), the play is a self-contained entity. The notion of a *Trilogie de Marseille* is retrospective. Like an Italian Neorealist movie, the conclusion of *Marius* is open-ended, fortuitously allowing Pagnol to create subsequent episodes, but nothing in the text or the circumstances of composition permits anticipation of a sequel. As a comedy of character, the play naturally puts less stress on structure, plot, and conclusion. As Molière's plays have sometimes to be concluded in an arbitrary fashion with the providential return of a long-lost relation, so the schooner *Malaisie* appears as a *navis ex machina* to take Marius away. To claim that as early as 1929 Pagnol foresaw sequels to the play and contrived a conclusion to *Marius* that would allow such development, is to make a big assumption. Charles Rostaing, *professeur titulaire* in Provençal studies at the University of Aix, has written a meticulous study of the so-called *Trilogie de Marseille*,[54] confirming that *Marius* is the most carefully written of the three plays; choosing, for example, the noninversion of the subject as a common form of solecism in French, he lists 42 examples in *Marius*, 62 in *Fanny*, and 179 examples in *César*. This proves perhaps no more than that plays are more literary than screenplays, *vérité de la Palissade*, but the implication of Rostaing's long analysis is that *Marius* is the original inspiration to which *Fanny* and *César* are hastily added as afterthoughts. The basic interest of the play is centered on the characters, thus the first priority of the dramatist is to maintain their consistency and continuity if he is to write further anecdotes, or *tiroirs*, which could be added almost *ad infinitum;* the term *comédie à tiroirs* might, therefore, be more appropriate than *trilogie* if the latter is taken to imply previous intent.

Marius is a romance in four acts centered on the opposing attractions for Marius of a life at sea and his love for Fanny. The scene for the four acts is César's Bar de la Marine on the *vieux-port* where Marius works as a bartender for his father and where Fanny looks after a fish stall just outside. From early in the play, Marius plans furtively with the mysterious Piquoiseau to run away to sea. Fanny, in an attempt to stimulate the interest of Marius, flirts with the sailmaker Panisse, a client and contemporary of César the widower father of Marius. Panisse has even gone so far as to broach the question of marriage with Fanny to her widowed mother Honorine, owner of the fish stall, who approves. Snared by her bluff and in a fit of jealous rage, Marius threatens to thrash Panisse at the end of Act 1. Fanny thus feels free to declare her love for Marius in Act 2: her declaration is not rebuffed by Marius but it causes him embarrassment since it coincides with his planned escape to sea. He had always loved Fanny but his plans to go to sea had prevented him from making her an honorable proposition; confronted by the choice between Fanny and the sea in the climax of Act 2, his anguish is solved by the return to ship of the man he was to replace.

Fanny and Marius thus remain provisionally free to love but they are living on borrowed time in the remaining two acts. Despite their ripening love, Marius is still attracted to a sea-faring life. Fanny realizes this and when, at the end of Act 3, she overhears a tormented Marius refusing a position on the *Malaisie* for love of her, she determines to sacrifice her love for him by inciting him to go to sea. The couple had been indiscreet and there is a strong rumor in the neighborhood that they are lovers, but Fanny is not pregnant (this is only established in *Fanny*, Act 1, Tableau 2, scene 6), and the only obstacle to the departure of Marius is Fanny's love for him, which he had always tried to discourage because of his passion for the sea. Fanny makes the necessary sacrifice but her plight is less tragic than that of Madame Butterfly, for example, since Marius is sure to return one day to his home in Marseilles; and there is always the consoling knowledge that he had loved only her and loved her enough to refuse to go to sea when an opportunity presented itself. Fanny thus registered a notable moral victory before surrendering her Marius and she was always sheltered by the permanent offer of marriage with the prosperous Panisse. The play ends with Fanny in Act 4 feigning indifference to Marius, who then feels free to escape to the *Malaisie* which is about to depart. The formal development of the plot hinges on the love affair of Marius and Fanny overshadowed by Marius's inevitable departure one day. It is not, however, in the melodramatic plot but in the incidental characters and episodes that the originality of the play is to be found.

As a synopsis reveals, the character of César is not a necessary part of the plot: Marius loves his father so César is not even a pretext for his son's escape to sea. César, however, on stage for most of the play, holds everything together, particularly when played by Raimu, supervising and dispensing justice with his highly colored exclamations; his gags (the fly-catcher liqueur bottle of Marius, his friend Landolfi in Paris) and his thunderous interventions dominate the play. The famous games of cards, first of *manille* which Panisse abandons because César cheats and then of *manille aux enchères* which Escartefigue abandons because César insults him, are among the high points of the play, so rich in warm, colorful humor. Objectionable but lovable, César reaches astonishingly lifelike proportions, as do his clients and accomplices: Panisse, the rotund sailmaker (a *panisse* is a small, squat loaf in Marseilles parlance);

Monsieur Brun, the dapper customs inspector from Lyons, and Escartefigue, *cocu* and skipper of the *fériboite* ("a buoy with two propellers," "a boat with two rear-ends") which plies across the *vieux-port*. Escartefigue's inflated view of his maritime functions provokes the merciless taunts of the other *habitués* of the Bar de la Marine.

Many of the actors who performed in these incidental rôles remained with Pagnol throughout his film-making career, guaranteeing a fresh, animated backcloth of *vraisemblance* to his work. The part of Fanny is the prototype for most of Pagnol's future female rôles: a willing martyr to love, often represented as a *mère célibataire*. Woman is the *primum mobile* of Pagnol's world, the ultimate sanction of man's success. She is never more deserving of love than when she assumes the responsibility of motherhood alone; only the forces of reaction condemn her. Conversely, the parable of Zoé runs through *Marius* as a warning against excessive license.

The remarkable strength and depth of the character portrayal is confirmed in a curious way. The unusually high number of private jokes among the characters creates a strong sense of inner complicity in the play. The stage joke is normally directed outwards to the audience for effect, but in *Marius* it is frequently directed inwards as a demonstration of the characters' full relationship with each other. Undoubtedly a consequence of the harmonious, corporate effort of Pagnol's *troupe*, the phenomenon is a striking example of the life and authenticity of the play. A selection of the numerous examples will suffice to make the point:

César: And you wouldn't see so many thankless, rebellious children.
Fanny: Well, if my mother were to slap me, I don't know what I'd do.
César: You don't know what you'd do? You would go and cry in a corner, that's all. And if your poor father were alive to give you a cuff from time to time, it wouldn't do you any harm. (*Marius and Fanny look conspiratorially at each other and laugh. César rumbles on*) Who'd have kids, the way they plague you![55]

The characters' "conspiracy" is sometimes linked to the traditional gag:

Cesar: . . . And that's why (*he tries to unstick his finger*) these bottles are easier to pick up than to put down! (*He manages to put the bottle down on the counter. Marius laughs*) And you laugh!

Marius: You're laughing too.
César: Maybe, but I'm laughing at my own patience. *(He goes to the window and watches the passers-by.)*[56]

Rostaing has also pointed out how Pagnol skillfully varies the dosage of *provençalismes* in the play according to milieu and mood. Of an inferior social background to Honorine, the chauffeur normally uses more *provençalismes*, but when Honorine loses her temper she relapses almost entirely into a Provençal dialect: "*Ma pitchouno couchado émè un homme, aquéou brigand de Marius*",[57] similarly Panisse erupts in Provençal when he catches César cheating at cards: "*Siou mestré Panisse et siès pas pron fin per m'aganta!*"[58]

The archetypal values implicit in *Marius* appear again in later works. The tension between the younger and older generations dominates and is conveyed effectively by the parallels established between the César - Marius and Honorine - Fanny couples. Insisting on a respect for traditional values of honor, industry, and respect for parents, parental authority is, however, softened by a sense of humor and real affection. The bonds between the two generations are closer than usual since both parents are alone: Honorine is a widow and César is a widower. As an *ensemble* they therefore form a natural family; Marius and Fanny were in this sense destined for each other. Both Honorine and César bridle when corrected by their children, even on the most elementary detail: "*Tu ne vas pas apprendre à ton père/ta mère*" is their reflex response. Survival of the family depends upon a proper understanding of parental authority but César and Honorine both have a bark that is worse than their bite.

They perhaps insist on proper forms of respect because they feel themselves to be so vulnerable, both having a deep affection for their children which they find hard to dissimulate. It is curious that they should feel the need to dissimulate at all, but displays of emotion between them and their children are treated with restraint and some embarrassment:

Marius: I love you.
César (quite moved
and shocked):   But I love you too. Why do you say that?
Marius: Because I can see that you are concerned about me and you worry about me. And it makes me think I love you.
César (very moved):   But of course, you chump.[59]

If firm parental control is accepted by adult children it is because it is recognized as an expression of real love. The parents reveal their concern for their children to others on a number of occasions; both Honorine and César are fierce in their defense, whether it is Honorine protesting at the suffering Marius inflicts on Fanny or César defending his son against Panisse. Pagnol presents these family relationships with deep insight and a great delicacy of feeling. The family framework is traditional, authoritarian but humane.

Equally traditional is the masculinity of *Marius:* since the play is set in a bar, the masculine values do not come as a surprise but they do mark future works of Pagnol. César takes a vicarious pride in his son's sexual prowess and Panisse's mourning for his widow is quite superficial. Pagnol exposes without complacency the frequently coarse attitude of bars' older *habitués* toward women. The finer feelings, sentiment and romance, are represented by the younger generation, Marius and Fanny, although the quandary of Marius and his eventual departure also symbolize a masculine revolt against domesticity. The rock-like permanence and familiarity of these old-fashioned values contribute as much to the play's continuing popularity as the ebullience and zest of its characters. The play itself is demonstrably one of the finest contemporary comedies of character, benefitting from a rare mass identification of the actors with their rôles, in the best traditions of the *commedia dell'arte.*

Marius had been accepted first of all by René Rocher, director of the Théâtre Antoine, but he had generously ceded it to Léon Volterra who was prepared to give Pagnol a large advance on the play.[60] As the initial contact with Antoine's *protégé* indicates, Pagnol's portrayal of a popular milieu corresponded as much as his previous satirical works to the early interests of Antoine and Socialist theater. The political commitment of the arts as exemplified in the work of Romain Rolland, Gémier, or even Jean Renoir (whose film *La Vie est à Nous* [1936] was made as publicity for the Socialist/Communist coalition government of the *Front Populaire*) was not, however, for Pagnol. He never carried a torch for any political party and the frequent parallels between his work and that of politically committed dramatists and *cinéastes* do not provide evidence to the contrary; his moral and aesthetic independence did not render him less sensitive to the tastes of the times, however. As his satire, based on elementary ethical premises, finds expression in plays whose allegorical caricature is reminiscent of Brecht and the Expressionists, so *Marius,* its sequels, and Pagnol's work in the cinema coincide with the works of politically activated advocates of the *Front Populaire* and Populism. There is, for example, a parallel between *Marius* and

Hôtel du Nord (1929), the masterpiece of Dabit, the Populist author who accompanied Gide to Russia and to whom Gide's *Retour de l'U.R.S.S.* is dedicated. As the somber northern hotel of Dabit's novel witnesses the differing fortunes of its often-unhappy occupants, so the sunlit Bar de la Marine of Pagnol's play is host to the gaiety and mirth of its various clients; the concept of both works coincides but Pagnol's humorous extrovert humanity is nonaligned.

Marius marks a watershed between the two modes of writing, the one satirical and theatrical and the other Naturalist (dubbed "Neorealist" by cinema critics). The satirical mode becomes an experience of the past but *Marius*, a deliberately contrasting form, was a topical experiment with an unmapped future before it. The logical conclusion to such a form was in the cinema and *Marius* itself was soon adapted to the screen, under the general direction of Alexander Korda (1931). The giant figure of Antoine stood astride both modes of expression. He had himself staged the satirical plays of Becque and encouraged Pagnol's theatrical début; he also had abandoned theater for the cinema and a more direct reconstruction of reality. By precept and by example, he would help Pagnol in the future as he had helped him in the past.

XII Fanny

Fanny does not belong to the world of theater where it was, however, first performed. It was written after the screen adaptation of *Marius* and after Pagnol's controversial irruption into the discussion of cinema theory in 1930. The movie version of *Marius* (1931) was made at the St. Maurice studios of the giant Paramount organization by Alexander Korda, in close consultation with Pagnol who followed the filming with a devouring interest; he was already converted to the movies as the ultimate form of dramatic art a full year before turning to the manuscript of *Fanny*. His friend Pierre Blanchard had told him of the new talking movies which could now be seen across the Channel in London; Pagnol made the trip to the London Palladium in 1930 just to see *Broadway Melody*, starring Bessie Love. Although he admits that the quality of sound reproduction left something to be desired, the film made such an impression upon him that he returned to Paris on May 17 to write in an article for *Le Journal* (for which Antoine wrote cinema reviews) that talking films were a more advanced form of dramatic art than theater. This was the beginning of a harrowing period when Pagnol was assailed on all sides for his controversial ideas on cinema. He had a good enough sense of humor to recall that his old ex-friend Stève Passeur called him to say: "I've just read your article. If it's not a practical joke, it's distressing; if it is a practical joke, it is still distressing."[61] Pagnol maintained his stand but did not become completely embroiled in the debate until after writing *Fanny* which was first performed at the Théâtre de Paris on December 5, 1931.

The plot and theatrical sense of structure are no less tenuous for being written with an awareness of movie techniques. Identical in concept to *Marius*, thus lending itself to movie adaptation, *Fanny* favors incidental anecdote and characterization. Continuity with the characters of *Marius* is maintained and their consistency is preserved. The premises of the original plot are respected insofar as the play opens with a grief-stricken Fanny and a bad-tempered César anxiously awaiting news from Marius, now at sea. Pagnol creates a poignant scene out of nothing when the letter finally arrives and Fanny and César combine to read it and reply to it. The letter (Act 1) contains little for Fanny but is significant to the development of the play. It transpires in the second tableau of Act 1 (scene 6) that Fanny is pregnant; deprived of news from Marius who, even in his letters to his father, reveals no sign of concern for her, Fanny resolves to accept Panisse's offer of marriage if he will accept both her and her unborn child.

Far from scorning the *fille-mère*, Panisse exultantly accepts Fanny in Act 2 in a scene which the Behrman, Logan, and Rome musical version of the entire trilogy captured nicely in the song "Panisse and Son." The joy of becoming a father at last was perhaps greater for Panisse than that of having such an attractive young bride as Fanny. The balance of Act 2 is spent in overcoming César's obstinate, proprietorial attitude toward Fanny. When she confesses to him also that she is to have a child, points out the uncertainty of Marius's return, and, with the approbation of Panisse, promises that the child will have César for a godfather and César for a name, then and only then does Raimu-César consent to her wedding. This scene represents a nice climax and an appropriate conclusion to the play but Pagnol adds another act to settle the question of Marius.

The third and final act is contrived and labored. It shows the return of Marius almost a year after the wedding of Fanny and the birth of Fanny's healthy son. Fanny is contented in her marriage with Panisse, a good man who has showered affection on her and her son. Although she loves Marius, there can be no question of deserting Panisse for him on his return to Marseilles; her respect for

Panisse and her love for Marius are a demonstration of the classic difference between *Agape* and *Eros*. Pagnol seems to be seeking a definitive ending by bringing back Marius. Since Fanny cannot leave Panisse, Marius will have to leave Marseilles again. If Marius is to leave Marseilles again, without marring the happy ending, he has to be shown in an unfavorable light. Harder and more bitter than in the previous play, Marius is now not only bold enough to silence his redoubtable father but is also selfish enough to thank Panisse for his caretaker operation and to envisage reclaiming Fanny and *his child*. There can be little sympathy for such an attitude and Fanny delivers a dignified remonstrance, reminding Marius of the importance of the family. It is thus with a sigh of relief that she and the spectators watch the archetypal male adjust to his situation and leave to catch the train back to his ship.

Despite the absence of Raimu, Alida Rouffe, and Pierre Fresnay from the stage version of *Fanny* (they returned to perform in the screen version in 1932), people flocked to the Théâtre de Paris to renew their acquaintance with the unforgettable characters Pagnol had created in *Marius* and whose identity he so brilliantly amplified in *Fanny*. With an undeniable genius for characterization, Pagnol succeeds in creating tender, touching scenes from the most banal circumstances: César's sense of loss at his son's departure and the letter he composes to him, his possessive pride in his grandson notwithstanding the adoption by Panisse, are among the most notable examples. Enlivened by moments of unrelated merriment such as Monsieur Brun's purchase of the *Pitalugue*, a secondhand boat with so marked a tendency to capsize as to be called *Le Sous-Marin*, the play follows the formula so successfully established by *Marius*. Like the scenes with the Arab carpet-vendor in *Marius*, the scene with the Annamite (Vietnamese) client of César in *Fanny* has, however, dated and could well be suppressed.

A particularly important scene is inserted in Act 1, like a giant "aside" from the author. As if to demonstrate the authenticity of his characters and their setting, Pagnol confronts them with a stock caricature of the Marseillais, as he is generally imagined to be in the dark, rainswept provinces north of the Loire. Marius Tartarin, ostensibly looking for Honorine, arrives in Act 1, scene 6, exclaiming "*Tron de l'air de bagasse!*" and talking about *bouillabaisse* (the famous fish soup of Marseilles). Following a hair-raising cluster of clichés and expressions of the stock Marseillais image, he gives his name and address as "M. Mariusse, 6, rue Cannebière, chez M.

Olive." Marius and Olive are two fictitious children of Marseilles about whom there is an unending stream of jokes similar to the Dai and Ianto stories of Welsh lore. The stupefaction and incomprehension of the genuine Marseillais when confronted with this parody of themselves makes a telling point; César's initial indifference, imagining Tartarin to have been a Parisian, gives way to a fierce outburst of civic pride: ". . . in Marseilles we build the tunnel du Rove and fifteen miles of docks to feed Europe with the strength of Africa!" The scene clearly states Pagnol's intention to be taken seriously in his reproduction of authentic scenes of Marseilles life.

XIII *A Change in Direction*

This is an appropriate point at which to underline the importance of a new direction taken by Pagnol. By way of a distraction from the composition of *Topaze*, he had rediscovered his native province and had realized his gift for vivid portrayal of scenes familiar to him. The reproduction of the settings he knew so well is too affective to be called "Naturalist." Rather than use the term "poetic realism" which is applied to Renoir's films, the definition "popular realism" will be adopted in the following analysis of Pagnol's career subsequent to *Fanny;* the implications of this term will be amplified in the next chapter. *Marius* was spontaneously a more humorous play than *Fanny* where the absence of the son and lover saddened everyone, but it only rarely sacrificed authenticity to laughter-making. The Marius Tartarin scene affirms a deliberate option for Popular Realism, which was already implicit in *Marius* and which prefigured the imminent, inevitable transfer to sound movies. After his apprenticeship with Paramount Studios and further reinforcement of his team of Marseillais secondary characters (Vilbert, Delmont, Dullac, Maupi, Vattier, and later Blavette were all to appear frequently in Pagnol's movies), Pagnol was ready to pack his bags and return south to Provence with his newly acquired filming equipment.

XIV *Postscript*

Fanny was Pagnol's last contribution to the theater for a quarter of a century; it concludes a cycle of plays which are homogeneous and in which the pattern of development is evident. *Marius* is linked by its deliberately contrasting form to *Topaze* which is, in turn, the climax to an earlier sequence of plays. Similarly, *Judas* is the *pièce à thèse* followed by *Fabien* which was supposed to have a more pop-

ular appeal, but the substance and style of both plays is quite different from any of Pagnol's previous work. Neither play had a good
reception and they both lack the sense of authority of the earlier
plays, but Pagnol's faith in *Judas*, at least, remained unshaken.

XV Judas

The play was dogged by bad luck from the beginning. Raymond
Pellegrin, who had played the part of Manon's suitor in *Manon des
Sources* (1952), was cast as Judas but he collapsed shortly after the
opening night on October 6, 1955, at the Théâtre de Paris. Roger
Rudel was his understudy but he, in turn, went down with appen-
dicitis. Despite the encouraging first performances, this second mis-
fortune was too much for the company's morale and Elvire Popesco
abandoned the production.

The play is based on the Bible story of Judas Iscariot who, according to Pagnol's thesis, was himself unlucky. In the preface to the
definitive version (Editions de Provence, 1968), Pagnol advances the
controversial thesis that, as a well-trusted disciple, Judas was given
the most difficult task, the denunciation of Christ; Judas, in this
sense played an essential rôle in the equally essential Crucifixion.
With a similar argument one could, of course, also justify the rôles of
Nebuchadnezzar, Herod, and Salomé, to name a few. Pagnol argues
that there is little condemnation of Judas in the Gospels, with the
notable exception of Saint John, whose testimony he criticizes.[62]
Mindful of the theological implications of the hypothesis, the
dramatist must also make the idea work on stage. In a careful adaptation of material contained in the Gospels, Pagnol creates a lively,
interesting text but the interest is not always dramatic; *Judas* is a
thought-provoking dramatization of a Bible story but it never attains
the heights of great theater. In comparison with the legendary
Topaze and *Marius*, it must inevitably have seemed like an anticlimax to many theater-goers. Had Pagnol, however, been interested in his reputation rather than in writing, he would simply not
have exposed himself to such impossible comparisons, particularly
when the Judas theme had already been presented to Parisian
audiences (Paul Raynal, *A Souffert sous Ponce Pilate*, 1939, and
Pierre Bost/André Puget, *Un Nommé Judas*, 1954).[63]

If examined on its own merits, always assuming a basic interest in
the interpretation of the New Testament, the play has qualities that
make it worth performing; depending upon the religious commitment of the audience, the thesis itself can be dramatic. Pagnol has

gone as far as possible in his dramatization; lively secondary
characters and the "hero's" plausible inner motivation are effective
vehicles for a plot which must, after all, conform to the outward
aspects of the original story.

The tragedy of Judas Iscariot is unravelled in five acts. The first
act shows him returning furtively to his family for the Passover
shortly after a squad of Roman soldiers had manhandled Simon, his
father, and Rebecca, his betrothed, in their search for him. Judas
does not, however, spend the Passover with his family but returns to
Jerusalem to celebrate the feast with Jesus and the other disciples.
Having extricated himself from his persistent, orthodox family who
are pained by his absence during the Passover, Judas returns to the
family home in the second act. He had, in effect, just attended the
Last Supper where he had learned that he would, or was supposed
to, betray Our Lord; highly distressed by this implication of guilt, he
returns to his home to contemplate. He arrives so late that he meets
only the mysterious, visiting stranger who has a bed downstairs.
They are discussing the implications of the prophecy when the
Roman search party returns under their colorful Provençal centurion
Marcius and the high priest Caiaphas. Reluctantly deciding to exe-
cute Christ's wishes and to fulfill the prophecy, Judas follows it so
scrupulously as to accept only the derisory sum of thirty pieces of
silver rather than the much greater amount offered by Caiaphas.

In Act 3 Judas has betrayed Christ and is brought before Pilate for
questioning: Pilate and his effete counselor, the Greek Phocas, were
inclined to treat the Jesus affair as an internal matter for the Jewish
magistrates until an inspired Judas spoke to them of his faith in
Jesus, in whom the people saw an unsurpassable hope and power. It
was thus not in pointing out Jesus in Gethsemane but in speaking of
his love for Him that Judas brought about the Crucifixion. In Act 4
we follow the distant, invisible Crucifixion with Judas; assuming all
the time that Jesus would eventually save Himself by a miracle, and
having accepted the ungracious rôle of traitor (better indeed, in the
eyes of posterity, that he had never been born) Judas collapses in
despair when Christ dies on the cross. Full of remorse, he is induced
by the death of Christ to believe that he betrayed, rather than executed, a divine prophecy. Marcius, the Roman centurion, who took
pity on Christ and abbreviated his agony, has been converted and
tries in vain to reason with the despairing Judas. The two meet again
in the fifth act at the sepulcher when Marcius is accompanied by a
number of the Apostles who show considerable hostility toward

Judas. After reaffirming his unique love and devotion to Christ, an uncomprehending Judas flees to find refuge in death while the former centurion Marcius prays for him.

The theological difficulties of Pagnol's version of Judas are obvious and numerous. Since he was unaware that he was to be an agent of Christ's death, Judas would seem to have been deceived. His suicide, which causes problems if Judas is to be rehabilitated, appears to be the fault of Somebody Else. Pagnol neglects to close the parenthesis he had opened on the question of predestination. The principal theatrical merit of the play is in the varied infrastructure of secondary characters, from the perplexed, old-fashioned father of Judas to the outspoken centurion Marcius and the callous spectators on Calvary. Christ is not portrayed. Topical parallels are drawn between German-occupied France and Roman-occupied Judea: Pagnol reminds his audience rather clumsily of the comparison at one point in Act 5 by having one of the German mercenaries of the Roman army exclaim "*Achtung!*" As in Camus's *Etat de Siège*, the search parties and the passive resistance of the population must still have had a particular significance for French theater audiences of the 1950's.

One of the famous, oft-repeated public performances of Maître Jacques Isorni, the eminent defense lawyer for Pétain[64] and other great losers, is the "Trial of Jesus." In his analysis of the evidence for the prosecution, Isorni finds a number of inconsistencies; he stresses in particular the constraint imposed upon the Sanhedrin by Roman occupation. The allegory with Pétain is never very far away. The "Trial of Jesus" is now almost a party-piece that Isorni has had in his repertoire for a sufficient number of years for Pagnol to have known of it when writing *Judas*. Had Pagnol in fact known of Maître Isorni's allegory, his adaptation to the more appropriate parallel with Judas is to be commended. However, opinions will always remain divided as to whether a new look at Judas and Pétain reveals a hero or a traitor. It does not much matter, one feels, to the contemplative *académicien* for whom the question is undoubtedly interesting but academic. *Judas* is a well-conducted excursion which offered its author the same scholarly distraction as that enjoyed by Claudel with his *Mort de Judas* (*Figures et Paraboles*, 1936).

XVI Fabien

This is the only play of Pagnol's to be called anything other than a *pièce:* Pagnol called it a *comédie gaie en quatre actes*. This definition suggests a carefree, uninhibited romp, written as much for the author's diversion as for that of the audience. The play never gets off the ground, however, and is the gloomiest piece of work ever written by Pagnol. It can be categorically defined as a mistake. The concept of the play suggests that it was designed for a wider, more popular appeal than *Judas:* this is confirmed by Pagnol's choice of director and theater, Albert Willemetz of the Théâtre des Bouffes Parisiens, where it opened on September 28, 1956. The Popular Realism of Pagnol's work is always best expressed through the settings and *milieu* of Provence that he knew so well: *Fabien* is a miscalculation in that Pagnol tried to transfer the simple, spontaneous merriment of Marseilles to a Parisian fairground. The play will probably never be revived and a swift synopsis should show why.

The setting is the home of Fabien, a philandering photographer (played by Philippe Nicaud) and his common-law wife Emily (played by Milly Mathis). Ruthlessly taking advantage of his *belle grosse caille,* the plump, plain but adoring Emily, the dashing Fabien ensures a comfortable home for himself without being tied by any obligations. He flirts freely and widely with all the women of the neighborhood and since he lives in a fairground (Luna Park is a French equivalent of Coney Island), he has a varied selection; his circle includes Madame Lodoiska, the bearded lady, and a Viennese skater. Every evening Fabien finds a pretext to go out and court one or other of his many paramours; his evening *sorties* suddenly abate at the end of Act 1, when Emily's younger sister, Marinette, comes to stay. Played by Odile Rodin, Marinette is attractive and naive. By the end of Act 2 Fabien has inveigled her into posing with him for tender Valentine pictures. Emily is the unsuspecting accomplice since she takes the pictures in the belief that they will be good for business; Fabien poses for them in the hope of seducing Marinette. The measure of his success is revealed in Act 3 when Marinette informs him that she is pregnant; the couple decides to confess everything to Emily in the hope that her frustrated maternal instinct and her endless goodwill may lead her to accept their marriage and to care for the child. The plan eventually works out after an unexpected display of emotion by Emily who had always trusted Fabien. She is finally not called upon to accept Fabien's marriage since in Act 4 Marinette's doctor reports a mistaken diagnosis. As callow as Fabien, Marinette waits no longer to depart; she had only consented to marriage with Fabien for the sake of expediency. Never a man to grieve over an unsuccessful affair, Fabien persuades the faithful, eager Emily that he loved her all the time, and resumes his evening outings. His total cynicism is well expressed at the end of the play when, during the supper that precedes the first of his resumed nocturnal *sorties*, he comments on Emily's spirit of self-sacrifice: "It's amazing! You only like the dregs of the wine bottle, the coarse end of the lettuce leaf, the cheese rind, and burned meat. You do have funny ways, but don't worry, dear, I won't deprive you."

Far from being a *comédie gaie* the play reads like a dark parable on the servility of woman and the egoism of man. Surrounded in Luna Park by freaks and victims of nature, the bird-man, the bearded lady, and the vicious Fabien, Emily is a pathetic figure. Her kindness and stupidity are both exploited and ridiculed by those who surround her; to them, warmth and generosity of spirit are unknown qualities. Designed to amuse, the play is like a nightmare landscape of Hieronymus Bosch.

Fabien was thrown off quite casually by Pagnol, who himself admits in his preface to the play that he no longer finds a likable character in it.[65] Short of abandoning his realist vein for the more figurative expression of the earlier satire, Pagnol could never have hoped to emulate the success of the trilogy, or subsequent work set in Provence, with *Fabien*, a curious mixture of dark, unintentional satire and Popular Realism. By a happy coincidence, Provence is a naturally picturesque part of the world, and it also happened to be the part of the world that Pagnol knew best; by setting his work in Provence, or in Marseilles, he automatically guaranteed an attractive setting, established reliable terms of reference and a sureness of touch. Provence, on the other hand, would have been converted into a prison for Pagnol if he had never been able to move outside its limits. The reluctance to have a label attached to his work and the freedom to write about whatever he pleased explain Pagnol's forays beyond his native heath. Without the freedom to range freely Pagnol might not have made such a serious error of judgment as with *Fabien* but, conversely, his main source of inspiration would have quickly run dry from overexploitation. It should be remembered that *Fabien* is only a minor postscript to an impressive career as a dramatist and that it is a marginal diversion from Pagnol's rich, original activity as a movie maker. It is now time to turn to those twenty-five eventful years which separate *Fanny* from *Fabien*.

CHAPTER 3

Pagnol in the Movies

DESPITE the glaring publicity and the clashing of cymbals with which Pagnol's entry into sound movies is usually associated, he began production of his own films only after a number of careful precautions. His first positive step toward work in the cinema followed the production of *Marius*. Similar in many respects to Jean Epstein's silent classic about Marseilles, *Coeur Fidèle* (1923), and coinciding with the coming of sound, the play attracted the attention of the European branch of Paramount Studios; as everyone knows, Pagnol then worked with Alexander Korda for the Paramount production of *Marius*. The three stages of Pagnol's introduction, apprenticeship, and independent production in the cinema industry begin with the adaptations by Paramount of *Marius* and then of *Topaze*; he next formed his own company and hired a director to make a film of *Fanny* (1932). From this first practical phase he moved into a period of noisy controversy (1933) about the conceptual, aesthetic ramifications of sound in the cinema. Quick to point out that the swaggering newcomer had yet to make a film himself, the critics were soon silenced in early 1934 by *Jofroi* which marked the emergence of Pagnol as a film maker. This chapter will follow the three phases of Pagnol's development as a *cinéaste* but something should first be said about a discreet but ever-present background figure in his career.

It has never been suggested that Pagnol's intention to make movies preceded *Marius*, although his theatrically dangerous path of increasing Naturalism runs parallel to the course previously taken by Antoine, "the first man to introduce door-handles into literature," as Cocteau unkindly quipped. Antoine, too, had turned from the theater to the cinema in a quest for realism but so little of his work has survived that it is virtually impossible to establish any patterns of influence. In his original articles on cinema theory entitled *Ciné-*

maturgie de Paris (of which more later) Pagnol alludes to Antoine's example. And if the absence of sound is thought to have discouraged the verbose Marseillais from going into movies, it should be recalled that *The Jazz Singer,* Warner Brothers's first "talkie" which starred Al Jolson, was made in 1927 and had reached Paris by 1929; it ran as a counterattraction, first to *Topaze* and then to *Marius*. Antoine's son, in his book *Antoine Père et Fils,* has devoted a number of interesting pages to the films made by his father; the last films of Antoine *père* included an adaptation of Zola's *La Terre* (1921) and an adaptation of Daudet's *L'Arlésienne* (1922) which was filmed in and around Arles and the Camargue with a cast of native Provençaux. Antoine was also film critic for *Le Journal* from 1930 to 1940, at precisely the time when Pagnol moved into cinema. If it is difficult to establish the precise relationship between Pagnol and Antoine, it seems fair to suppose that Antoine's presence and previous example were at the very least a moral support for Pagnol in trying times. Whatever the case may be, Antoine's film career in this context deserves the attention of future researchers.

I *Phase I: Paramount Studios*

The coming of sound to the cinema provoked a commercial war in Europe in the early 1930's between German and American interests. American production had swamped the European market in the days of silent films but, with the coming of sound, language barriers were established. In order to preserve its considerable European market, the American movie industry increased its production, imposed conditions on the foreign purchase of projection and sound-recording equipment, and, in the case of Paramount Studios, established subsidiaries in Europe. The Germans alone developed the expertise necessary to confront the Americans. The Tobis-Klang film company was formed with the help of Dutch bankers to meet the challenge of the American Vitaphone, Western Electric, and R.C.A. competitors. Tobis-Klangfilm then combined with the U.F.A. (*Universum Film Allgemeine* [Aktien] *Gesellschaft*) to make "talkies" and to market the equipment necessary for the projection of these movies. Western Electric combined with Paramount for identical reasons. By 1930 Western Electric had established a French subsidiary named *la Société de Matériel Acoustique* whose principal target was an American-controlled sound film industry in Europe, based on the newly constructed Paramount studios at St. Maurice-Joinville. No expense was too great to preserve the European market which had traditionally brought huge profits to American films whose expenses had already been covered on the domestic U.S.A. circuit. The St. Maurice-Joinville studios were equipped to make 150 films simultaneously in fourteen different languages (French, Swedish, German, Spanish, Italian, Portuguese, Czech, Danish, Hungarian, Rumanian, Yugoslav, Polish, Norwegian, and Russian).[1] The might of the American electro-technical industry, with American Telegraph and Telephone backing Western Electric, General Electric combining with Westinghouse to support R.C.A. and R.K.O., was matched at every step by the Germans. *Les Films Sonores Tobis* and *Filmsonor* were German-controlled agencies in Paris and Tobis-Klangfilm also took over the old Menchen studios at Epinay to create a film-producing complex as well equipped as that of Paramount at St. Maurice. The net result of this situation was that most French film makers were indirectly employed by either the Germans or the Americans. René Clair was a notable capture for the German U.F.A. while the Americans secured the services of Pagnol and Cavalcanti.

French distributors and French sound reproduction systems maintained a marginal existence during this period. Gaumont had perfected a sound reproduction system that employed records like the "Vitaphone" system; the Petersen-Poulsen system, similar to Western Electric's "Movietone," had also been used in French films. Distributors like Gaumont, Aubert, Braunberger-Richebé, and Pathé-Natan also maintained their activity which began gradually to increase as the American onslaught waned. The Germans were able to rent their equipment at substantially lower rates than Western Electric and the public, becoming more discriminating as the novelty of the "talkies" wore off, attended the hastily produced Paramount movies less frequently. Finally, with the development of "dubbing," *doublage*, Paramount no longer needed to maintain its increasingly costly European operation: they were able to return to Hollywood where, with Metro-Goldwyn, Fox, and Warner Brothers, they produced dubbed foreign versions in sufficient numbers to recapture their world hegemony. By far the most successful film produced by Paramount during its opulent period of residence in Paris was *Marius*. The film version of Pagnol's play is perhaps the most successful Franco-American production ever.

By selling the rights of adaptation of *Marius* to Paramount Studios, Pagnol became an employee of a giant multinational corporation. He had mixed feelings about his new status and describes

them in his memoirs of this period which are misleadingly called
Cinématurgie de Paris.[2] The original, authentic *Cinématurgie de
Paris* consists of the three articles written for *Les Cahiers du Film* in
1933 - 34; it is not easily accessible since *Les Cahiers du Film* can
only be consulted at the annex of the Bibliothèque Nationale in Ver-
sailles. The second version of *Cinématurgie de Paris*, as published by
the *Editions de Provence* in 1967, contains quotations from the
original, theoretic work but it consists for the most part of Pagnol's
recollections of his early apprenticeship in the cinema. Both works
have their own value but they are entirely different documents.
Although the memoirs are the most useful reference for the moment,
the original *Cinématurgie* provides the topic of the next section.

Pagnol was first of all awestruck by the size and efficiency of the
Paramount organization but, as the best-known French dramatist of
the period, he also felt humiliated by the secondary rôle he was
given in the adaptation of his own play. It was only through Korda's
personal initiative that Pagnol played the part he did in the adaptation of *Marius*. There is still a note of resentment in his later parody
of the values of Paramount Studios written in 1965 for *Le Figaro Littéraire*. For this retrospective caricature of the artistic values of
Paramount, Pagnol has simply reversed the values that had
prevailed in his own studios, *La Société des Films Marcel Pagnol*.
For him, the author was always the indisputable inspiration and
maker of the film but the relations between himself and his filming
units were always marked by the most affable informality.[3] If Pagnol
was contemptuous of the Paramount approach and felt humiliated
by it, he had nothing but admiration for the technical expertise of
the company. He was able to swallow his pride and learn much from
the Americans; although repeatedly rude about Kane's insensitivity
to human and artistic considerations, Pagnol admired his overall
control of the operation from the financial transactions to synchronization: "If it was later possible for me to make my own films
and also to direct a laboratory, studios, and distribution agencies, it
is thanks to the friendship of Robert T. Kane."[4] Pagnol also realized
that, before reaching this level of authority in his own self-sufficient
studios, he would have to learn and master the tasks of each member
of the film unit. He served as an attentive apprentice to Korda from
whom he learned much and he has also had the delicacy to
remember and to thank the otherwise-forgotten Garry Schwartz,
laboratory director of Paramount's St. Maurice Studios in 1930;[5]
working with Schwartz in the laboratory, Pagnol learned to cope
with all the technical problems of film-making.

This intelligent, active cooperation with the American technicians of Paramount not only provided Pagnol with an outlet for his qualifications in English, and for his constant interest in mechanics, but also equipped him to make his own films. The determination to do just that was probably confirmed by the tactlessness of the Scenario Department in the arrangements it made for the adaptation of *Topaze*, the rights to which had been bought by Paramount shortly after the release of *Marius*. After the successful completion of *Marius*, Pagnol had believed that he and Paramount would reach a new understanding; he was encouraged in this belief by Bob Kane's initiative in forming a committee of authors. There were to be ten members of the committee selected by Pagnol and André Daven and it was Pagnol's understanding "that Paramount had at last understood and my dream was now coming true: we were going to establish a French film industry which would no longer produce base imitations of Hollywood."[6] He was all the more disappointed eventually to observe that Kane's committee of authors never played a rôle of any significance whatsoever in studio planning. It was the last straw, then, for Pagnol to learn, without any previous consultation, that Louis Gasnier was being flown back from Hollywood to direct *Topaze* and that Léopold Marchand, an old associate of *Les Moins de Trente Ans*, had been retained to rewrite the dialogue for the film version of *Topaze*. With encouragement of this kind it was inevitable that Pagnol should contemplate making his own films; his taste for self-sufficiency has already been noted.

The continuing stage and screen success of *Marius* had secured for Pagnol the means to produce his own films but, although initiated by Garry Schwartz into the technical problems of film-making, he was still unfamiliar with the problems of distribution. Determined to assume and maintain responsibility for his own films, Pagnol went into partnership with a French distribution company, Braunberger-Richebé, and hired Marc Allégret in order to make the film version of *Fanny* (1932). He reassembled the ever-faithful cast of *Marius*, thus ensuring continuity in the screen version of his play, and demonstrated that the massive machinery of Paramount was not indispensable. It is interesting to note in Claude Beylie's filmography[7] that the script-girl's pseudonym of "Gourdji" conceals the identity of Mme Françoise Giroud, Minister for Women's Affairs in the Chirac government, 1975.

Pagnol was thus able to continue his apprenticeship in the cinema while assuming greater independence. It was in this spirit that he contented himself with sharing responsibility for two more films: *Un*

Direct au Coeur (1932) and *L'Agonie des Aigles* (1933). For the film adaptation of his own play, Pagnol worked with the producer Raymond Boulay and hired Roger Lion to direct it. He was clearly anxious to demonstrate his independence of Paramount since he used an R.C.A. sound recording unit for the film. Pagnol's artistic involvement increased only slightly with *L'Agonie des Aigles*, directed and produced by Richebé; it was Pagnol himself who prepared the dialogue and scenario from the novel, entitled *Les demi-soldes*, by Georges Esparbès. An historical drama set in Napoleonic France, *L'Agonie des Aigles* is as modest a part of Pagnol's artistic creation as *Un Direct au Coeur* but, inasmuch as both films provided a valuable proving ground, they are included in the filmography.

It was only in late 1933 that Pagnol finally committed himself to a career as a movie maker, but he moved all the more decisively for having laid his plans carefully. His preparations had not gone unnoticed; the article in *Le Journal* (1930) and his subsequent association with Paramount Studios had been considered treacherous by people of the theater and even dangerous by the surviving partisans of silent movies. He was a marked man. The movie and theater journals of the time reported frequently on Pagnol's activity; a number of small incidents, such as his eulogy of talking films at his presentation of the film *Marius* to the *Marseillais de Paris* (October, 1931)[8], served to confirm his identity as a heretic of the *théâtre en conserve* school. The tone of discussion was, however, as decorous as that of an English garden party, compared with the veritable scandal provoked by Pagnol's massive, provocatively publicized mobilization of resources in late 1933 when he founded his own complete film industry.

II   *Background to Debate*

The tension created in the movie industry by the coming of sound prevented many people from looking beyond their own immediate interests; although providing an independent French alternative to German and American control of the French movie industry, Pagnol met with almost universal opposition. The most loyal, disinterested challenge to Pagnol's views on cinema came from René Clair, who represented those who were genuinely interested in the future of cinema as an independent art. Other more virulent critics attacked Pagnol in proportion to the extent they felt themselves threatened by the changes he was prophesying; their animosity reached its final paroxysm with the publication in 1933 of the first installment of *Cinématurgie de Paris*.

Even before the publication of his movie manifesto, Pagnol's theory of cinema was easily identifiable and just as easily deformed; it was labelled *théâtre en conserve* (canned theater) by his detractors. While the charge is inaccurate, it is not entirely undeserved. With only his theater career behind him, Pagnol had presumed to revise contemporary thinking on the cinema in his article in *Le Journal*. Furthermore, the first films with which he was associated were simple adaptations by others of his plays *Marius* and *Topaze*. Although Raimu's massive authenticity creates some wonderful moments of cinema in *Marius* (in the game of *manille*, for example), critics could justifiably write: "I saw the same actors on the screen as for the stage version, there was the same succulent dialogue with its hyperbole, realism, and simplicity and I really thought I was seeing the play all over again, so close is the resemblance between it and the scenario."[9] Pagnol was not, of course, directly responsible for these early movies, but he has never made a secret of the importance for him of the archival value of film; thanks to the film version of *Marius*, future generations will see the great performance of Raimu as César. This was far from being Pagnol's only interest in the cinema and he spent many years trying unnecessarily to refute the charges of *théâtre en conserve* which were levelled by committed opponents who simply used the expression as a term of abuse.

The best and most accessible record of the polemic is to be found in René Clair's book, *Réflexion Faite*.[10] The book consists of a collection of notes compiled in the course of his association with the cinema; the jottings which date from the period 1922 - 1935 are published in italicized print and Clair's method is to comment on these in the light of his subsequent experience. Much of the book deals with the controversy of "*théâtre filmé*." Far from objecting to the coming of sound, Clair welcomed it as a further aid in the growth of the new art form; his main fear was that talking films would be abused as an adjunct to theater. Many of the differences between Pagnol and Clair arose out of simple misunderstandings which they have long since settled satisfactorily. They always maintained cordial relations throughout the most difficult phases of the protracted debate; as the first two movie makers ever elected to the *Académie Française* they became fast friends. Clair quotes Pagnol as saying: "Without admitting it, we have convinced each other. He started to make talkative movies and because of him [Clair], I started to stress plastic qualities in my work. If our quarrel continues, and I believe it will endure as long as our friendship (which is indestructible), I'll end up making silents and he'll wind up doing talk-shows on the radio."[11] Clair's grave-side oration at Pagnol's funeral is eloquent proof of their reconciliation.

In the wide coverage given to the controversy by the popular press, the tone of discussion varied from the comprehensive calmness of René Clair to outright scurrility. The most responsible journalists wrote for *Le Temps, Comoedia,* and *Pour Vous* (a weekly cinema journal created in 1928 by the daily *L'Intransigeant*) which opened its columns to the most distinguished commentators of the time (both Clair and Renoir contributed to it). Vuillermoz of *Le Temps* and René Bizet of *Pour Vous* criticized Pagnol's opinions but they remained dispassionate and recognized his good faith. The provincial press was the most hostile, but it was spurred into activity only after publication of *La Cinématurgie de Paris*.

It is hard to understand the venom of the exchanges reported in the contemporary press unless one takes into account the threat which the "talkies" seemed to represent to large vested interests; both the theater and the silent film industries saw their future jeopardized. The sense of impending change created scenes in the cultural life of the capital which were as dramatic as anything witnessed since Victor Hugo's youth. At a *Banquet des Poètes,* sponsored by *Comoedia* in 1930 in honor of Le Goffic's election to the *Académie Française,* Gaston Rageot (President of the *Société des Gens de Lettres*) took the opportunity to speak of the possibilities of the cinema. Georges Ricou (co-director of the Opera) followed this up, unsolicited, with an even warmer panegyric of "talkies." This caused pandemonium through which the stentorian voice of René Fauchois was heard bellowing: "Down with the cinema! We are here for poetry, not for cinema!" Fauchois and Ricou continued their dispute in the pages of *Comoedia*[12] (despite this, within two years Jean Renoir would make the film *Boudu Sauvé des Eaux* starring Michel Simon, from the play by Fauchois). Calmer, more farseeing critics recognized that the theater could not really be harmed by the "talkies." Achard himself wrote that "an increasingly sharp line of demarcation will be drawn between theater and sound cinema. The two art forms will coexist. If I may say so, I think it will be of great benefit to pure theater."[13]

The silent film industry had much greater cause for alarm; what seems so surprising forty-five years later is that there should have been anybody in the silent film industry who thought it could survive the coming of sound. Those who had presumed that all movies were the same, with or without sound-tracks, were soon proved wrong. The gift of speech was frankly embarrassing to the silent-film maker. The disarray in the industry was such that people of the theater — actors, directors, and authors alike — were drafted to make the "talkies" that the makers of silent movies could simply not understand, either conceptually or technically. The early talking film industry in Hollywood and Paris produced many movies that were either marked by the theatrical influence or were just straight musical comedy. It was undoubtedly this interim rôle of the theater and vaudeville which led many to fear that the theater business, as well as the silent film industry, would soon be gobbled up by the "talkies." Few people in the world of entertainment felt in any way charitably disposed toward Pagnol when he actually predicted such an apocalyptic development. *"Le muet est mort, le théâtre est à l'agonie"* (Silent cinema is dead and the theater is dying) was the inflammatory, incredible caption adopted by Pagnol for the first chapter of *La Cinématurgie de Paris*. It was published in the first number of *Les Cahiers du Film* (December 15, 1933), founded by Pagnol as the organ of publicity for his newly created film industry.

III   *Phase 2:* La Cinématurgie de Paris

Like most manifestos, Pagnol's tract offended perhaps more in its timing and style than in its content, which was not properly understood. The tone of the manifesto suggests that, after three years under sniper fire, Pagnol had deliberately (or even mischievously) opted for a big bang which would satisfy honor and snuff out his critics at the same time. Such tactics could only prolong the controversy and the misunderstanding, blinding people to the merits of Pagnol's case. Defused by the passage of time, *La Cinématurgie de Paris* (1933) is a more reasonable document than it originally appeared to be.

There is little need to point out any further just how provocative the timing of the article was; bristling with sharp-edged slogans, the style, too, is far from conciliatory. The title was chosen to echo that of Lessing's work of drama criticism, *Dramaturgie de Hambourg.* The analogy with the German critic's work (also admired by Antoine) was tantamount to the assimilation of theater to film theory. In the unlikely event of this willful provocation escaping the attention of the hypersensitive readers of the time, Pagnol immediately followed up with the unforgettable line: *"Le muet est mort, le théâtre est à l'agonie."*

As it happens, the Romantic alexandrine is entirely appropriate for such a splendid gesture of heroism: generous, thoughtless but sincere, Pagnol charged the enemy with the ardor of a *cadet de Gascogne*. For want of a more tactfully turned phrase he had made an implacable enemy out of each of the theater and silent movie employees whom he was consigning to unemployment. In the most harsh, basic terms, Pagnol was absolutely right to announce the end of the silent film industry; it would, however, have been more diplomatic simply to point out the need for careful adaptation to sound. He was also right in pointing out that the best sound movies to date had been made by people who had transferred from the theater; the success of *Marius* was, of course, implicit in these remarks but he also quoted as an example Achard's dialogue for the movie version of *Jean de la Lune*. Then, with a faith in the future of "talkies" that could not be reasoned with, he went on to argue that the silent film industry's ineptitude combined with the theater's relative comprehension announced a new art form. The "talkies" were indeed a new art form, different from silents, but they would never, of course, totally absorb the theater.

In a statement of principles drawn up as a conclusion to the article, Pagnol stated that "the talking film is the art of printing, fixing, and propagating theater"; he immediately covered himself against the charge of *théâtre en conserve* by adding a little-heeded qualification that "the talking film will re-invent the theater by bringing new resources to it." This is the substance of the first chapter of the original *Cinématurgie de Paris*. Two more chapters were added in the successive numbers of *Les Cahiers du Film*, January 15 and March 1, 1934; they were written in response to the nationwide reaction to the first installment and consist, for the most part, of detailed answers to specific points. Reading like notes to directors, they were incorporated in a little-known revision of Pagnol's film theory entitled: "Réflexions sur l'Art Cinématographique" *(Revue Politique et Parlementaire*, February, 1964) and will be studied as a reference to Pagnol's filming technique in a later section.

The first chapter of *La Cinématurgie* is both a gesture of defiance and an intuitive statement of faith; contributing even further to the soured polemical tone of discussion, it deprived itself of the calmer, more sympathetic reading that it required to be properly understood. The passion with which Pagnol stated his case augured an inspiring commitment to sound movies but did nothing to render his argument more lucid; and he had, of course, been injudicious in claiming that the future of the theater lay in sound cinema. His mistake was to take the part for the whole. Both the "talkies" and the theater are sub-categories of dramatic art: they both require interpretation, performance, and directorial orchestration but their qualities are different. Pagnol himself specified this distinction in 1964, long after his last movie, in "Réflexions sur l'Art Cinématographique," when he drafted a list of seven sub-categories of dramatic art: a) theater, b) pantomime, c) opera and oratorio, d) choreography, e) puppetry, f) radio readings, g) "talkies" (he could also have added silent movies to the list!).[14] This restatement of Pagnol's view corresponds with the practical example of his own films but it was only after *Jofroi* that he could demonstrate that "re-invented theater" was not very different from what René Clair meant by "*cinéma pur.*" It was not unnaturally assumed until then that by "re-invented theater" Pagnol meant the film versions of his own stage plays, for there was nothing else to serve as a yardstick. In his answers to the charges of *théâtre en conserve*, inevitably provoked by the misunderstanding of his premature article, Pagnol reveals that, *a priori*, qualities of realism are inseparable from his concept of dramatic art.

The second chapter of *La Cinématurgie* is entirely devoted to a refutation of the accusation of *théâtre en conserve;* Pagnol is at pains to point out that, both technically and conceptually, cinema is more than a camera dumped in the *trou du souffleur* (prompter's box). He refers directly to the theatrical experiments of "*notre maître Antoine*" who, embarrassed by the conflicting presence of real actors on an artificial set, tries to make the set more real. Since this is but a poor imitation of reality itself, however naturalistic the set, the alternative is to make the actors as artificial and figurative as the décor; this was what the Greeks tried to achieve with the mask and the buskin. Pagnol argues that, in a more naturalistic context, this is the same kind of conceptual harmony and reality attained by the cinema. "A shadow among shadows, a picture among pictures, the actor becomes as real or as false as his surroundings. His voice is no longer the voice of a man but the voice of a character who will live beyond the actor, freed from the vicissitudes of the human condition."[15]

Pagnol's new dramaturgy — *la cinématurgie* — used the photograph, a reproduction of reality which introduces or reduces everything to the same perspective, as its basic unit. It was thus that in the name of dramatic art he incorporated the landscape of

Provence, with the voices of its inhabitants, as stage props in his celluloid plays. Both in his association with Jean Giono, one of the greatest of contemporary storytellers, and in his assertion of complete control as author and director, Pagnol the movie maker explicitly imposed a shape on reality. The difference between his films and those of the Italian Neorealists is that the latter abandon the dictates of dramatic art and present reality in its most noncommittal, documentary form; their films have no formal conclusions.

Pagnol's forthright, authoritarian concept of his rôle is characteristic of the man who severed contact with Paramount when they usurped his right to adapt the text of *Topaze*. His decisiveness has not dated in an age when the documentary trends of cinema recognize reality in each man's truth. It is a pity that this controversial moment in Pagnol's career has so often been neglected; the admirable work of rehabilitation by Claude Beylie glosses over the episode and therefore does nothing to dispel the prevalent impression that there is something to hide. Pagnol admittedly lacked tàct and stumbled in his argument but his instinct was right; he was amply justified when, defiantly, he announced with *Jofroi:* "Nous voici loin du trou du souffleur" (we're a long way from the prompter's box here).[16] Far from being an episode to forget, the very conviction with which Pagnol went thundering into the fray, courting certain unpopularity, is a landmark in modern French cinema. He rallied a flagging industry, giving a new sense of direction to those hitherto discouraged by the purely commercial concerns of such huge organizations as Paramount.

Jean Renoir himself derived benefit from Pagnol's independent enterprise to make *Toni*, and wrote later: "I lived as best I could, making poor films from time to time until Marcel Pagnol gave me the opportunity to make *Toni*. With *Toni* I learned much: it was a film that gave me the courage which was necessary to try something new in different directions."[17] Renoir's testimony is a particularly appropriate vindication; the acknowledged master of "poetic realism" adapted plays to sound cinema with only mixed success until Pagnol gave him the inspiration to make a full-blooded movie. It is amusing to see the later Renoir flexing his muscles, as it were, by including theatrical scenes (the army vaudeville in *La Grande Illusion* and the charades in *La Règle du Jeu*) which prove his control of the medium of cinema. Pagnol's studios, however, were more than midwife to the work of others; Claude Beylie presents the films of

Pagnol as deserving of a place alongside the work of Renoir. Through *Toni,* for which Visconti worked as Renoir's assistant, there is also a link with postwar Italian movies.

IV *Phase 3: Pagnol Makes Movies*

Similar to the strong, central direction of Paramount, Pagnol's movie organization was, however, based on the assumption of the author's preeminence. In 1933 he formed a production company named *Les Auteurs Associés* which, as the name implies, derived the great majority of its screenplays from extant plays and novels. The company was headed by a very close-knit group; Pagnol himself, as founder, was *President-Directeur Général;* his brother René and old friends from school and *Fortunio,* Charles Arno-Brun and Marcel Gras, were directors.[18] The company had its own journal entitled *Les Cahiers du Film* whose early numbers carried the well-publicized *La Cinématurgie de Paris.* The company bought its own equipment which was installed in its own studios in the impasse des Peupliers in Marseilles; Pagnol also guaranteed an outlet for his movies by buying a number of cinemas in Marseilles and equipping them for sound movie projection. There was as little doubt about the company's ambition as about who was in charge. Pagnol had perhaps hoped for better cooperation from literary people in the preparation of their work for the screen but his position in the company, combined with his ultimate rôle as adapter of Augier, Courteline, Daudet, and Giono, provokes a piquant comparison with Robert T. Kane. Pagnol's increasingly preponderant rôle is symbolized by the production company's change of name in 1934 from *Auteurs Associés* to *La Société des Films Marcel Pagnol;* the important difference from Paramount was that, himself a well-tried dramatist with a clear idea in his own mind of what "talkies" should be, Pagnol turned almost exclusively to novels for the substance of his films. Details of the sources for all the films directed or produced by Pagnol are included in the filmography but the present study deals only with the work of which Pagnol assumed artistic control as director; of the films for which he was directly responsible, those which were derived from the work of Jean Giono are the most important. Derivation from Giono is of two kinds; first there are the films adapted from his work *(Jofroi, Angèle, Regain,* and *La Femme du Boulanger);* then there are some later films, original works of Pagnol, but marked by the pattern of the first phase adaptations *(La*

Fille du Puisatier, Naïs, and *Manon des Sources).* The remaining films are generally inferior and will be examined after those which derive directly or indirectly from Giono's novels and short stories.

V   *Collaboration with Giono 1932 - 1941*

In keeping with the early activity of *Les Auteurs Associés,* Pagnol made arrangements with Giono in 1932 to adapt some of his work for the screen. In a letter sent to Giono on September 30, 1932, Pagnol sought adaptation rights for *Colline, Un de Baumugnes, Regain, Jean le Bleu,* and *Le Serpent d'Etoiles;* Giono replied in the affirmative and with alacrity on October 1. The mutual agreement was ratified in a formal contract, dated November 8, 1932, which specified that, in return for collaboration on the screenplays, Giono would receive six percent of the income from each screen adaptation; since the contract was *synallagmatique,* non-observation of its terms by one party automatically released the other party from all obligations. It is evident from the date of the contract and from the number of adaptations envisaged that the future of *Les Auteurs Associés* (i.e., Pagnol's movie career) depended heavily upon Giono at the outset. This association with Pagnol made a contribution to the cinema which bears comparison with the work of the great director-scenarist teams of Renoir-Charles Spaak and de Sica-Cesare Zavattini, but it ended unhappily in October, 1941, with a court case brought by Giono for alleged neglect of the November, 1932, contract.[19] Since Giono's charges (which proved to have little substance) mark the end of a rich moment in the history of cinema, the court case will be examined in due course; because they were probably only a pretext for more personal, private differences, the details of the case will not, however, be given a preponderant place in this study.[20]

Although alike in their love of the Provençal landscape and in their gift for storytelling, Pagnol and Giono were temperamentally different. As Norbert Calmels expressed it: "Mistral sings, Daudet narrates, Giono declaims, and Pagnol chats."[21] Whereas Giono's muse has the power of untamed, elemental passion, Pagnol is inspired by a more gentle, gregarious sense of continuity in human relations. They both express the landscape that shaped them. Remote in the fastnesses of upper Provence, Giono is dominated in a near-mystic way by external nature incarnate in the presence of the pagan god Pan; his lyrical epics are Homeric. Pagnol's Latin world is more intimate and urbane; he is of the ancient Roman civilization of coastal *Provincia* where the population and the landscape have long since established familiar relations. The unassuming simplicity of the characters who people Pagnol's films, combined with the natural background before which their lives unfold, creates a sense of Popular Realism which is lighter than Naturalist documentary yet less fanciful than Renoir's "poetic realism." The world of Pagnol's films and later work is as pagan as that of Giono since man's ambition for, and attainment of, earthly happiness is a persistent theme. It is thus hardly surprising that Giono's texts should often undergo a substantial transformation in adaptation to the cinema by Pagnol. As if to confirm the conversion to the values of his own world, Pagnol filmed all his adaptations from Giono's work near his birthplace at Aubagne; a striking example is the reconstruction in the Barres Rocheuses du Saint Esprit (near La Treille) of Aubignane, the hill village of upper Provence in Giono's *Regain*.

The tendency is always toward humanization of Giono's lofty, lyric strain; this conforms entirely, of course, to Pagnol's concept of cinema as the most realistic form of dramatic art. In the place of Giono's poetry, one finds humor; Pierre Leprohon suggests: "Pagnol takes from Giono the anecdote which amuses him. In *Un de Baumugnes*, for example, it is the core of melodrama around which Giono constructed his beautiful poem of redeeming Earth: Pagnol brings his own inspiration to this central anecdote and he infuses his own personality to the point where all trace of Giono disappears and there remains only the work of Pagnol."[22] However far Pagnol may sometimes go in his transformation of Giono's original, it is important to recognize that Giono's was the original inspiration; his stories set in the natural landscape of Provence provided Pagnol with the final cue to return to his native environment.

VI Jofroi

The first movie for which Pagnol assumed total artistic control was *Jofroi;* it was also his first adaptation from the work of Giono. Derived from one of a collection of short stories published by Gallimard under the title of *La Solitude de la Pitié* in 1932, adaptation rights were granted by Giono in a separate contract from the principal one of November 8. Pagnol's hour-long movie is based on a twenty-page short story entitled *Jofroi de la Maussan;*[23] the nature of the text required very few changes for the movie adaptation. Giono's story, a simple tale of a peasant's attachment to his land, is in a lower key than much of his work; marked by realistic observation of human behavior, frequent dialogue, and warm humor, it was so close to Pagnol's own world as to represent a natural starting point for collaboration. Pagnol's subsequent adaptations strayed progressively so far from Giono's original that, after *La Femme du Boulanger,* their legal differences simply recognized an already existing, *de facto* separation. With *Jofroi* Pagnol remained faithful to Giono's relatively untypical original.

The story is of the sale of Jofroi's orchard at La Maussan to Fonse. Pagnol characteristically switches the scene of the sale from upper Provence to Aubagne but the remaining detail is observed faithfully, to the point of reproducing some of Giono's dialogue. Fonse planned to replant the orchard after uprooting the aging fruit trees originally planted by Jofroi; no sooner does he begin to uproot the trees than Jofroi (whose house commanded a view of the orchard) emerges with a shot-gun to warn off Fonse, threatening to shoot him if he touches the fruit trees again. Having paid good money for the property which he is now not allowed to cultivate, Fonse is naturally upset. The elderly Jofroi regards the fruit trees as the children he never had; on the other hand, he is unable to reimburse Fonse since he had immediately put the proceeds of his sale into a pension fund. The pressures of the villagers, insisting on his lack of reason, drive Jofroi to threaten suicide. The ample advance publicity given by Jofroi to each and every one of his suicide attempts discourages the villagers from taking him seriously until he accidentally succeeds in calling their bluff by very nearly hanging himself from one of his beloved fruit trees. While his wife Barbe was alerting the villagers to his latest suicide attempt, Jofroi slipped from a branch during the preparation of yet another *mise-en-scène* and was only saved *in extremis.* Grieving over his wasted investment and genuinely fearful of a successful suicide attempt by Jofroi, for which he would be blamed, Fonse himself becomes very ill. He is only cured by news of Jofroi's natural death in his bed. In Giono's version Fonse immediately rises to go and tend his orchard at La Maussan; in Pagnol's version he postpones his expedition to La Maussan out of deference for Jofroi and at the advice of the *curé* whom Pagnol had created, together with the *instituteur,* as an element of increased reality.

The reticent humor and humanity of the peasants, interpreted by Vincent Scotto, Poupon, and Blavette, blend naturally with the beauty of the landscape in the hills behind Marseilles; the dusty roads, the music of the cicadas, and the rustling of the wind in the leaves of the *micocoulier* trees are incorporated as stage props to the central human drama. The background and landscape are not exploited for their own sake but are simply included as an authentic backdrop to the story which happens to be set in Provence. As Antoine once visited London's Whitechapel district in order to find information for an English laundry scene in a play he was to produce at the Théâtre Libre, so Pagnol created authentic settings for the stories of Provence which he liked to screen; the control of the Southern actors and the restraint with which the natural background is introduced eliminate any question of deliberate exploitation of a picturesque, marketable environment. As André Bazin, the great French movie critic, once wrote: "Whether it be *Angèle, Jofroi, Regain,* or *La Femme du Boulanger,* there are three basic ingredients for success in Pagnol's better films: their actors (e.g., Raimu and Fernandel), the text, and Provence. It should be stressed that the regionalism is never exploited by the descriptive possibilities of the production but it is incorporated into the dialogue and casting."[24] It is thus that Pagnol's belief in the preeminence of the scenario created, paradoxically, the great qualities of outdoor realism for which his work is renowned.

The team for *Jofroi* (see filmography) was to change little in subsequent productions. The cameraman, Willy Faktorovitch, was rarely absent from Pagnol's future movie sets; his apparently relaxed style was a direct consequence of the emphasis placed by Pagnol on the reproduction of the actors' performance. Aiming the camera in the general direction of the actors, Willy alternated between the close-up (which Pagnol treasured as a dramatic ploy) and longer shots which allowed the audience to register a change in scenery (Fonse's bedroom to Jofroi's orchard, for example). In Renoir's films, the long shot is hailed as a technical innovation; it is baptized "depth of field" and acclaimed as the first introduction of outdoor realism into sound movies in France. It should be recalled that these techniques were only developed after Renoir made *Toni* (1934) in Pagnol's studios with Pagnol's troupe of actors and with Pagnol's technical team who had already made *Jofroi* and *Angèle.*

Although working instinctively rather than with a clearly articulated concept, Pagnol showed in the generously acclaimed *Jofroi* how seriously he had been misunderstood in the polemics of *La Cinématurgie de Paris.* Many years later, in 1950, Vincent Scotto won an Oscar for his performance as Jofroi when the film was first revealed to American critics. The great Marseilles songwriter had agreed to perform in the film only to please his persuasive friend Pagnol. He also wrote the music for the film, thus heading a distinguished list of musical collaborators which included Darius Milhaud, Arthur Honegger, and Tino Rossi.

VII   Angèle

Although *Angèle* was adapted from his novel *Un de Baumugnes* under the agreement of November, 1932, Giono abandoned in March, 1934, both his involvement in preparation of the scenario and his right to inclusion in the film credits.[25] The adaptation is thus entirely Pagnol's own work and presents a number of changes from the original story, the central novel of Giono's *Trilogie de Pan (Colline, Un de Baumugnes,* and *Regain).* Unlike *Jofroi de la Maussan, Un de Baumugnes* has lyric flights and poetic qualities of language; they were reduced by Pagnol to more banal proportions in the interests of realism. The original story is of Albin, the pure young peasant of the northern hills, who returns to woo Angèle Barbaroux, the daughter of the farm called "la Douloire" where he had worked one previous summer. He returns to be told by her father Clarius that she is no longer there; a wiser, older friend, Amédée (who could almost be included in the family of Giono's supernatural "healers"), learns that, seduced and dishonored by Louis, a visiting stranger from Marseilles, Angèle is indeed at the farm but kept in conditions of strict imprisonment by her father, who wishes to hide her child and shame. With a capacity to convey his love and the natural, forgiving cycle of the seasons through the thrilling music of his harmonica, Albin locates Angèle's prison and serenades her nightly. With the able help of Amédée, the couple manages to flee with Angèle's illegitimate child; once free, however, they return for the father's blessing. With the involuntary mistakes of the past naturally forgiven, the couple return to Baumugnes to begin a new life. Amédée, who tells the story, stands back in a touchingly reticent conclusion to allow his friend Albin to depart without remorse: "The moorings of friendship which joined us were stretched taut: one more step and they would snap. I took that one backward step and departed."[26] Pagnol does not attempt to match this conclusion but finds an alternative in the distracting badinage of Saturnin.

In Pagnol's version, the change of title from *Un de Baumugnes* to *Angèle* is the first step in the necessary reduction of Giono's poetic pantheism. The theme of the *fille-mère* (or *mère célibataire*) replaces Giono's deeper sense of communion with nature without destroying the pagan overtones. A rôle of comic relief is created for Fernandel in the character of Saturnin who, in a touching scene invented by Pagnol, goes to Marseilles to retrieve Angèle from her sordid existence there. The opposition between country life and the city, a veritable *refugium peccatorum*, is stressed by Pagnol and in this sense he echoes Sicard's *La Fille de la Terre*. Clarius Barbaroux's sense of besmirched honor is played down; we see a tyrannical father rather than the distraught custodian of the family's good name. Similarly, the massive dignity of Albin the mountaineer is lessened. This is not a criticism of Pagnol's version whose warmth and poignancy are by now well known. Giono's rough-hewn eloquence creates figures of superhuman stature who are incompatible with Pagnol's gift for humorous character portrayal.

Even more successful than *Jofroi*, *Angèle* was also more ambitious. True to his belief in an authentic setting for his scenario, Pagnol set his construction team (composed of childhood friends at La Treille) to the task of building "La Douloire" from a deserted farmhouse east of Les Bellons and blasting out access roads with dynamite. All this in the name of dramatic art.

Jofroi and *Angèle*, both made in 1934, were pace-setters in French sound cinema. As the filmography shows, the film team for *Angèle* remained essentially the same as for *Jofroi*, with the significant additions of Fernand Contandin (Fernandel) as Saturnin and Orane Demazis as Angèle, a rustic Fanny awaiting her Marius.

VIII   Regain

As Beylie has pointed out, *Angèle* and *Regain* form a diptych; both far removed from city life, one is the story of "a broken contract which can only be renewed by the intervention of an honest young man from the hills, the other is the slow, fertile reanimation by an obstinate couple of a home and land which had been dying."[27] Despite the similarity of theme, there is a space of three years between *Angèle* and *Regain* (1937). Pagnol had, in the meantime, made *Merlusse, Cigalon, Topaze* (2nd version), and *César*. After falling out with Charles Arno-Brun of the production team, Giono once more abandoned adaptation of the scenario to Pagnol who made fewer alterations to the story than in *Angèle*.

Aubignane, a semideserted village of upper Provence, has only one remaining able-bodied inhabitant, Panturle. La Mamèche, an aging nomad woman blessed with the same semipsychic insight as Amédée in *Angèle*, undertakes to help Panturle restore life to the dying village; she realizes that with a woman and a home the giant Panturle could succeed in the great task which he has blindly, instinctively, set himself. In a series of apparitions, she manages to frighten the tinker/knife-sharpener Gédémus and his slave mistress Arsule away from their usual itinerary across the high plateau, diverting them to Aubignane. Once at Aubignane, Arsule meets Panturle who rescues her from her bondage to Gédémus whom he drives away. As with Albin, Panturle is moved by emotions that are situated somewhere between love and lust; in the extremity of their need for help, companionship, and sympathy in their heroic labors, love is a superfluous luxury. The natural dignity of Albin and Panturle renders them incapable, on the other hand, of lust or abuse of woman's physical frailty; Angèle-Albin and Panturle-Arsule want each other with an honest directness which is proscribed by the protocol of society salons. As if she were the instrument of some obscure force of nature, La Mamèche had accomplished all that was necessary for the renewal of life in the village.[28] The inevitable pregnancy of Arsule corresponds with the first wheat harvest of Aubignane which is so prodigious as to provoke wonder and high-bidding among the buyers of the agricultural fair at Banon. This success incites other couples to return to Aubignane, which is thus reborn, regained.

Pagnol's concern to have the composer Arthur Honegger write and direct the background music is evidence of his desire to recapture the lyric sweep of the novel, yet he is irresistibly drawn to the creation of supernumerary characters and witty dialogue. Pagnol retells Giono's story accurately but finds different points to stress. The theme of natural motherhood dates from *Fanny* and Pagnol's consort, Orane Demazis, became a specialist in it with her rôle of Arsule following on the parts of Angèle and Fanny; besides being close to Pagnol's own self-expression, the theme of natural, uninhibited love serves as a useful focal point for Giono's more intangible sense of closeness to nature. Despite this semicorrespondence of views, it is strange that critics like Beylie and Delahaye should describe this relatively faithful adaptation of Giono's original as the most literary of Pagnol's films. The majesty of *Regain*, far from inducing a stilted copy, encouraged Pagnol to make one of his most cinematic movies; he matches Giono's grandiose conclusion in a beautiful sequence which shows first a look of understanding and triumph exchanged between Panturle and Arsule and then lengthens into a shot of them resuming the sowing for the following year's harvest in their freshly tilled field, cradled by the surrounding hills. It is a rare moment in Pagnol's movies for not a word is spoken in this time. To guarantee the technical and conceptual synchronization of *Regain Symphonie*, Pagnol had Honegger and his orchestra live for several months on location near La Treille, recording as the film was made.

The technical ambition of the film marks a climax in Pagnol's career. He began by taking his childhood friend Marius Brouquier, a stonemason, to examine the upper Provence village of Redortiers which was the model for Giono's Aubignane; they then returned to La Treille to build a replica of the deserted village, ruin for ruin, in the Barres du Saint Esprit. In addition to the extravagance of building a ruined village, which required as many stonemasons, craftsmen, and odd-jobbers as an intact village, Pagnol also maintained in the field an orchestra, his actors, and the sound-recording unit, in itself a luxury in those days, as Lecocq the sound engineer appreciated.[29] Such numbers, in addition to the usual team of movie technicians, required further platoons of catering and kitchen staff. In this vast camp, living and working in his native landscape, Pagnol fostered a cheerful, relaxed atmosphere where the cook-out and games of bowls assumed almost as much importance as the film sequences; everybody who participated in the adventure was mentioned in the credits. Like Giono at Le Contadour, Pagnol was virtually living his own creative experience. Such a deployment of enthusiasm and energy seems almost to have won over Giono himself; he wrote guardedly in the preface to the published scenario: "Thanks to Pagnol's love of the uplands which he had recently discovered, the transplanted décor became a human experience." Commitment on such a massive scale inevitably produces a work of much conviction, with scenes such as the lyric finale, the sale of the miracle crop at Banon, and the departing Gaubert's legacy of a plough to the now-solitary Panturle, all fused by Honegger's music and the landscape into a sober, well-measured *dénouement*. Strong and cinematically mature, the film would have been even greater had Pagnol been able to render the style and appearance of his leading actors a little less well groomed.

IX   La Femme du Boulanger

Pagnol's best-known film in America, *La Femme du Boulanger* ran for seventy-five weeks in New York and in 1940 won the award of the National Board of Film Criticism as the best film of the year to be produced in a foreign language.[30] An apparent high point in

Pagnol's cinema career, it announces a certain number of changes. His relationship with Orane Demazis ended with the immediately previous film, *Le Schpountz* (1938); it has not yet been demonstrated that this event directed any change in Pagnol's themes but, more significantly, the rift with Giono dates from this film which was adapted from *Jean le Bleu.* As the court case will show, a certain number of misunderstandings had arisen during the previous joint ventures. To make matters worse, Pagnol went ahead with *La Femme du Boulanger* in 1938 before these misunderstandings could be settled to Giono's satisfaction. Under the terms of the contract of November, 1932, Pagnol was, of course, entitled to make a film adaptation of *Jean le Bleu;* at the trial in 1941, he was even able to produce an undated letter from Giono which said: "*Prends ce que tu veux, je t'ai télégraphié dans ce sens.*" But if Giono had disassociated himself yet again from the preparation of the scenario, it must have been for a reason. Rather than plunge into production, Pagnol might have been better advised to wait and to consult his friend more closely, but he interpreted Giono's disassociation as a vote of confidence in himself and went ahead with an adaptation which is even further removed from the original than *Angèle* from *Un de Baumugnes.* Furthermore, Giono felt that the title of *La Femme du Boulanger* belonged to him. Pagnol based his two-hour movie on a seventeen-page chapter of *Jean le Bleu* entitled "Le Boulanger, le Berger, Aurélie," but Giono had derived this chapter from a short story entitled "La Femme du Boulanger" which he had contributed to the *N.R.F.* in 1932.[31] Such freedom with his text and his title was the breaking point for Giono; had the two authors been on anything like cordial terms during the preparation of *La Femme du Boulanger* such a misunderstanding would not have arisen.

The original episode in Giono's autobiographical novel concerned the dimly recollected elopement of Aurélie, the baker's wife, with a local shepherd, but it is easy to understand how much new detail there must logically be in a two-hour movie which is based on seventeen pages of text. It will suffice to list the basic innovations in Pagnol's version to show how different it is from the original chapter in *Jean Le Bleu:*

i) The baker stops baking as soon as he hears of his wife's departure with the shepherd; the village bread supply is thus directly linked to the baker's marital plight and the villagers have a powerful incentive to mobilize in support of the baker.

ii) The baker refuses to admit his wife's adultery and to believe that he is a *cocu;* he persists in repeating that Aurélie is visiting her mother. His willful incredulity matches the obstinate character of Raimu, who plays the part of the baker, and it also prepares for the memorable conclusion when Aurélie is welcomed back by him as if nothing had happened. But Pomponette the cat is given a terrible scolding for her absence.

iii) Pagnol's baker is normally a teetotaler but he often drinks to excess during his wife's absence; his drunkenness, allied with his obstinate incredulity, creates a number of scenes of high comedy.

iv) The baker at one point tries to hang himself; there is nothing so dramatic in Giono's version.

v) The baker falls out with the *curé* who, besides being celibate, seems to him to be too young to understand the plight of a *cocu.*

vi) Pagnol creates a *curé* and an *instituteur* and exploits all the comic possibilities of the small-village rivalry between the two.

With the corpulent and bald Raimu playing the part of Giono's thin, red-haired baker, Pagnol clearly follows his own path in this film; much of the innovation is inspired by Raimu's participation, rendering the tone even more remote from Giono's original. *La Femme du Boulanger* is a descent in mood from the high plateau of *Regain* to a lowland village with a more animated social life. The exchanges between the old troupers, Raimu the baker and Charpin playing the Marquis de Venelles, recall the *Trilogie de Marseille* with de Venelles, like Panisse, still coming to Raimu but this time at the bakery, which is as great a center of social activity in the village as the Bar de la Marine in Marseilles. Raimu's relationship with the *curé*, whose sermon deeply offends him, is frankly comical: "Don't call me your son when I'm old enough to be your father," growls Raimu to the priest in the tone he used to adopt to scold Marius. With these relationships and that of the *curé-instituteur* inherent in his own work, it is surprising that Pagnol should have maintained an association with Giono's text which he manifestly did not need.

The theme has a fleeting resemblance to the two previous Giono adaptations but the elopement of Aurélie (Ginette Leclerc) is a caprice of which Angèle and Arsule, for all their sensuality, would have been incapable. With the departure of Orane Demazis and the return of Raimu there is, in every sense, a shift in the center of gravity. Pagnol himself admitted that Raimu played a preponderant rôle in the *mise-en-scène;*[32] as he had developed many gags in the trilogy, so his clumsy attempts to roll a cigarette and his scolding of Pomponette the cat, which returns at the same time as Aurélie, mark the distinctive contribution of Raimu to *La Femme du Boulanger*. The usual cameraman, Willy, was unavailable at the last moment but Pagnol's standing order to film the actors and to include the setting only as incidental seems to have been well understood by Georges Benoist, the replacement; he had the opportunity to film a memorable outdoor scene in the marshes where Aurélie and the shepherd have their hideout and where the *curé* has to accept a ride on the back of his enemy, the *instituteur*. Scotto's background music is not completely successful; as a composer of romantic ballads he had more success in his composition of the shepherd's serenade to Aurélie. Less fresh than *Angèle* and less elevated than *Regain*, *La Femme du Boulanger* is an admirably balanced film which, over and above the episode from which it takes its title, illustrates some of the concerns and rivalries of provincial France under the Third Republic; the Provençal setting brings a large dose of color and spontaneous mirth to the subject. It was Pagnol's tenth film since *Jofroi* and the last time he was to "collaborate" with Giono.

X   *The Trial Scene*

Pagnol appeared as the defendant in the Troisième Chambre du Tribunal Civil of Marseilles at 8:15 A.M. on October 14, 1941. Charging breach of contract, Giono and his lawyer Bodin pressed for:

1) Seizure of all films adapted from his work.
ii) A ban on all sales of editions based on these films.
iii) Damages of one million francs.
iv) Establishment of a commission charged with the assessment of worldwide revenue from films adapted from Giono's work.
v) Publication of the verdict in the French and foreign press at the expense of the defendant, otherwise a supplement to the damages should be paid *"pour le préjudice moral subi par lui"* (Giono).
vi) Costs to be met by defendant.[33]

Pagnol's defense countered by claiming that since Giono had never participated in the preparation of a scenario he had forfeited his rights to six percent royalties, as specified in the *contrat synallagmatique* of November 8, 1932. Whatever the previous personal understanding between Pagnol and Giono may have been, the latter was entirely unable to establish evidence of his participation in the adaptations from his work which would have entitled him to royalties; Giono's case was thus dismissed and he was summoned to pay nine-tenths of the costs. On the other hand, Pagnol's request that the case be put *hors de cause* was also dismissed; it was established that, in the terms of an agreement reached between Fasquelle and Grasset on October 20, 1937, Pagnol owed Giono two percent of the income from the sale of published editions of the scenarii of *Regain* and *La Femme du Boulanger*. The sum amounted to three thousand francs but Giono's lawyer had not been aware that his client was entitled to it; Pagnol thus had to pay one-tenth of the costs and three thousand francs. The real differences between Giono and Pagnol lay, one feels, elsewhere, and the untidy legal cases in which neither party was entirely in the right were only pretexts for more personal problems.

There were some concrete results to the hearing of October, 1941. They arose from:

i) Pagnol's right, as a result of Giono's noncooperation, to have *Angèle* published as his own work without reference to its origin.

ii) Giono's co-ownership of the title *La Femme du Boulanger* was established by virtue of the short story of that title which he had published in the *N.R.F.* in August, 1932 (N° 227), and from which he derived the chapter in *Jean le Bleu* from which Pagnol adapted the scenario of the movie.

Pagnol has thus always published *Angèle* as his own work without the acknowledgment to Giono which *La Femme du Boulanger* and *Regain*, for example, obligatorily carry; this situation is quite paradoxical since *La Femme du Boulanger* is much less faithful to the original than *Angèle*. Giono, for his part, used his co-ownership of the title *La Femme du Boulanger* to write a play with that title almost immediately after the hearing. Giono produced no evidence of a play or scenario entitled *La Femme du Boulanger* in court in 1941 and the play's completion date, given in a short foreword, is January 1, 1942.[34] Incorporating Pagnol's innovations to *Jean le Bleu*, Giono's later play follows the movie version and is thus a curious example of an adaptation of an adaptation, by the author of the original!

In its long-term effects the case marked an end, of course, to the outwardly successful collaboration of Giono and Pagnol. Furthermore, it probably contributed to the end of Pagnol's production company, *La Société des Films Marcel Pagnol*, which he sold to Gaumont in May, 1942, for an unspecified sum.[35] The burden of the director/studio administrator had been made even heavier after the capitulation of France to the Germans in June, 1940. Even though the terms of the surrender respected the territorial integrity of Southern France *(la zone libre)* under the government of Marshal Pétain in Vichy, there were serious problems of organization and conscience involved in continuing film production. Some of these difficulties will be examined in the next section dealing with *La Fille du Puisatier*, the only film completed by Pagnol during the 1939 - 1945 war. These difficulties, together with his romantic idyll with Josette Day (the leading lady of *La Fille du Puisatier)*[36] and the disagreement with Giono, are all contributory factors to Pagnol's virtual retirement until 1945.

XI   *Pagnol Solo*

Besides his movie adaptations of Giono's novels, Pagnol had, of course, made a number of other films in the period 1932 - 1941; with the exception of *César* (1936), the last "play" of the Marseilles trilogy but written expressly for the cinema, they were not generally successful. It is no coincidence that they have little in common with the memorable Giono adaptations. Although filmed in Provence at the Marseilles studios, they move too rarely out of the studio. There are a considerable number of external shots in these films, it is true, but the actors and the dialogue are often given a semitheatrical preponderance. *Le Gendre de Monsieur Poirier* (Augier and Sandeau), *L'Article 330* (Courteline), and *Topaze* were, after all, directly derived from plays. There were thus lessons to be drawn from the four Giono-based movies which were acclaimed as masterpieces.

XII   La Fille du Puisatier

Completed in late 1940, after the French capitulation to Germany, and just before the legal proceedings with Giono, *La Fille du Puisatier* is the first original creation of Pagnol to incorporate the lessons derived from the film adaptations of Giono's work. Like *Jofroi* and *La Femme du Boulanger*, which bears only the scantiest resemblance to Giono's original, *La Fille du Puisatier* allows expression of Pagnol's gregariousness by admitting the wider village community but it is firmly rooted in rural Provence. With the discreet transfer of the setting to Pagnol's lower Provence, the social and moral values of the scenario are normalized but external nature and the related themes of natural love and motherhood remain.

It was the first and only time that Pagnol cast rôles for Fernandel and Raimu together; in addition, Charpin was once more present as Raimu's opposite number. Since Pagnol's custom was to create rôles for his actors, it is difficult to establish beyond doubt whether the parts of authoritarian father and simple go-between were developed before or after Raimu and Fernandel signed their contracts: Raimu's part develops the one played by Henri Poupon as Clarius Barbaroux, the harsh father of *Angèle*, while Fernandel improvises on the part he played as Saturnin in *Angèle*. This revamped version of *Angèle* takes into account both the greater importance attached to the widower father's rôle, now played by César-Raimu, and the different orientation given to the part of the *fille-mère*, played by Josette Day, more *mondaine* than Orane Demazis.

The time is 1939 in Provence, near Salon, at the outbreak of hostilities with Germany. The film opens with Patricia swinging through the fields and olive groves, with a food hamper for her father. She is the daughter of Pascal Amoretti, a widower well-digger, played by Raimu; his naïve assistant, Félipe, is played by Fernandel. On her way to the site where the men are working, Patricia meets a handsome young poacher who helps her across the stream he is fishing. Upon introduction, she learns that the young man is none other than Jacques Mazel, an officer in the French Air Force and son of the owner of the Salon Emporium.

A few days later, it is Patricia's birthday: old Amoretti gives her a new hat and Félipe, an eager suitor, offers to take her to the Air Force Display in his newly acquired automobile — an opportunity to show off her millinery and his motor. Needless to say, Patricia meets the young Mazel, played by Georges Grey, who successfully draws her away from Félipe. After unsuccessfully trying to seduce her in his apartment, a remorseful Mazel leads Patricia back to the rendez-vous with Félipe, who has become drunk while waiting for her. He is incapable of taking Patricia home, so Mazel takes her on his motor-cycle. They stop on the way home, with catastrophic results for Patricia. Mazel arranges a meeting with her for the following day: he returns to his parents' home to find he has been posted overseas and must depart immediately. He gives an explanatory note to his mother, to be handed to Patricia at the rendezvous. Madame Mazel, who is a snob, attends the rendezvous, decides that Patricia looks too impoverished to be worthy of her son, so passes by without delivering the message.

Patricia becomes pregnant as a result of that journey home with

Jacques and confesses all to her father. Pascal, his honor shaken to the core, takes her to the Mazel parents to explain the situation. They scoff at him. Madame Mazel even boasts of her son's conquests. Pascal behaves with dignity and does not beg. The consequences for him, however, are that he must send away his daughter, to have her baby with his sister Nathalie; to keep Patricia at home would not only bring dishonor to his family, it would be a bad influence on his five other daughters.

Patricia goes to Nathalie where she has a son who takes her family name of Amoretti. Acting the rôle of a warm-hearted man beneath a gruff exterior, Raimu portrays his inner conflict in the same way as César in the scene in *Fanny* where he receives a letter from his son which, for form's sake, he refuses to read. Spurred on by Félipe (who betrays no animosity or resentment toward either Patricia or Mazel), Amoretti senior finally decides to visit Amoretti junior. His taciturnity always belied by his actions, the well-digger takes his daughter and grandson back to his home.

Shortly afterwards, there is news that the Mazel's son has been killed in action. There is a good scene where Monsieur and Madame Mazel, in town clothes, toil up a hillside through the olive groves, ostensibly to consult Pascal about a well but really to see the baby whom they are now eager to recognize as their own grandson. The proud and dapper Mazel, played by Charpin, is shown up by the rustic surroundings, for which he is badly clothed, and by the contrast with Raimu. The moment of revenge is a triumph for the well-digger who enjoys humiliating Mazel:

Pascal: I think, I think . . . I think nothing at all. I think the baby is called
            Amoretti and he is my grandson.
Mazel: Of course he is your grandson. But what are we for him?
Pascal: Passers-by.[38]

Madame Mazel also reveals that she neither delivered Jacques' letter to Patricia nor informed him of the birth of the baby. Pascal is blunt: "That's another dirty trick. Typical of a shopkeeper."[38]

Jacques Mazel eventually returns from the dead, however. He had been shot down and held prisoner. Once more Raimu reveals an almost feminine sensitivity beneath his craggy exterior. Pushing his delicacy to an extreme, he keeps Patricia at home as soon as he learns of Jacques' return. Patricia takes her cue from Pascal. The Mazel family arrive to apologize to Pascal for the wrong they did him, and to make reparation by preparing the marriage of Jacques and Patricia. The latter intervenes to point out that it is not a question of reparation, but of love between herself and Jacques. She will only marry him if he wants her. He does. Félipe, in the tradition of classical comedy, follows this romantic, idealized example with a comic proposal shorn of all sentiment. He asks Jacques if he may marry Patricia's sister, Amanda: "Would you be very upset to have a brother-in-law as stupid as me?" On this note, the film ends.

The film shows Pagnol working comfortably with the medium of cinema. The skills of the noble craft of the well-digger (Raimu was also the purveyor of necessary resources as César, the barman, and Aimable Castanier, the baker) are well documented; the Provençal environment and the political problems of the time fall easily into place as the necessary accompaniment to events. If Patricia's refusal to marry Félipe-Fernandel seems inconsistent with Pagnol's implicit approbation of Amoretti's life near the land, it should be remembered that Jacques Mazel returns wounded from the war unable to pursue his military career and ready to accept Patricia's advice to cultivate some land that belonged to his family. There is a suspicion of sentimentality in the relations between Pascal Amoretti and his daughter Patricia but, like the Parisian schooling of Patricia, much of this can be attributed to the need to explain how a humble widower well-digger like Raimu could have as elegant and well-spoken a daughter as Josette Day. The film has humor, pathos, and conviction; it is also visually beautiful and the striking opening will always linger in the memory.

XIII *Political Recriminations*

Critical appraisal of the film is still marked by the political passions aroused by Marshal Pétain's armistice in 1940. Astonishing to relate, the files of the French *Institut des Hautes Études Cinématographiques* (I.D.H.E.C.) still carry an assessment of *La Fille du Puisatier* as "political propaganda in favor of Vichy and Pétain."[39] It was bad enough to construe the film in this way in 1940 but feelings should have long since cooled sufficiently to enable the injustice to be corrected. The doctrine of Marshal Pétain, *l'espirit Maréchal* as it was bad enough to construe the film in this way in 1940 but feelings should have long since cooled sufficiently to enable the injustice to be corrected. The doctrine of Marshal Pétain, *l'esprit Maréchal* as it was called, can be summed up in the national motto *Travail, Famille, Patrie* which he devised to replace the historic *Liberté, Egalité,*

Fraternité. At the end of the 1939 - 1945 war everything associated with Pétain and his uneasy alliance with Nazi Germany came under deep suspicion; innumerable brutalities were committed as reprisals after the liberation of France and many French men of letters were shot or quarantined by their avenging countrymen. Pagnol himself was on the liberation black list, as were Giono and many other writers. *La Fille du Puisatier* may coincidentally evoke the Marshal's doctrine but Pagnol had been making films about people living close to the land, concerned with the integrity and survival of their families, ever since *Jofroi;* his heroines had been martyrs to love since *Marius*. There may have been some tactless allusions in the film publicity of the time but these do not render the elements of *famille* and *travail* in the film in any way sinister; they simply recapitulate the familiar themes of Giono's work. As for the element of *patrie*, it plays an entirely natural part in a film which was, after all, made during the momentous events of 1940.

It is clearly nonsense for Gaullist fanatics to reproach Pagnol for including the scene in the Mazel's house where some friends gather to listen to the Marshal's armistice speech on the radio. The events of the film are situated in 1939 - 1940 and the Marshal did make the speech. It would have been far more reprehensible for Pagnol to show his Provençaux complacently enjoying their own little lives while the war was still continuing, before the armistice was signed. The inclusion of the Marshal's speech enables Jacques Mazel, who had been shot down in combat, and Félipe, who had been awarded the *Médaille Militaire* as a sergeant in the front line, to think about their own personal lives. The real debating point is whether or not French people had the right to accept the Marshal's armistice as the last word before ever hearing of anyone named de Gaulle.

Even if it is considered separately from the context of previously expressed values, the solution Pagnol offers in *La Fille du Puisatier* could scarcely be called propaganda. In addition, Pagnol declined as inappropriate during the national crisis an invitation, extended by Pierre Benoit and Maurice Donnay in 1942, to stand for election to the *Académie Française*.[40] Pagnol's reluctance to serve the Vichy régime can also be seen in his resignation from the C.O.I.C. (*Comité d'Organisation de L'Industrie Cinématographique*) in 1941.[41] Created in October, 1940, and composed initially of Raoul Ploquin, Marcel Pagnol, Roger Richebé, Jean Painlevé, Léo Joannon, and Jean Galland, theoretically responsible to Jean Prouvost, Vichy minister of Information, the C.O.I.C. (like every other Vichy organisation) was in fact answerable to the Germans. Over the C.O.I.C. and its Vichy superior, the German distributing agency *Kontinental* exercised total control. By resigning from the C.O.I.C. after the successful completion of *La Fille du Puisatier* and by halting work on a project entitled *La Prière aux Étoiles*,[42] Pagnol ensured that he never worked for the Nazis. He survived the black period of doubt following the liberation of France but it now seems ridiculous that he should ever have been submitted to such humiliation; it is absolutely absurd that echoes of unreasoning, postwar vindictiveness should survive into the last quarter of the twentieth century.

XIV Naïs

The persistence and strength of the themes which run through the Giono adaptations survived Pagnol's temporary retirement from film-making and re-emerged in 1945 in *Naïs*. Although the film was directed by Raymond Leboursier and adapted from the Zola short story *Naïs Micoulin*, it should be mentioned in an examination of work inspired directly or indirectly by cooperation with Giono. Pagnol wrote the scenario and produced the film with *La Société Nouvelle des Films Marcel Pagnol*. As was his wont, he demonstrated his solidarity by marrying his leading lady who was now, after Josette Day, Jacqueline Bouvier.

Naïs marks the saturation point of the earlier themes but it also initiates a change and progression toward the great *Manon des Sources*. Saturnin-Félipe becomes Toine played, of course, by Fernandel; Toine is the hired hand on the farm which is ruled with a rod of iron by old Micoulin (Barbaroux-Amoretti) played by Henri Poupon. Toine, a hunchback, adores at a respectful distance the beautiful daughter of Micoulin, Naïs, played by Jacqueline Bouvier-Pagnol but, like Patricia, Angèle, and the heroine of Sicard's *La Fille de la Terre*, Naïs falls for a slick city-dweller; he is Frédéric Rostaing, a law student and son of a family as bourgeois as the Mazels. Toine, as always, helps the young lovers and protects them from the severity of the old patriarch. It is at this point that the predictable pattern of events changes, for Naïs leaves the land to be reunited with Frédéric in the city; in gratitude for his help, she abandons her heritage to Toine. This innovation can be dismissed as a variation on a theme; Pagnol's women always, it is true, sacrifice all to love but Naïs shows more initiative than her predecessors.

The development of the female rôle, from Fanny via Patricia to

Naïs, corresponds to the differing temperaments of the actresses who not only interpreted the parts but were also a part of Pagnol's own life: Orane Demazis, Josette Day and Jacqueline Bouvier-Pagnol. Pagnol's dramatizations of his relations with the women he loved explains the note of increasing lyricism which reached a magnificent climax in *Manon des Sources*. It was as if he had rediscovered the romantic ardor of his youth when he married in middle age a remarkable beauty some twenty years his junior; no less a critic than Claude Mauriac wrote of Jacqueline Pagnol, as she appeared in *La Belle Meunière*, that she exhaled "an aura of youth, grace and love."[43] If the commercial and artistic success of *Naïs* remains limited, the work retains interest as a prelude to *Manon des Sources* and as an important turning point in Pagnol's theme and approach. The cinema underwent a change in definition from dramatic art to lyric self-expression with the story of Naïs fleeing the land to rejoin her lover in the city; it echoes Jacqueline Pagnol's own romantic progress from her childhood near the Camargue, where she sometimes tended the sheep,[44] to marriage with Pagnol in Paris. Pagnol's second and last wife, Jacqueline Bouvier, bore him a son, Frédéric, and a daughter, Estelle, who died in infancy in Monte Carlo.

XV Manon des Sources

Most of Pagnol's better movies were adapted from novels but *Manon des Sources* began as a movie in 1952 and was converted only later into the novel cycle of *L'Eau des Collines*. The climax to Pagnol's career as a film maker, it combines homage to Jacqueline Pagnol with a revival of some Giono and pre-Giono themes. The synopsis shows how.

The background to the film is presented in rapid flashbacks; it is later developed in the novel *Jean de Florette*. Manon's hunchback father, Jean, son of Florette who married outside her native village, moved into a farm bequeathed by his late mother. Although his mother was from the district, Jean himself comes as an interloper to Les Bastides Blanches. Resentful of a stranger's intrusion into their neighborhood, and coveting his land, Ugolin Soubeyran and his grandfather conspire to starve hunchback Jean de Florette out of his farm. By sealing and hiding a spring, his principal source of water, they drive Jean to an exhausting routine of water carrying. Jean is physically incapable of carrying sufficient water for his crops and soon follows Manon's young brother to the grave. Manon and her

mother, a former opera singer, take to the hills where they are
sheltered by a woodcutter's wife, Baptistine. Manon's natural antipathy toward Ugolin leads to the suspicion that he was in some way
connected with her father's death. He, in turn, feels an inarticulate
love for her.

There are five sections to the three-hour movie; each corresponds
approximately to the changes in décor. Hunted by gendarmes in the
hills where she lives and tends her goats, Manon is put on trial in the
village of La Treille, disguised this time as Les Bastides Blanches, for
stealing melons. From the courtroom, the scene switches to the hills
where Ugolin's love gropes vainly for response from Manon. She
repudiates him, feeling even more disgust for him after his obscene
amorousness. Convinced of their responsibility for her father's
death, Manon blocks the spring which provides the villagers with
water. The fountain in Les Bastides Blanches dries up and the effects
of this are shown in the third section. An undefined sense of guilt for
Jean's death is crystallized by this apparent curse. Hounded by a
sense of divine retribution and worried by his emotional setback,
Ugolin confesses all and commits suicide in sordid circumstances in
the fourth part. This deals a severe blow to his grandfather, *le Papet*
César, but its effects on the villagers are beneficial since a mollified
Manon unblocks the spring. She has been encouraged to relent by
the young village schoolteacher who met her in the course of his
geological expeditions. The fifth and final section concerns Manon's
marriage to the young teacher, played by Raymond Pellegrin; this
follows the "miracle" of restoration of water, which the priest was
able to accomplish after Manon had provided some necessary information.

There is an evident resemblance between Pagnol's Manon and the
heroine of the abbé Prévost: as the latter recognized only the dictates of nature, the rule of her instincts, so Pagnol's heroine runs
wild and free like an elusive wood nymph. For Marcel Pagnol-
Raymond Pellegrin, who played the part of her schoolteacher suitor
(and that of Frédéric in *Naïs*), she also resembles Célimène in the
désert. *Manon des Sources* is manifestly *Naïs* rewritten; no longer
constrained to leave her native environment, the heroine exercises a
unique authority by receiving her suitor on her own territory. In a
highly romantic dramatization Pagnol created a place for his last
love in the world of his childhood poems and revitalized the bookish,
Virgilian sylphs and dryads who had hitherto peopled it. The story
also echoes Jean Giono's *Colline* which Pagnol had once planned to

adapt to the screen. The villagers of Les Bastides, in Giono's version, are warned in a mystic communication from the aging Janet of the dangers of alienation from nature; shortly afterwards, when the village water supply runs dry, they associate Janet and his communication with a hostile external nature and prepare to kill him. Janet dies and the water returns before the villagers can put their plan into effect, but his warning has been heeded. Like Janet, Manon is associated in the minds of Pagnol's villagers (in Les Bastides Blanches) with the obscure force of external nature; the superstition and guilt aroused by the dried-up village fountain are exorcised by the priest (who has benefitted from a rational explanation), but the warning is once more heeded.

The film is astonishingly rich (the original version was over four hours long) and has a passionate prolixity; Pagnol's verve sweeps him on to create a lyric epic which sometimes stumbles but which also attains a grandeur matched by no other film he made. As Pierre Leprohon commented, "His mistakes, his foibles and his naiveté are more endearing than faultless techniques of soulless adaptations. He expresses his strong, rich personality and that's what counts."[45] For the great André Bazin, Manon came close to being the finest French film epic ever; it was Pagnol's incapacity "to isolate his theatrical formation from his cinematic flair"[46] which prevented the film from reaching the greatest heights. The poetry of Manon des Sources is, however, too important a feature to be disregarded and Pagnol forces critical reappraisal in a film where, paradoxically, he seems not to care what the critics may think. Sweeping aside decorum, Pagnol creates a giant vision of his world; he has, perhaps, too much to say.

It is hard to isolate the high points of such an experience, particularly when it is projected in versions of varying lengths. Manon's rejection of Ugolin, the inspired ad-libbing of the habitués of the village bar, and the twenty-minute sermon of the curé, portrayed with gentle malice, stand out but the vast canvas of Manon des Sources transcends the momentary appeal of isolated scenes. Filmed at La Treille in the summer of 1952, it was a last call to arms for many members of the team who had worked with Pagnol since Jofroi and Angèle, nearly twenty years before. Willy Faktorovitch was still behind his cameras, the loyal Blavette, Rellys, Vattier, Henri Poupon, Delmont, and Milly Mathis also answered the roll call under the Barres Rocheuses where the ruins of Aubignane still stand, just down the road from Angèle's farm: for Pagnol, a summer filming among such friends, with his wife as the star-lead acting out a dramatization of her youth in a landscape that was part of his own life and childhood, scene of past triumphs, the world of everyday merged with the circumambient fantasy and fiction of the cinema.

XVI   *Other Films*

Despite the pejorative implication of the subtitle, some of Pagnol's "other films" were the equal of any of those already described, but some were very bad. Since the plan of this book is to cover Pagnol's most valuable, enduring achievements, only the better and more interesting films in this category will be examined. They are: *Merlusse, Cigalon, César,* and *Le Schpountz. Topaze* is a notable absentee but, of the three versions, the one starring Jouvet as Topaze (which Pagnol did not make) remains the best. As for the adaptation of three of Daudet's *Lettres de Mon Moulin (Les Trois Messes Basses; L'Elixir du Père Gaucher; Le Secret de Maître Cornille),* the film never jells and lapses into a tired, lackluster parade of characters out of everyone's dictionary of Provençal folklore.

Merlusse is the screen adaptation of the short story which Pagnol contributed to *Fortunio* in January, 1922, under the title of "L'Infâme Truc." The change from short story to screenplay leads inevitably to alterations but much of the text of "L'Infâme Truc" remains in the shooting directions of the scenario and the plot remains intact. The hero is an impassive, veteran schoolteacher named Blanchard who has the appearance of an ogre for the young boys in his charge; "cruel, hairy and one-eyed," he recalls Nickleby's tyrant at Dotheboys Hall, Wackford Squeers, who had but "one eye which was unquestionably useful, but decidedly not ornamental." Blanchard, taunt the boys, stinks of fish, hence his nickname *(merluche* — hake). As the Christmas term is nearing its end, arrangements are made for those boys who, for varying reasons, have to spend Christmas at the school; they include Macaque the Annamite, because he lives too far away, and Villepontoux, because his mother is otherwise engaged. At the last minute the father (or mother, in *Merlusse)* of Cernin, who was to supervise the dormitory, falls ill. Blanchard is the only replacement available and, to accommodate the *censeur,* he agrees to replace Cernin in the dormitory. At the same time, a possibility of promotion for Blanchard is in the offing. A conversation between the *proviseur* and the *censeur* reveals the antipathy of the latter toward Blanchard and his marked preference for the other candidate. Successive scenes progress from Blanchard's strict surveillance of the *étude,* where his unpopularity is revealed by a *pique-cul* planted on his chair, to the dormitory. On Christmas morning the boys awake to find that each has a present in his shoes. From a box of paints and a bag of Cochin China rice for the Vietnamese to four packets of "Celtic" cigarettes for Galubert, one of the bigger boys, each gift matches the taste of the recipient. They realize that only "L'Infâme Truc" (or "Merlusse") could have been responsible for this. Ashamed of their previous contempt for him, they hastily fill up his shoes with their most treasured possessions while he is shaving in the dormitory bathroom. One boy gives a metal-edged ruler, another an old packet of toffees, while Galubert gives him his prized love letter. The *censeur,* in the meantime, has looked in and witnessed this unusual exchange of gifts. It is sufficient to alter his opinion of Blanchard. After a scene of mock disapproval from the *proviseur* and retraction by the *censeur* from his previous dislike of Blanchard, the experienced old teacher is summoned to the office to hear welcome news. He is to be recommended for promotion and the *palmes académiques.*

The sentimentality of the reconciliation and the discovery of the basic good nature of all concerned are quite Dickensian. As strong a contrast as possible is drawn between Blanchard's true nature and that suggested by his repelling physiognomy. He never attempts to endear himself to the pupils although he is extremely sensitive to their every reaction. His sensitivity is further revealed in this final interview with the *proviseur* when he mentions that he has never punished a pupil, in spite of his threats. Pagnol creates an authentic background of schoolboy behavior and school jargon for his story. Not even his schoolroom classic *Topaze* reproduces with more accuracy the psychology of the pupils and the mood of boarding school life.

Pagnol filmed his short story in 1934 and then made a second version in 1935 at the Lycée Thiers in Marseilles. The plight of the boys left behind at Christmas is presented with knowing compassion by Pagnol, former *pion* of the Lycée Thiers, and Poupon gives a memorable performance as "Merlusse." In setting and length Pagnol's generous film invites comparison with *Zéro de Conduite* (1933) but does not have the same stature as Vigo's masterpiece; *Merlusse* was, however, highly enough regarded to be revived in 1965 for a French TV production directed by Georges Folgoas with Georges Wilson in the lead.

Made in the same year, planned as the other half of a double bill with *Merlusse, Cigalon,* according to Blavette, is based on a real incident which occurred during filming in Provence.[47] Cigalon is a chef of great ability, whose unfrequented restaurant is in a small Provençal village. The restaurant is unfrequented because Cigalon is a lover of *farniente.* It requires the competition of a former laundress, Madame Toffi, who also opens a restaurant, to goad Cigalon into culinary activity. Before the formal opening of the two restaurants, Madame Toffi declares: "If your takings are the half of mine, I'll marry you." On the opening day Madame Toffi has many more clients than Cigalon. He, however, has an opulent-seeming client who eats a meal of "grand luxe." The customer turns out to be a professional *griveleur,* a man who eats and then does not pay. To preserve his reputation and to avoid the ridicule of the crowd attracted by the unusual nature of the competition between the two *restaurateurs,* Cigalon gives the *griveleur* the money needed to pay for the meal. So, apparently having earned less with her many parsimonious customers than Cigalon with his one magnificent gourmet, Madame Toffi has to keep her promise to marry Cigalon. The film never won as many plaudits as *Merlusse* but it remained one of Pagnol's favorite films because everyone involved had such fun making it.

César, as the last episode of the trilogy and starring the redoubtable team of Raimu, Fresnay, Charpin, and Demazis, was destined for a box-office success whatever its qualities may have been; as Pagnol relates in his preface to the last edition of *César,* the distribution chief of his film company estimated that "the film of *César,* with the original cast, was worth about ten million francs before it was even made."[48] As with *Marius* and *Fanny,* the incident is more important than the plot; in *César* it is simply designed to bring about the reconciliation of Marius and Fanny. Panisse dies early in the film, expressing the wish that Fanny remarry without waiting too long. Fanny's son Césariot is eighteen years of age, a student at the École Polytechnique in Paris. Two years after the funeral of Panisse, Fanny informs Césariot of his true civil status and he, unknown to his mother, goes to Toulon to pay an incognito visit to Marius, who owns a garage there. Césariot enjoys meeting Marius but he returns from Toulon the victim of a tasteless practical joke of Fernand, an associate of Marius, who had taken advantage of Césariot's stiff, naive sense of social superiority. The misunderstanding is later settled to everyone's satisfaction when Marius and Fernand visit the

Bar de la Marine during a business trip to Marseilles. As the film draws to a close, Césariot reconciles himself to the probability of his mother's remarriage with Marius. The latter, having sold his garage at Toulon to open a marine motor business at Cassis near Marseilles, returns to visit Fanny, head of Panisse's shipchandler's business, in order to put a business proposition to her. His proposition turns into a much bigger undertaking and the film ends with the couple in each other's arms.

With the same familiar characters, M. Brun, Escartifigue, and *le chauffeur,* loitering around the Bar de la Marine and the family of Honorine, *Tante* Claudine, César, and Fanny, massed to cope with the death of Panisse and the return of Marius, the film offers a reassuring sense of continuity. The characters are not as lively as they were, however; in his famous monologue on comparative religion, César's complacency is sufficiently shaken for him to envisage the fact that God may not be a Marseillais. As in *Marius* and *Fanny,* the richness of invention and the humor remain powerful antidotes to developing melodrama. No longer rooted to the Bar de la Marine by the exigencies of stage management, the scene darts in a bewildering sequence of *fondus enchaînés* from trains to funeral parlors, from Césariot's fishing expedition with Marius at Toulon to the *arrière-boutique* of the late Panisse's shop. The ever-inventive Pagnol devises a poignant game of cards started by César, Escartefigue, and Monsieur Brun shortly after Panisse's funeral; it is only on seeing his hand of cards unclaimed on the table in front of his empty chair that his companions appreciate what the death of Panisse means. The game of *trompe-couillon* (or *casse-guibolle)* where a large brick is put under a bowler hat in the middle of the street for the benefit of all would-be kickers, becomes the substitute distraction for the amiable loafers of the Bar de la Marine. The film has the charm and warmth of the other two plays in the "trilogy." With a life of its own it is always entertaining and Willy was no less effective behind his cameras in evoking the animation and color of Marseilles. The theme and location suit Scotto's style and his background music is consequently well matched.

Le Schpountz was made in 1937, at the same time as *Regain;* it owes its unusual title to a Slav term of abuse used by cameraman Willy to describe cinema fans whose enthusiasm was excessive and uncritical. Apparently based on a real event, the film portrays a moviestruck grocer's assistant, Irénée Fabre, played by Fernandel, who haunts the film set on location in Provence. Irénée pesters for a screen test which is laughingly granted to him in Paris. To the dismay of his uncle, played by Charpin, Irénée takes the offer seriously and departs for Paris for his screen test; his arrival at the studios causes mirthful incredulity and his reception is not at all what he expected. Irénée secures a job as "props" manager through the kindly intervention of Françoise, an actress played by Orane Demazis. She intervenes again on Irénée's behalf to secure him a minor, supporting rôle in a film. Irénée, who believes he has a gift for tragedy, turns out to be a revelation as a comic actor in the small part he played. There follows a delicate moment of readjustment when Irénée has to swallow his dignity and accept the fact that he makes people laugh. He is helped, with great discretion, by Françoise. Reconciled to the fact that he is a comic, Irénée accepts the many contracts which are now genuinely offered him. He has succeeded — even more so when he wins the hand of Françoise. Together they return to the Midi to meet the uncle and cousin Casimir. The awestruck family is gently informed of Irénée's success as a comedian and then of his marriage with Françoise. Such scenes as these succeed admirably but the love plot between Françoise and the buffoon Irénée is completely implausible.

One of the most interesting points in the film is the discussion of comedy between Françoise and Irénée. It includes some of Bergson's and some of Pagnol's own ideas, which are taken up later in his *Notes sur le Rire*. Rabelais and Bergson are repeated in Françoise's apology for comedians: "Laughter is a quality which belongs only to Man and which God perhaps gave him as consolation for being intelligent."[49]

Pagnol's basic thesis in *Notes sur le Rire* is that laughter is a victory hymn: it represents one man's sense of superiority over another. This is how he explains the phenomenal success, early in the century, of the *Pétomane*. It is this theory that Irénée puts forward in his chagrin at being discovered as a comic, rather than tragic, actor: "Come on, Françoise; if you laugh at someone it's because you think you're superior."[50]

Irénée's dilemma is identical to that of Merton Gill, played by Red Skelton, in Robert Alton's *Merton of the Movies;* convinced of his talent as a tragic actor, he wins through as a great comic. *Make Me a Star* (Paramount, 1922) was the original version of the Skelton movie and was probably Pagnol's model too. The topic is also the movies and movie-making; the panorama of studio life gives Pagnol the opportunity to take swipes at some of the attitudes he least appreciated at Paramount. By satirizing the stiff sense of hierarchy fostered by the administrative directors of the studios, Pagnol is able to underline the fact that on *his* sets the creative process is democratic and fraternal. The film is very definitely a "talkie" but Fernandel's great performance, Pagnol's commentary on contemporary moviemaking, Gauteur's detailed analysis,[51] and the recent appearance of *Le Schpountz* in *Livre de Poche* contribute to make it a film well worth examining.

XVII   *Of the Cinema*

A series of consecutive film synopses creates a literary tone which is not always appropriate in film criticism. The much-vaunted *auteur* theory was originally based upon a notion of thematic consistency which is itself suspiciously redolent of literature. When cinema is defined as dramatic art there is an even greater risk of incomplete appraisal by the inadequate apparatus of literary analysis, which does not account sufficiently for the organization of the industry and the demands of the camera.

The themes of Pagnol's films and the organization of his business have been sufficiently documented to demonstrate that, as director and producer, he enjoyed a unique freedom from external restraint in his decision-making. Such a freedom is only relative, however, to the working conditions under which other directors labored; in absolute terms, the financial commitment required by each film must have created some pressure on Pagnol to find a winning formula. This constraint is common to all makers of movies: artist and businessman, even the most scrupulous movie maker must, perforce, become an entertainer. It is true that the *Société des Films Marcel Pagnol* was run on a small budget like a family business; Blavette talks at length of the loyalty commanded by Pagnol among his team of actors and technicians. The directors of the company were either members of the Pagnol family or long-standing friends from Marseilles school days. Such conditions serve to liberate the artist but it is difficult to minimize the cost of some of Pagnol's large-budget movies; the sound recording unit in *Regain* and the color film process (RouxColor, the first French process) employed in the unsuccessful *La Belle Meunière* were costly luxuries. It is also probable that the profit margin of *Les Cahiers du Film* was negligible. It is thus reasonable to suppose that the recurrence in Pagnol's work of the themes of the Giono adaptations owes at least something to box-office success; having become over the years part of Pagnol's metaphorical Provence, these themes found natural expression in the much more personal statement, a virtual testament, of *Manon des Sources*.

Pagnol's selection of means and material was much more free from constraint. He was in the enviable position of being both reforming theorist and practitioner; having the privilege to practice what he had preached in *La Cinématurgie de Paris*, Pagnol developed a filming technique that was consistent with his concept of the cinema as dramatic art. In a final revision[52] of his film theory Pagnol retained the following four main points:

a) The film offered the dramatist the opportunity to impose his perspective, his way of seeing the action. Like a play seen through one pair of eyes in the best seats, the film, claimed Pagnol, imposed a single superior perspective on the whole audience wherever they may be seated; by looking into the single eye of the camera lens, the actor looked into the eyes of everyone in the audience.

b) The actors and the setting of the film were guaranteed to be the best available; the economics of the cinema allowed a unique junction of talents seen (and subsidized) by an audience of millions. A similar production, including such a combination of all the talents, would require a guaranteed full house for decades if it were to be an economically viable stage play.

c) Where dramatic action is slowed in a stage play by the need to announce entries and changes of scenery, the camera registers these movements in a self-evident way, as they take place. Pagnol estimated that, in a two-hour movie, the time saved by being able to attack a scene directly amounts to as much as a half-hour.[53]

d) The close-up *(gros-plan)* offers the dramatist a wonderful opportunity to heighten dramatic effect and Pagnol used the *gros-plan* with delight. A close-up of Raimu's benign, patriarchal countenance is particularly rewarding; it belies his gruff manner and demonstrates that if he barks he has no bite. An accumulation of scenes is required in the stage play before the spectator can learn as much about one of the characters. Furthermore, sound movies also create the possibility of a close-up in sound; the throwaway line, the whisper, is audible throughout the auditorium and is as effective as its visual counterpart, the fleeting, telltale facial expression seen in close-up.

Pagnol argued and demonstrated persuasively that cinema is a dramatic art but he used all the technical gadgetry at his disposal to create a particularly cinematic form of dramatic art. In a series of interviews with some of his technicians , a special number of *Cahiers du Cinéma*[54] offers valuable insight into the film techniques derived from the above principles. The dialogue was all-important and Pagnol, after preparing the sequence to be filmed, would supervise shooting from a sound unit from where the actual scene could not always be seen. The camerawork, entrusted invariably to Willy Faktorovitch, consisted of following Pagnol's instructions and of reproducing the actors' performance. Suzanne de Troye, *montage* girl for *Angèle* and other films, recalled that "Pagnol left a lot of liberty to the actors and the cameraman hardly had the right to intrude. Pagnol wanted his actors to have at all costs freedom of movement, and when he was told 'so-and-so has moved out of range' he would reply 'that doesn't matter, we'll shoot again from a different angle!'" Although Pagnol could apparently sense from the sound recording if there was difficulty or embarrassment of any kind on the set outside, Willy always insisted on a 'retake,' which he called a *sécurité*, of each sequence. It was characteristic of Pagnol's style to place such confidence in the actors; it enabled them to relax more comfortably into their parts and to move more naturally in their surroundings. As part of the vast natural stage, the landscape of Provence figured as much as the décor of a play; given the nature of cinema, this was not always sufficient but Pagnol was between the Scylla of *théâtre filmé* and the Charybdis of overexploitation of his setting. The shooting sequences, worked out beforehand with Willy, included not only a number of *gros-plans* but also frequent lengthening or zooming shots which included the background scenery. These *travellings* always register and set the scene, serving as the equivalent of a scene change on the stage. It was thus, paradoxically, the adaptation of a theatrical device which contributed to Pagnol's cinematic success, for Willy's camera rarely dwells on a background scene if it is not dramatically functional. The screenplays of Pagnol's films are all published as stage plays with stage directions, set descriptions, and dialogue, but never include shooting sequences.

It is probably not possible to include the shooting sequences because of Pagnol's readiness to use so much film in reshooting and *sécurités*; the proportion of unused footage is very high. Such extravagance was the price that had to be paid for the easy, unhurried tempo and the warm performances which came to be associated with Provençal Popular Realism. This could not have been achieved by a director anxious to economize on film and a cameraman hustling for new angles; it is the creation of a *coopérative provençale* at play.

CHAPTER 4

Pagnol Immortel

DESPITE its great prestige, election to the *Académie Française*
is always a little sinister since it suggests that one's finest
achievements are behind one. Pagnol's early years as an *académicien*
only served to confirm this impression. He was elected to companionship with the thirty-nine other *Immortels* on April 4, 1946;
the official ceremony of reception was held on March 27, 1947, and
it was the regional novelist Jérôme Tharaud who delivered the address of welcome.[1] He stressed the Provençal origins and cinematic
achievements of the new *académicien*. Pagnol's reply paid homage,
as the tradition demands, to his predecessor. Since he had been
elected to the seat of Maurice Donnay, who had had a long association with Le Chat Noir (a Parisian night club famous for its shadow
theater), Pagnol was able to develop a link between the early projection of silhouettes and modern cinema; studiously avoiding
reference to Marseilles, he confined his remarks to matters of
literature and cinema. Tharaud had welcomed Pagnol as the first
cinéaste to enter the Academy but Pagnol extended the context to
embrace dramatic art in general; he pointed out that there was not a
single dramatist in the depleted ranks of the postwar *Académie* and
modestly added that, but for their deaths during the war, Bourdet
and Giraudoux would almost certainly have become members instead of him.[2] To confirm his semiofficial representation of the
dramatic arts, Pagnol was able to inform his audience that, like
Maurice Donnay himself and thirty-seven previous members of the
Académie Française, he was a past president of the *Société des
Auteurs et Compositeurs Dramatiques*. Nothing new was said and
nothing recent had been accomplished; turning back the clock to
prewar days, the *Académié Française* recognized Pagnol for achievements of a previous decade. This is not to say that his election was

not deserved; it was retrospective and, as such, it was no longer any more relevant than the *Académie Française* itself.

I   *A Time of Change*

The long hibernation in Pagnol's creative life had begun in 1941 and it continued for some time after his election to the *Académie Française*. It was due to the impulsion of Jacqueline Bouvier that he had made *Naïs* in 1945 and written *Le Premier Amour* (1946), a naive scenario about the birth of spiritual love between man and woman in primitive times; it was also, of course, thanks to Jacqueline Bouvier, who had since become his wife, that he finally put a definitive end to his creative torpor by making *Manon des Sources* in 1952. A high point in his career, *Manon des Sources* also marks a change in Pagnol's style from dramatic to poetic; as if encouraged by the success of a more personal vein in the film, he abandoned Naturalist drama for intimate prose. The reasons for this slow change in Pagnol's approach are both social and personal. The aftermath of the 1939 - 1945 war was unpleasant in France; recrimination and reprisal threatened everyone. As President of the *Société des Auteurs* at the time of liberation, Pagnol assumed responsibility for the defense of its members in addition to justifying his own wartime activity to the ever-vigilant committees of inquiry. In a letter to Pagnol dated February 3, 1958, Pierre Benoit applauded him for his leadership of *La Société des Auteurs*, adding that Pagnol touched greatness in his dignified impartiality during those troubled times.[3] The avenging zeal of the repatriates was incentive enough to keep a low profile, particularly when one's richest themes were qualified as Vichy propaganda.

In addition to the *règlements de comptes* and more enduring, the grim new postwar mood of political and philosophical commitment imposed silence on Pagnol, the prewar advocate of *laissez-faire;* even his satires of municipal corruption seemed dated and dwarfed by the massive issues at stake in a realigned Europe. The wheel has since turned full circle in France with the austere determination of the postwar years relaxing into a search for solace in nature on the one hand and a rash of local real-estate frauds on the other. Temporarily outstripped by events, Pagnol was also overtaken by major changes in his personal life; he remarried in 1945 at the age of fifty after thirty years of uninhibited freedom and then, in the following year, lost his closest associate with the death of Raimu.

II *Adaptation*

The period 1945 - 1952 was clearly a time of difficult readjustment; the work Pagnol accomplished in that time reveals a man striving conscientiously to complete an uncongenial task. The serious company he now kept and the absence, or prescription, of his personal inspiration are reflected in *Notes sur le Rire* (1947), *La Belle Meunière* (1948), *Critique des Critiques* (1949). A compensation for the laboring author was the official encouragement he could now give, as an *académicien*, to the literary ventures of friends and acquaintances; he prefaced a full dozen works during this time, proving to be as generous a godfather as Molière. The total number of Pagnol's prefaces, often reproduced in his beautiful copperplate script, greatly exceeded this number; similarly, the work of obligation undertaken directly or indirectly for the *Académie Française* can be taken to continue collaterally with other, more interesting ventures long after the triumphant emergence in 1952 from his somber retreat. Thus *Le Rapport sur les Prix de Vertu* (1956), his translations of Shakespeare's *Hamlet* (1947) and Virgil's *Bucolics* (1958), the historical essays on *Le Masque de Fer* and Michel de Montaigne in 1964 are all included in this section. Pagnol's happiest association with the *Académie Française* was undoubtedly at the time of Marcel Achard's official reception *sous la Coupole* in 1959; it was Pagnol himself who delivered the formal address of welcome to his close friend and, as could be anticipated by the intimacy of two such great comic talents, he created an unprecedented atmosphere of merriment in the solemn surroundings.

III *Academic Duties*

With titles which suggest an exploration of ideas, both *Notes sur le Rire* and *Critique des Critiques* lapse into a surprisingly large amount of personal opinion. Despite the deficiencies of its argument, *Les Notes sur le Rire* is an amusing text; asserting his intention to define the laws of laughter and to develop Bergson's famous thesis of the *"mécanique plaqué sur du vivant,"* Pagnol in fact contents himself with a well-illustrated demonstration of his own preconceived notion of the victory hymn. Laughter, for Pagnol, is an assertion of superiority, an expression of self-congratulation. Thus the phenomenal success in France of the *Pétomane* (an entertainer who made his fortune at the turn of the century by passing wind in an astonishing number of improvised modes) is explained by the audience's satisfaction at seeing (and hearing) someone make the worst kind of social faux pas; the members of the audience laugh because they did not do it. The theory undoubtedly holds true for slapstick comedy but it is inappropriate as an analysis of humor. Pagnol's own brand of humor remains unaccounted for; the success of his character portrayal is not to be measured, for example, in the decibels of the laughter it provokes but rather by the constancy of the quiet smile elicited by the silent pleasure of recognizing familiar things. The Anglo-Saxon sense of humor, the capacity to take a joke against oneself, is shared only with one's closest, most trusted friends, according to the Latin Pagnol. This helps to explain the vehemence of the vituperative *Critique des Critiques;* undoubtedly nettled by the stinging reception the critics gave the disastrous *La Belle Meunière* in 1948, Pagnol responded with this work which he dedicated to the former *Moins de trente ans,* Roger Ferdinand, "in memory of our joint struggles against Ignorance, Injustice, Snobbishness and Envy." Pagnol highlights the discrepancies between popular success and critical acclaim, arguing that the small-mindedness of critics is responsible for this state of affairs; with the specifically named exceptions of Lucien Dubech, Pawlowski, Henry Bidon, André Antoine, Pierre Brisson, Robert Kemp, J-J. Gauthier, Georges Pioch, Léon Treich, Gabriel Boissy, Paul Achard, André Warnod, and Paul Léautaud, Pagnol accuses critics of being "*dangereux écriveurs*" who should have a special permit before being allowed to practice. When he delivered the annual *Rapport sur les Prix de Vertu* to the Academy in 1956, Pagnol was still rumbling; with mock seriousness he began his speech by declaring that he was just as qualified to speak of virtue and its rewards as all "the art critics, literary critics, theater critics and sports critics who unhesitatingly pronounced judgment on works or exploits of which they themselves were incapable."

Pagnol's academic activity was more constructively employed in his translations and in some ventures into history. The first translation he undertook was that of Shakespeare's *Hamlet.* For his introduction to the translation he included some of the more judicious comments from a *Fortunio* article he had written in January, 1924, and added some well-chosen remarks on stage production. Pagnol argued in a scholarly way that Gertrude's infidelity contributes as much as his father's murder to Hamlet's anguish and he underlines this interpretation when rendering the play into French prose. The translation itself is very free as a result of Pagnol's desire to clarify some of the more dense passages of the play; however important the lucidity of a text may be to stage production, some of the liberties taken by Pagnol would stun the purists. "This distracted globe" becomes *"le crâne de fou"* and "Go get thee to Yaughan, fetch me a stoup of liquor" is translated as: *"Allons, va donc, jusqu'au bistro me chercher un petit vin blanc."* Pagnol's stage sense was vindicated at the 1954 Angers Festival when Serge Reggiani played the lead in a production which was praised by Lindsay Anderson for "its directness, its lucidity, its consistent sense of the dramatic" and for the use of "contemporary theatrical speech."[4] It is the only dramatic composition of Marcel Pagnol to be accepted in the repertoire of the *Comédie Française* where, as the height of irony, it has never been performed.[5]

The translation of Virgil's *Bucolics* was introduced in *Chapter 1* as a particularly revealing example of Pagnol's deep spiritual attachment to his native Roman Provence; written in 1958 after his intellectual "return" to Provence, the alexandrines and *rimes riches* of the French version are at one and the same time a personal statement and a sensitive rendering of Virgil's original mood.

The historical disquisitions on *Le Masque de Fer* and Montaigne break new ground. The article on Montaigne was commissioned by the *Académie Française* for a work entitled *Gloires de France* to which all forty *académiciens* had to contribute; Pagnol chose to investigate the nature of Montaigne's religion. He dutifully examines the text, consults the accredited authorities on the question, Dom Devienne, La Bouderie, Maturin Dréano, and reaches the pedestrian conclusion that Montaigne was just religious enough to ensure himself. Where the Montaigne article was a *pensum, Le Masque de Fer* reveals by its liveliness and its very length that Pagnol took a genuine interest in the subject. Pagnol's book is an investigation into the true identity of Cinq-Mars' legendary captive at Pignerol. Known for convenience as Eustache Dauger, many different identities have been imputed to him. Pagnol's book, dedicated to André Chamson, discusses in the entertaining style of an enthusiastic amateur the theories that have previously been put forward. The Duc de Beaufort, Monmouth, and Richard Cromwell are but a few of the better-known names that have been put to the face behind the iron mask. Pagnol's own intriguing explanation is that it was Louis XIV's young twin brother, born only a few hours after him. Always a potential rallying point since the differences in age could be disputed, Louis had to have him hidden away, with those distinctive features forever concealed. The great importance of the prisoner is reflected in the deference shown to him at all times by his warders. In a subsequent review of the book, Georges Mongrédien, an eminent seventeenth-century scholar, approved of Pagnol's summary of the case but very gently suggested the suppression of the last thirty pages which put forward Voltaire's thesis of Louis XIV's twin brother.[6]

Pagnol only fully asserted himself as an *académicien* after the resounding success of the first two books of his *Souvenirs d'Enfance*. Given this confidence, he loosened his starched collar and relaxed into the warm, easy humor for which he is better known. This is typified in his speech of reception for Marcel Achard, December 3, 1959, probably one of Pagnol's happiest moments in the Academy. Master of the situation, speaking to his most intimate friend, Pagnol delivered what is supposed to have been the funniest formal speech ever given at the Academy. He began with a charming, untranslatable elegance: "Voltre exorde, qui eût voulu que je renonçasse aux critiques traditionelles exprimait donc le souhait qu'à l'éloge funèbre d'André Chevrillon, je répondisse par le vôtre. Ne soyez donc pas si pressé. Il est certain qu'un jour cet hommage vous sera rendu; mais j'espère que celui qui aura le chagrin de le prononcer est encore sur les bancs du lycée."[7]

The expectations of his audience, whetted by such an unorthodox beginning, were not disappointed. The skill and daring of the speech exact admiration. Pagnol pointed out that the Academy had never forgiven Molière for being an actor, yet Achard had been an actor: worse, he had even played an undignified clown: "I know very well," says Pagnol, "for I have seen you with your powdered face and fake chin, walking pigeon-toed, provoking gales of laughter and prolonged applause by getting yourself kicked! . . .

— And kicked where, sir?"

The apprehensive hush which followed this rhetorical question, was shattered by the laughter which erupted from the sedate assembly as Pagnol, with brilliant timing, paused, turned over the page, and resumed: "In the *Théâtre de l'Atelier* before an audience of as big. . . ."[8] Even Mauriac laughed, related a delighted Madame Pagnol.[9] Henri Bordeaux, it should be added, went home to mutter into his *mémoires* that these new fellows were turning the Academy into a circus.[10] Pagnol, however, was now immune from such crustiness, having discovered the previous year a rich new seam in his literary work, the subject of the following chapter.

CHAPTER 5

The Return of the Native

A S the constant background to his artistic work and as a regular summer retreat in real life, the setting of Pagnol's childhood remained with him for ever. Thus it is only in relative terms that one can speak of *Souvenirs d'Enfance* as a return. With *Manon des Sources*, Pagnol had developed a more explicit link between his real and artistic lives than in the previous scenarii acted out in Provence; in *Souvenirs d'Enfance* the link becomes almost absolute despite a certain dramatization. It is not without some diffidence, expressed in the introduction to *La Gloire de Mon Père*, that Pagnol submits his younger self to the scrutiny of the reading public. His prose in the three volumes of *Souvenirs d'Enfance* is thus his most intimate work with the landmark events of his childhood etched as clearly as if they had only just occurred. The two other prose works, *Pirouettes* and *L'Eau des Collines*, which will be studied in this chapter, are hardly less intimate. As an account of adolescent life, *Pirouettes* is a natural pendant to *Souvenirs d'Enfance;* since the first draft dates from 1920, the novel can be regarded as close to the mood of the young high-school graduate. The scenario of *Manon des Sources*, incorporated with some alterations as a novel with *Jean de Florette* in the cycle of *L'Eau des Collines*, is a manifestation of the *genius loci* which, in the eyes of the romantic Latin scholar, became incarnate in the person of Manon - Jacqueline Bouvier, the golden-skinned sprite of the hills of La Treille, *la blonde chasseresse* of Pagnol's schoolboy poems (see quotation on p. 23).

I Souvenirs d'Enfance

Written in three volumes, *La Gloire de Mon Père, Le Château de Ma Mère*, and *Le Temps des Secrets, Souvenirs d'Enfance* ranges over Pagnol's recollections of childhood from earliest infancy to the first years at high school when he was nearing the age of twelve. It

133

should be stressed at the outset that the work is not an autobiography; it has some documentary value but, strictly speaking, it is
not so much about Pagnol as about his parents. He writes his *"petite
chanson de piété filiale"* with an appearance of easy, guileless spon-
taneity which is deceptive for, elaborating on his own childhood, he
creates an immensely rich and understanding tribute to the often-
ignored lessons of childhood in general. Although his successive
memories are given an artificial, dramatic life with much dialogue
and detail, there is no plot imposed upon the broadly accurate
chronological sequence of events. This method is particularly well
adapted to the theme of childhood and ensures a lively evocation not
only of the events but of the mood of a child's life. The principal
episodes follow each other in the book in the same way as each new,
daily phenomenon presents itself to a child; with his well-known
dramatic flair, Pagnol successfully captures the all-important note of
spontaneous surprise and wonder by dispensing, as a doubly omniscient author, a series of unexpected events. Each of these episodes
is linked by the imperfect tense, narrated in the unfussy, expeditious
past-historic tense and further animated by dialogue and an impressive, but theoretically implausible, amount of detail. How could he
remember it all? This episodic treatment is blended into an overall
unity by the consistency of the author's tone and style; time overlaps
itself and the anecdotes of *Souvenirs d'Enfance* run into each other
in the same way as the idyllic days of a Provençal summer which,
like the book, suddenly ends without having gathered a wrinkle.

Ever-present at work and totally absent at play, the calendar is
only the vaguest of guides to the subdivision of the work; the three
volumes hasten over school and linger over the long, glorious summers spent in the hills of La Treille where everything happens in a
rich, timeless profusion. An important example, indicative of
Pagnol's overall approach, is the telescoping of two summers into
one in the first two volumes, *La Gloire de Mon Père* and *Le Château
de Ma Mère*. It is known for a fact that the Pagnol family spent their
first summer at La Treille in 1903; Pagnol confirms this in *La Gloire
de Mon Père* when, at eight years of age, he protested his right to accompany his father and Uncle Jules on their first hunting expedition.[1] *La Gloire de Mon Père* ends after the triumphant hunting
exploit of Pagnol's father but the same summer continues in *Le
Château de Ma Mère* where young Marcel inexplicably attains the
age of nine.[2] Pagnol's own archive reveals that he was in *6e primaire*
at the elementary school of Chartreux-Longchamp during the year

prior to the first summer in La Treille, 1902 - 03, yet he returns from his summer holidays, according to *Le Château de Ma Mère*, not to *5e primaire* but to *4e primaire*.[3] Since he did not, in fact, enter *4e primaire* until October, 1904, it is evident that the two summers of 1903 and 1904 are compressed into one to provide the substance of *La Gloire de Mon Père* and the opening pages of *Le Château de Ma Mère*. The chronology reverts to normal in the following volume, *Le Temps des Secrets*. It was at the end of the academic year 1904 - 05 that Pagnol passed the public entrance examination for the Lycée Thiers which he entered in October, 1905, at the age of ten; this is confirmed in Marcel's first encounter with Isabelle Cassignol in *Le Temps des Secrets:*

Isabelle:	Do you go to school in town?
Marcel:	Yes. I start high school in October. In sixth grade. I'm going to learn Latin.
Isabelle:	I've been at high school for a long time. And I'm going into fifth grade next year. How old are you?
Marcel:	I'll soon be eleven.
Isabelle:	Well, I'll soon be eleven and a half, and I'm a year ahead of you. . . .[4]

The events recalled by Pagnol have their origins in his own childhood but he submits them to a refining process in order to extract the purest essence of memory and mood: the dramatization and elaboration of the isolated episodes reach beyond the particular detail of his own autobiography to universal aspects of childhood in general. It is important to stress the universality of the theme for there are critics who relegate *Souvenirs d'Enfance* to a restricted, local area of interest. It is only the thematic analysis of universal values that can account for the subdivision of the three volumes of *Souvenirs d'Enfance;* although highlighting each incident, charging it with life, "loading every rift with ore," and even using the episode rather than the theme as the basis for the titles (especially in *La Gloire de Mon Père* and *Le Château de Ma Mère*), Pagnol's trilogy of childhood follows the eternal cycle of the infant growing away from home. Entirely dependent upon his parents and close family in *La Gloire de Mon Père*, the child finds his own recreative resources when he learns to hunt, so to speak, with another boy of his own age (Lili des Bellons) at the beginning of *Le Château de Ma Mère*. Even his friend Lili is abandoned in *Le Temps des Secrets* when Marcel's awakening adolescent interest in girls alienates him from everybody and when, at the *lycée,* he learns to fight his own battles.

A   *The Author's Perspective*

With the gentle irony implicit in the surprised revelation of details in his own life, Pagnol establishes an impression of objectivity in the distance put between himself, the narrator, and himself, the child-subject. The first person singular pronoun is only a thin disguise for another identity, which Pagnol studies with as much curiosity as Anatole France contemplating his younger self: "The little fellow really interests me: I didn't pay too much attention to him when he existed but now that he has gone I like him a lot. He was a lot better than all the other 'me's' that came afterwards. He was certainly scatterbrained but not malicious, and I must give him credit for not leaving me with a single unhappy memory. His was an innocence I have lost and which I naturally miss."[5] Pagnol's younger, other self, as dramatized by the author, assumes responsibility for the narrative in the set pieces but he is relieved of his responsibility in the linking passages by the guiding hand of the omniscient author.

B   *The Universality of* Souvenirs d'Enfance

The perspective chosen by Pagnol alternates between that of the dramatist and the natural, omnipotent storyteller, preparing surprises (the plans to rent a villa), maintaining suspense (the long walk along the canal), and hinting darkly at distant threats (bad weather bringing the end of the summer holidays). The qualities of the storyteller are shared by most Franco-Provençal writers from Mistral to Giono and Bosco and are particularly well adapted to the evocation of childhood when combined with the mock-seriousness and humor of Paul Arène or Marcel Pagnol. Arène's account of his childhood in *Jean des Figues* offers many parallels to *Souvenirs d'Enfance* and must have been known to Pagnol whose *Pirouettes* (1932) was published by Fasquelle only a few years after the same editor had reprinted *Jean des Figues* in *La Gueuse Parfumée* (1929). Both Arène and Pagnol begin their stories, naturally enough, with their birth; the parallel becomes significant when the elements of comedy and coincidence are compared. Accidentally exposed to the full heat of the sun by the inconsiderate movement of the family donkey, in whose shade he had been resting, the baby Jean des Figues is possessed by a spirit of unpredictable fantasy as a result of the sunstroke suffered at the start of his life. Chance plays as comic a rôle in the circumstances of Pagnol's birth, as related at the opening of *La Gloire de Mon Père*, when the unborn baby participates, with the use of the first person plural, in his and his mother's race against the clock from La Ciotat to Aubagne, where he was born.

It was a capricious destiny which had ordained that Marcel should, like the *abbé* Barthélemy before him, prepare his *entrée* into the outside world on the Aubagne - La Ciotat road, for both were elected to the same chair of the *Académie Française* on March 5, after an interval of a few hundred years. Pagnol tampers a little with the dates to achieve this coincidence but the most important point to retain is that he wants to begin his life, in the book at least, under the sign of unpredictable chance. Both he and Arène refuse to admit into their childhood a system which smacks as much of logic as Naturalism. Arène's rejection is quite explicit: "Have you never seen the dissecting-room of the real modern author? Have you not seen him in his blood-stained apron, working in his shirt-sleeves with his gleaming scalpels. . . . ?"[6] Pagnol's approach to childhood is an implicit rejection of Naturalism; instead of reasoning from the dead past to the present (like Guéhenno and Sartre in a predominantly imperfect tense) in order to explain his adult self, he renounces the present to return to the reanimated past. Beyond certain specific moments in his own life he seeks the flavor of childhood for its own sake. As the author of a child's life he thus maintains the unpredictability of tomorrow.

C Pagnol the Moralist

No more than Alain Fournier, Twain, Carson McCullers, or Salinger does Pagnol allow excessive, grown-up rationalization to dim the perception of a fresh, first experience. The juggernaut of casuality destroys the simple wisdom of childhood which he is seeking; he frequently reverses the rôle of adult authority: "Since they always come too late to do anything about it, children have to accept the incurable habits of their parents and try not to upset them"[7] and "I at last understood that grown-ups are silly and never do as they please."[8] The use of the plural in Pagnol's frequent aphorisms on childhood reveals an ambition to generalize on the experiences of a younger, other self; by underlining the relativity of adult values, as seen through a child's eyes, he assumes the stature of a moralist. Many of the lessons are explicit, the beauty of friendship and the formative value of play, but, like Anatole France, he also establishes by irony and inference a set of fundamental counter-values: the discussions between his republican father and Catholic uncle Jules demonstrate the need for tolerance; his father's occasional need to posture before his own rigid sense of probity teaches Marcel to make allowances for human frailty. The deep prevailing undercurrent of the *Souvenirs d'Enfance* carries the reader to an awareness of his own vanity and of the tyranny of his social obligations. For Pagnol the *primitif* childhood and nature represent between them a state of innocence and freedom which adults, in their wisdom, seek only when it is irretrievably lost.

D   *Language and Style*

The passing of childhood is also to be regretted from an aesthetic point of view: "Until the sad phase of puberty, the world of children is different from ours: they possess the wonderful gift of imaginative ubiquity."[9] The child's capacity to wonder and to see things as if for the first time are among the most precious attributes of the artist and the simple, direct language of *Souvenirs d'Enfance* conveys the clear, bright vision of infancy. Both in the description of objects that surround him and in his understanding of a child's mode of perception, Pagnol's correct, concrete language is always admirably adapted to the subject. Such is the quality of the language in the three volumes that their constant high sales are often attributed to their use in French schools for traditional dictation exercises — *c'est plein de dictées!* Interested enough in words as a child to compose vocabulary lists, dazzling Lili with *anti-constitutionnellement*, Pagnol continues to indulge the same habit as an adult author. *Souvenirs d'Enfance* contains a statistically high number of concrete nouns; the visits to the *brocanteur* in *La Gloire de Mon Père* provide Pagnol with a pretext for a veritable orgy of nouns in the description of the flotsam and jetsam brought home by his father.

The child's keen curiosity and the observation of the world around him are also evident in the descriptions of the Provençal countryside where everything has a name, both in French and in Provençal; his extraordinary knowledge of the flora and fauna of Provence also demonstrates his love of the countryside. The plants and shrubs he mentions are all found in the *garrigues*, the heath-lands of inner Provence which are so fragrant with wild thyme, fennel, sage, and rosemary. They are:

l'argeras	a type of thorny gorse
la baouco	a coarse, durable variety of grass, growing wild, usually yellow in color
le cade	juniper
la coucourde	pumpkin

la farigoule	a type of thyme
les messugues, or *mussugues*	the wild cistus which prefers sunny slopes; *messugues* can also mean the cistus-covered slopes (pink or white flowers in May/June)
le pétélin	the terebinth tree
la pigne	fir-cone

The fauna are equally well documented:

une agasse	magpie
une alude	a variety of large, winged ant
une bartavelle	although in *Larousse*, the *bartavelle* has too prominent a rôle not to be explained. It is the largest type of partridge, known as a rock partridge and is found only in S. Europe.
une bedouïde	a crested lark *(cochevis huppé)* See Mistral's *Mireille*, Chant II — *couquihado.*
une bouscarle	wagtail *(bergeronnette* or *hochequeue)*
un cabridan	a large wasp
un cul-blanc	(Italian *culbianco)* a wheatear
un darnaga	crossbill (type of finch)
un passe-solitaire	a rock thrush *(merle de roche)*, a migratory, Mediterranean bird of solitary habits
une larmeuse	a lizard peculiar to S. France
un limbert	a lizard peculiar to S. France
un pregadiou	*(prie-dieu)* a praying mantis, so called because of the shape of its forelegs (See also Gide, *Si Le Grain Ne Meurt*, O.U.P., 1946, p. 55)
une ratepénade	a type of bat
sayre	types of thrush. The *sayre* known in the North of
tordre	France as a *grive litorne*, is the common fieldfare. Together with the rarer but larger *tordre* (Latin *Turdus*, French *Draine*, English *Mistle Thrush*), it is much prized by French hunters and gastronomes.[10]

Allied to the enumeration and naming of the objects that surround him, the child's specific use of language reveals both his interest in concrete things and his incapacity to manipulate abstract concepts. Whether describing one of Lili's traps or the gory battle between the *pregadiou* and the ants, the language always remains precise enough to pick up the finest material detail.

Pagnol adds the qualities of a shrewd psychologist to his linguistic control when he deals with a child's mode of perception; adapting his gift for the *bon mot*, he sprinkles his text with *faux-naif* truths and infantile maxims: "My father was always twenty-five years older than me and it's always stayed that way";[11] "when the baby sister Germaine began to totter and to stutter, she revealed our own strength and wisdom to us, and we accepted her for good";[12] "and that day I discovered that grown-ups could tell lies as well as I could, and I no longer felt I could trust them";[13] "tools are very cunning; as soon as you look for one it understands and hides."[14] The adult Pagnol sometimes intrudes explicitly in his *mise-en-scène* with more sophisticated homilies: "And so they [girls] separate us from our friends by laughing on swings which soon stop when there is no boy there to push them";[15] "such is the frailty of our reason; it's usually only used to justify our beliefs."[16] There is often a dry, *pince-sans-rire* barb in the homily and it can be positively cutting: "Success often creates talent."[17]

Since *Souvenirs d'Enfance* does not purport to be an autobiography, it would be futile to try to reach the original, individual child Pagnol through the trappings in which he is presented by his older self. In matters of style, perspective, and moral lessons, Pagnol, the adult author, intrudes to expand the narrative into a view of children as they are generally assumed, or supposed, to be; as regards incident, the selection of the material is also the decision of the author. The whole text is so drenched with Pagnol's present personality that his other little self is drowned; even a documentary autobiography must inflict the same fate on the author's past self. Since autobiography can only ever be ourselves as we want to be seen, why not present a frankly personal view? As with his movies, Pagnol's fiction is strangely truer than fact. In any event, the portrait of the artist as he wishes to see himself, whether as a young man or as a boy, has the intimacy of a self-confession. It is rewarding to penetrate into the intimacy of the self-portrait and this can best be accomplished, in the case of Pagnol, by following more closely the episodes of each of the three volumes. The chronology followed by Pagnol has been confirmed against external evidence and it is substantially correct but this, of course, bears no relation to his unverifiable character portrayal.

E   La Gloire de Mon Père

Covering the period 1895 - 1903, the first volume of *Souvenirs d'Enfance* deals with random recollections until Marcel reached the age of six. An incident to which much significance was subsequently attached occurred while the family still lived in the Marseilles suburb of St. Loup. Left temporarily in the care of his father at work while his mother was shopping, the three-year-old Marcel accidentally revealed that he could read; on the strength of this achievement, the *lycée* which was opened at St. Loup in 1962 took the name of Marcel Pagnol. By the time he was six Pagnol was a pupil at the *école communale*, the district grade school, of Chartreux-Longchamp, where his father taught. It is from this age that the memories around which Pagnol weaves a cocoon of adult afterthought assume any density; the principal events in the book relate in consecutive order to his progress in school, the courtship of his mother's sister, aunt Rose, by the future uncle "Jules," the birth of sister Germaine and cousin Pierre, the plans to rent a villa, the visits to the *brocanteur* to find furniture for it, the long voyage to La Treille, his childhood games in the country, and the great hunting expedition. Apparently unconnected, the events lead naturally into each other: it was because Thomas Jaubert from Perpignan, the Catholic 'r'-rolling uncle "Jules," became his brother-in-law that Joseph Pagnol was able, by sharing the cost, to rent a villa in the country. There are two basic leitmotivs which draw the loosely connected anecdotes together.

The addition of uncle "Jules" to the family is the cause of never-ending sectarian dispute: Catholic, expansive, and possibly Monarchist, uncle "Jules" has political views which are diametrically opposed to the republican, anti-Catholic austerity of Joseph Pagnol, who was probably an adherent to the radical party. The two men have much esteem for each other but they never overlook an opportunity to score doctrinal points off each other. It is this sectarian background that explains the delicious irony of the conclusion. Having, on an earlier occasion, deplored the vanity of a colleague who had had himself photographed (at a time when photographs were rare) with a fishing prize, Joseph furtively seeks to have himself photographed in La Treille with his two *bartavelles*. The irony of fate dictated that it was the arch-enemy, the *curé*, who had the camera and who provided the much-desired service. Joseph's lame excuse to his son for a) having his photograph taken and b) having it taken by the *curé*, was that the *curé* really wanted him to refuse in order to be able to accuse the *instituteur* of sectarianism, "but," says Joseph, "we were smarter than he was!" It was thus that the child saw the human side to his father, *"surpris en flagrant délit d'humanité."* Although this episode gives its title to the book, the events leading up to it are introduced only halfway through the narrative when, around August 15, uncle "Jules" "cooked" the cartridge wadding in grease.[18]

The second leitmotiv is provided by the private life of the child's imagination. This is constant to all three volumes and, it has been seen, dictates the choice of language and the author's perspective. In his description of Marcel's activity in *La Gloire de Mon Père*, Pagnol shows more specifically the excitement of first contact with external nature and the influence of a child's reading matter on his play and games. The impact of the space and freedom offered by the countryside was immense. Pagnol's own succinct analysis is eloquent enough testimony; on emerging from La Treille, advancing into the countryside for the first time, "the fairy tale began and I felt my life-long love beginning to burgeon."[19] Throughout the book, from the *Pieds Nickelés*, in the comic bathroom passage where Marcel gives a demonstration of how to "wash" without getting wet,[20] to the works of Gustave Aymard and the translations of Fenimore Cooper,[21] Marcel's leisure reading provides him with fortifying examples to emulate. The classroom texts, Andersen and Daudet, are never regenerated in recreation: child psychologists would be more qualified to decide if this is a consequence of the inhibiting context of the class or of a preference for the violent themes of the recreational books. There is always much cruelty in Marcel's games, as Pagnol admits: "I think man is naturally cruel; children and savages prove it every day."[22] Little brother Paul and Marcel devastate the insect population surrounding La Bastide Neuve but uncle "Jules" and Joseph are responsible for a veritable hecatomb of fur and feather in the surrounding hills. It would be wrong, however, to pass any judgment on such pre-ecological pastimes; more significant is Marcel's freedom to act out his private life and to establish his own kind of contact with the natural world about him. This emancipation from parental apron-strings was a necessary preparation for the arduous daily adventures with Lili des Bellons, the hardy peasant boy, and it forms an interesting contrast to the activity of the child Gide during his summer holidays at Uzès, just across the Rhône.[23]

F   Le Château de Ma Mère

Although opening as a sequel to *La Gloire de Mon Père*, the book is a self-contained, thematic whole. From beginning to end it deals with Marcel's ripening friendship with Lili des Bellons, a local lad whose real name was David Magnan and who was killed in the 1914 - 18 war. The episode of *le château de ma mère*, which lends its title to the book, comes as a final climax, an ultimate obstacle to the resumption of the previous, halcyon summer's routine which Marcel and Lili had shared. As has been observed, that same summer, which occupies the first half of *Le Château de Ma Mère*, is a compression of two years into one; the vivid concentration arising from this serves to convey most appropriately the state of heightened consciousness in which Marcel visited the enchanted new world to which Lili introduced him: "with the friendship of Lili, a new life began for me"[24] and "I had never been so happy in all my life."[25] The first extraordinary tour of Lili's traps, the visits to la Chantepierre and to the cave of the *"grosibou,"* all demonstrate that *"Lili savait tout."*[26] The identification of everything that surrounded them and the plentiful use of proper names create a sense of loving intimacy with nature: "He introduced me to the old jujube-tree of La Pondrane, to the service-tree of the Gour de Roubaud, the four fig-trees of Précatory and the black bearberries of La Garette. . . ."[27] The descriptions of the landscape in *Le Château de Ma Mère* are the most poetic of the three volumes of *Souvenirs d'Enfance* but the robust, practical Lili does not respond in the same ecstatic way as Marcel to La Chantepierre, for example, the singing rock whose melody changes according to the direction of the wind.[28] Although rooted in reality, Lili is capable of finer sentiments and Pagnol composes a memorable, solecism-riddled letter from him[29] which stands as a touching tribute to friendship. Marcel's friendship with Lili isolates him from his family; the increasing self-sufficiency of the young Pagnol can be seen in his refusal to go hunting with his father ("If they want to leave tomorrow, they can hunt alone"[30]) and in his subsequent decision to run away, announced to his parents in another grammatically horrible note.

The structure of the book follows the simple cycle of the seasons. The happy memories are always sunlit, but when the time comes to return to school, then clouds, both literal and figurative, appear. The first summer(s) of 1903 and 1904 end(s) in the middle of the book with a rainstorm. Marcel and Lili were reunited at La Treille for the Christmas holiday in 1904 and then the family began weekend excursions to the hills: "The mud of February splashed and squirted under our feet. Then, in April, the foliage sprang from the tops of the walls, arching over our heads."[31] Living impatiently for the following summer of 1905, Marcel had two important obstacles, two anecdotes, to overcome — his examinations and the custodian of *le château de ma mère*. The latter needs no explanation but the examinations that Marcel passed in June, 1904, should be situated in their context.

As a pupil at an *école communale*, a state primary school, Marcel enjoyed free tuition. Under the Third Republic all primary education was free; Marcel could have remained at the *école primaire communale* until the age of thirteen and then continued, until the age of eighteen, and at state expense, either at an *école primaire supérieure* or an *école normale*. It was not, however, possible to continue studies at university level from this stream; only the fee-paying *lycée* (which admitted students to the *petites classes* at the age of six or to the mainstream at the age of ten) prepared students for entry to the university and thus to the liberal professions. In order to remedy the injustice that this represented to poor families who could not afford the fees of the *lycée*, the state offered a limited number of scholarships to the brightest pupils of the *école primaire*. The scholarship, which guaranteed free tuition and materials at the *lycée* for the duration of their studies, was awarded annually to the limited number of pupils from the *écoles primaires* who passed the *concours des bourses* at the age of ten to eleven. It was for this examination that Marcel was working in the long June "without Sundays" of 1905. There was both an honor and a stigma attached to the successful candidates who became *boursiers de l'Etat*. In the social rivalry between the streams of the *lycée* (especially in the *petit lycée*, the fee-paying parallel to *école communale*) and the *communale*, it was a point of honor for the latter to demonstrate that, less privileged, it could produce students who were able to cope with the *lycée* program. It was thus that, by taking the scholarship examination, Marcel became "*le champion qui allait défendre l'honneur de l'Ecole du Chemin des Chartreux.*"[32] Despite the undoubted quality of the young students who passed the *concours*, there remained the hurdle of social prejudice to overcome. Since children are no less cruel than their parents, who are sometimes capable of sneering at those so unfortunate as to be "on welfare," the *boursier* at the *lycée* had sometimes to endure the taunts of his more fortunate classmates. Bright enough to pass the examination and tough enough to ride the difficulties of an arduous initiation, the traditional *bizutage*, the *boursier* Pagnol tells his story in *Le Temps des Secrets*.

G   Le Temps des Secrets

Marcel has the summer of 1905 before him at the opening of the book and he prepares to relax into his holiday routine once the problem of the odious custodian of the *château* is settled. It cannot be said that he rested on the laurels of his success in the *concours des bourses* for he was disappointed at not passing top of the list into the *lycée*. Tante Fifi's arrival at La Bastide Neuve early in the story introduces the parable of the grandmother's jealous love for her husband; thus the principal theme of the book is broached. Young Marcel is inspired by the mysterious concept of love to reflect on the curious behavior and sexual precocity of Clementine, the school concierge's daughter. This new preoccupation coincides with a period of "dangerous" inactivity. No longer able to set his traps with the same frequency as the previous summer since Lili is detained by his father to help in the fields, Marcel sometimes wanders aimlessly around les Bellons where he finally meets the attractive, capricious young Isabelle. She is presented with the same aura of spellbound unattainability as Reine Cabridens, the first love of Jean des Figues; the unpolished Marcel with his dirty hands has the same sense of inferiority as Jean des Figues before the accomplishments and social superiority of his first love: "My love was as natural as the dew and the cicada's song; it had to be that way for would it not have been foolish of me, Jean des Figues, a peasant and son of peasants to presume to enter the Cabridens' house . . . ?"[33]

It was with a swelling sense of pride that the tousled Marcel became the *cavalier servant* of Isabelle, destroying the spiders that terrified her and earning the name of Bellerophon conferred with semiseriousness by her father. Enslaved by Isabelle who inhabits a magic, ethereal world, whose father is a poet with the noble name of Loïs de Montmajour and speaks in verse, Marcel neglects his friend Lili and withdraws into the privacy of his dreams and make-believe world; uncommunicative at meals, he retires hastily to his room "running to my nightly rendez-vous with my memories of the day."[34] The spell of his infatuation is broken by a combination of parental intervention and physical accident. There is a comic contrast between Bellerophon's previous vision and the crude reality to which Marcel suddenly awakens: he learns simultaneously that Isabelle's father, who was a drunkard, was really called Cassignol and that she herself was not immune to the most vulgar of gastric complaints.[35] As Arène only recognized his real love for Roset, the gypsy girl, after abandoning the unreal perfection which he had attributed to Reine Cabridens, so it may be said that Marcel, after a much longer interval, turned from Isabelle to Manon des Sources. The wistful, Renoiresque memories of the little girl on the rustic swing were not immediately effaced, however, and the expeditions with Lili are colored by the chaste romance of Bellerophon. Their remaining exploits together are condensed into the incident of the giant Chimaera-headed snake which had invaded their Garden of Eden and which, singlehanded but too late, they slew. The changing weather announced the impending start of a new school year and Marcel returned to Marseilles. Independent as of that summer, he was now alone in a new world at the *lycée*.

Although the last third of the book, which deals with initiation to the *lycée*, is a change in scene, the progression of the theme continues. The isolation of the adolescent is completed "and I realize today that the *lycée* had practically detached us from our families about whom we never spoke."[36] Free from adult constraint, engrossed in his private world with its own protocol, Marcel once more develops his other identity of Bellerophon which had lived so intensely in the summer. His cause is now more realistic than at the time of his previous manifestation: he goes to battle for Oliva, a *boursier de l'Etat*, who had been terrorized by Pégomas, a big, bourgeois bully in the same class. With all the odds against him, "*forcé de prendre des risques pour l'honneur du nom*,"[37] Marcel perseveres in his plan to provoke Pégomas, and triumphs. Reconciled with his own myth, Marcel is at last able to assert his personality in a class which was already rich in original characters. Many of them reappear in *Pirouettes* at the end of their school careers.

The encroaching adolescence of his own son Frédéric, to whom *Le Temps des Secrets* is dedicated, was undoubtedly a contributing factor in Pagnol's choice of subject but *Souvenirs d'Enfance* also provides a stage for the themes which constantly reappear in Pagnol's work. Far from taking a new direction, the three books are confirmation of a talent that is situated fairly and squarely in the tradition of the great Provençal *naïfs*, Frédéric Mistral, Paul Arène, and Jean Giono. *Mémoires et Récits* and *Mes Origines* (Mistral), *Jean des Figues* (Arène), *Jean le Bleu* (Giono), and *Souvenirs d'Enfance* have much in common and represent a distinctively southern style of playful, poetic recollection.

H   Pirouettes

The story of *Pirouettes* was originally published as a serial in ten episodes (October 1, 1923, to February 15, 1924) in *Fortunio* and bore the title *Le Mariage de Peluque*. The first half of the book constitutes a re-presentation of a serial entitled *Les Mémoires de Jacques Panier* which dates back to 1920. Jacques Panier is still the narrator in the first person singular and the essence of the story still concerns the marriage plans of Panier's unpredictable companion, Louis-Irénée Peluque. In fact, Panier is as much a self-portrait of the author as little Marcel of the *Souvenirs d'Enfance* and he invites the reader to "guess what I look like from the sound of my voice";[38] in his 1932 preface to *Pirouettes*, Pagnol wrote that he did not change the 1924 manuscript of the young man he was because "he perhaps had his reasons, reasons which I have now forgotten. And I did not want to touch these posthumous pages." Like *Souvenirs d'Enfance*, *Pirouettes* is also an evocation of a mood, a phase in the author's life. The specific story concerns Peluque's plans to marry Lucie Ledru who imagines him to be rich and whom he imagines to be an heiress; both parties are in fact penniless and in its final phases the *dénouement* is quite theatrical. Although providing a comical twist to the story, Peluque's marriage plans are only part of the broader canvas of carefree, eighteen-year-old flirtation. Moving from the countryside of Provence to a friendly neighborhood in Marseilles, near the *lycée* he was attending, Pagnol has a new playground, "the Plaine St. Michel [now place Jean-Jaurès] where I spent the happiest days of my youth, in the company of Felix-Antoine Grasset, the pessimist poet, and Louis-Irénée Peluque, baptized 'Emperor' by the street-kids and 'Philosopher' by his class-mates."[39]

Lounging in the square or in the bar of Hippolyte (an interesting pre-figuration of César) during their after-school hours, the self-possessed Panier and his companion Grasset are periodically galvanized into action by the sentimental escapades of Peluque. Unable to resist a pretty face, Peluque is frequently unfaithful to his heiress and calls on his friends to extricate him from his embarrassing commitments. The behavior of the young trio is marked by the naive enthusiasm of youth and the unpredictability of a Gidean *être d'inconséquence*. Their conversation is spiced with pastiche and parody of the school *baccalauréat* curriculum which they, and the other *habitués* of Hippolyte's bar, are studying. Inhabiting the social vacuum which is the privilege of all students, they are free from social classification and constraint. The student's sense of total freedom contributes to their unpredictability: the whirlwind decisions of Peluque and the total absence of a sense of responsibility explain the title of the book and are an exhilarating expression of freedom. So it is that, in the third chapter, Panier surrenders the narrative to Grasset who, as the victim, is best placed to describe an astonishing, unexpected act of aggression by Peluque. Unlike *Souvenirs d'Enfance*, the story is divided into chapters; these can be explained in relation to each monthly episode of the serial that Pagnol contributed to *Fortunio*. The last prank, or episode, is the most comical, a good climax to an amusing book. With princely largesse, Peluque invites the clients of Hippolyte to the home of his father-in-law-to-be who, during the family's absence, had entrusted his keys to the "wealthy" son-in-law-to-be. The havoc involuntarily wreaked by the redoubtable Lagneau in the Ledru home puts an end to Peluque's hopes of marrying an heiress but, on learning that the father of his intended was bankrupt, the lively student philosopher turned without regret to his next conquest.

Fast-moving, funny, and irreverent, *Pirouettes* is a worthy sequel to *Souvenirs d'Enfance*, anachronistic as such an appraisal may seem. It is to be hoped that, with the reprinting of a number of Pagnol's works in *Livre de Poche*, it will soon become more easily available to the general reader.

II   L'Eau des Collines

There are fleeting glimpses of the native population of Provence in *Souvenirs d'Enfance;* Lili des Bellons reveals the peasant's close, distrustful instinct of hostility to strangers when he refuses to tell the Pagnol family of all the fresh-water springs he knows; his *esprit de clocher* also moved him to rule categorically that "all the poachers of La Treille were hunters and all the hunters from Allauch and the city were poachers."[40] The two novels of *L'Eau des Collines* deal more specifically with the mentality of the Provençal peasant whose unrelenting acquisitiveness leads to dark, long-lasting disputes of succession and inheritance. The original screenplay of *Manon des Sources* is amplified to the proportions of a fresco of rural life, dominated by the saga of the Soubeyran family. The first volume, *Jean de Florette*, sets the scene and the second volume, *Manon des Sources*, covers the swift, dramatic sequence of events which finally resolves the disputed succession of Florette Cadoret.

A Jean de Florette

After an introduction to the villagers of Les Bastides Blanches, Pagnol introduces the story of Pique-Bouffigue which exposes the social context into which the original fairy tale of *Manon des Sources* is now inserted. Marius Camoins, known as Pique-Bouffigues, is the owner of "Les Romarins," a farm with its own water supply which he leaves to his sister Florette who dies shortly after receiving the inheritance and thus never returns to her birthplace. Shortly before his death, Pique-Bouffigue refused to sell his land to his neighbor, Ugolin of the *mas de Massacan*, last of the influential Soubeyran family, who needed the valuable water supply of "Les Romarins" to realize his plan to grow carnations. Naturally hostile to the idea of anyone moving into the property which they coveted, Ugolin and his uncle, old César Soubeyran, blocked the precious spring of "Les Romarins" to discourage purchasers. They reckoned without the existence and character of Florette's son, Jean Cadoret the hunchback, who took over the property with his wife Aimée and pretty daughter Manon. Determined to discourage them from staying, neither Ugolin nor César revealed the existence of the spring which Jean needed for the vegetables he was cultivating for the rabbits he planned to raise. The villagers of Les Bastides Blanches knew of the source but, because Jean was apparently a stranger, they saw no need to tell him of it. Only César and Ugolin knew, after discreet inquiries, that Jean was the son of Florette Camoins who had left Les Bastides Blanches to marry Lionel Cadoret from the village of Crespin; even though such a desertion of her native village smacked of treachery, the Bastidiens would not have considered Jean de Florette as a stranger had they known his origins. César Soubeyran, who knew Jean's origins, was all the more hostile to him since he had once loved Florette and had hoped to marry her on his return from military service from North Africa; Florette's "treacherous" marriage had made a personal victim of him and he was happy to repay the score.

With the greatest duplicity, Ugolin feigns friendship for Jean de Florette but never reveals the existence of a spring; he goes so far as to give advice on where to find water in places where he knows it cannot be found. Jean's life becomes an exhausting routine of manual water-carrying from the hills where he befriended a Piedmontese woodcutter, Giuseppe and his wife Baptistine. Even with the help of these friends, Jean's task is impossible; his tribulations are finally cut short when he is killed trying to excavate a well on his property with explosives. It is the long, avaricious wait of Ugolin and his uncle that dominates the book; for a whole summer they follow with increasing glee the futile agony of Jean de Florette. The longer his labors endure, the more criminal Ugolin, le Papet César, and, indirectly, the passive villagers appear. After his death his bereaved daughter and wife withdraw from the scene of so much suffering to live with Giuseppe in the hills; Ugolin and César quickly acquire the worthless, waterless property of "Les Romarins" and free the blocked spring for which Jean had sought so long. The discovery of a spring soon after her father's death seems to Manon to be more than a coincidence and, vaguely conscious of the injustice her family has suffered, her alienation and exile from the inhuman community of Les Bastides are confirmed. The book ends with the Papet triumphantly baptizing his nephew "King of the Carnations."

B   Manon des Sources

With a succession of dramatic discoveries and decisions, the action of the second volume accelerates from the long, unremitting labor of Jean and the equally long anticipation of Ugolin slowly circling his prey. Substantially similar to the screenplay, Manon des Sources also resolves the family issues raised in Jean de Florette. Anxious for the last of the Soubeyrans to take a wife, the aging bachelor César is relatively pleased to learn that his nephew Ugolin has fallen in love with Manon; unknown to her, Ugolin, dog-like, follows Manon in the hills where she tends her goats. He neglects his lucrative carnations to spy on her but, unfortunately for him, he had always inspired Manon with revulsion and she had also had confirmation of her worst suspicions regarding the spring of "Les Romarins." Irritated by the avarice of the Soubeyran men and by the increasing prosperity of their carnation-growing, the Bastidiens begin to talk of the mysterious, temporary disappearance of the water supply during the Cadoret family's period of residence at "Les Romarins." Manon overhears two hunters speaking of this and she plans a terrible revenge on Ugolin. It goes without saying that she spurns his pathetic, desperate advances but she wishes to destroy him altogether.

Unsuccessful in her plan to burn down Ugolin's house with him inside, she finally blocks his water supply which is indispensable to the cultivation of his carnations. It is the very spring which Ugolin had himself once blocked that Manon seals, but she seals it at its source together with the village water supply. The absence of water and the continuing hot weather threaten the crops with extinction and the villagers' consternation is shrewdly exploited by the parish priest who creates a vague sense of communal guilt among them. In a state of mind similar to that of Giono's villagers in *Colline*, the Bastidiens look for a scapegoat; they do not suspect Manon of cutting off their water supply but they are troubled by her refusal to pray for the return of the water.

After the adroit intervention of the young village schoolteacher and the exposure of the Soubeyran conspiracy, Manon relents. Her original intention had been to punish Ugolin but after his suicide she sees less reason to deprive the village of water; with the schoolteacher's help, she clears the underground lake which feeds all the springs of the district. Encouraged by events to take an interest in Manon, the villagers learn, to their dismay, that she, via her late father, was a descendant of Florette Camoins and was thus, whoever Florette's husband may have been, from Les Bastides Blanches. Adopted by the villagers and finally married to the schoolteacher, Manon is reintegrated into the community. Her son Jean is born at Christmas; at the same time César Soubeyran dies broken-hearted. He had learned that Jean de Florette was his son and that Florette had married another in order to legitimize the child; he who had loved Florette and wanted the Soubeyran family to survive had persecuted his own son. César's last act is to leave all his property to Manon's child whom he had expected to be a son. Thus the Soubeyran line continues through Manon, its principal victim. The story ends on this note of expiation and regeneration.

It would be a mistake to call *L'Eau des Collines* a regional novel with all that the term implies of local color exploited for its own sake. There is none of this self-consciousness in Pagnol's rich, compelling tale which is situated in the surroundings he knew from childhood and in which he moved with easy self-assurance. *L'Eau des Collines* is dedicated to Jacqueline Bouvier and, as has already been observed *à propos* of the movie version, it is built around a very personal rôle created by Pagnol for his wife, "with her shoulder-length hair gilded by the sun and dried in the wind";[41] nobody has yet successfully argued that a lyric poem does not have some universal value.

The harsh world of the peasants enhances the passages that describe the activity of the shy goatherd Manon. The contrast is nowhere greater than in her confrontations with Ugolin when they seem to be matched as Beauty and the Beast. A particularly effective example occurs when, having bathed in a mountain pool, Manon emerges to dance naked before her flock and the hidden Ugolin who, dull and clumsy as he was, "felt somehow that this girlish dancer, still glistening with the cleansing rain-water, was the goddess of the hills, the pine forest and spring-time."[42] Jean-Louis Vaudoyer might have been describing Pagnol's novel when he wrote of Arène's work that "nature presses in on all sides, reigning supreme in an uninhibited pastoral domain where Virgilian shepherds and the minor deities of the Anthology still survive."[43] There is, once more, much to remind the reader of Paul Arène in this novel; the lively tone, which stresses by inference the most somber moments of the story, is to be found in *La Chèvre d'Or* and *Domnine;* the names of Soubeyran, the Bastidien Cabridan and Anglade's property at Canteperdrix[44] are also in *Jean des Figues.*

The traditional remedy for sunstroke which Baptistine applies to Jean de Florette[45] duplicates the one applied to Jean des Figues[46] and to Mistral's Mireille in *Mireille* (Chant II):

> O belèu uno souleiado,
> Faguè Vincèn, vous a'mbriado.
> Sabe, dis, uno vièio, aperamount i Bau
> (Ié dison Taven): vous asaigo
> Bèn sus lou front un got plen d'aigo,
> Elèu, di cervello embriaigo,
> Li rai escounjura gisclon dins lou cristau.

Translation: Or perhaps a touch of the sun — said Vincent, has affected you — I know, he said, an old woman in the hills of Les Baux — (she's called Taven): she applies — right on your forehead a glass full of water, — and immediately, from your dazed mind — the offending rays are driven by magic into the glass.

Arène established in *La Chèvre d'Or*, a novel about the legendary hidden treasure of the Saracens, that the Provençal, far from being a light-hearted buffoon, can be close, mean, and greedy. Pagnol, too, contradicts the popular, marketable image. The poetic presence of Manon is surrounded by coarse, rough people who are described in an authoritative way. The descriptions of the landscape, the detail of Cadoret's attempts to raise rabbits and Ugolin's difficulties in cultivating carnations all reveal Pagnol's knowledge of his subject. He also parodies the conservatism of country wisdom which, con-

densed and preserved in proverbs, is often self-contradictory, as this
sequence shows:

"*S'il pleut pour la Saint-Paterne*
  L'été sèche ta citerne."[47]

"*S'il pleut pour le jour d'Ascension*
  Tout s'en va en perdition."[48]

"*S'il pleut en juin*
  Mange ton poing."[49]

"*S'il ne pleut pas pour Sainte Anne*
  N'espère que Sainte Jeanne."[50]

To the lightness and fantasy of *Souvenirs d'Enfance* Pagnol brings
the earthiness of peasant attitudes, conspiracy hatched and avenged
on an epic scale and, as an inveterate believer in happy endings, the
familiar theme of regeneration. *L'Eau des Collines* is Pagnol's own
spiritual version of *Regain:* the existence of Les Bastides Blanches
was threatened by greed and selfishness, but it and the Soubeyran
family were redeemed by the return of Manon. *Plus ça change. . . .*

Pagnol's development as a novelist is a natural consequence of his
experience in the cinema; the screenplay, as dialogue with set
description and actors' directions, prefigures the novels he was to
write. Rich in dialogue, human anecdote, and concrete description,
Pagnol's novels are also written in a lively, humorous style with the
familiar *formules à l'emporte-pièce* reappearing as a quip or maxim.
Souvenirs d'Enfance, Pirouettes, and *L'Eau des Collines* are also
very close to Pagnol's most intimate experience; as he says in the introduction to *La Gloire de Mon Père:* "It's no longer Raimu who is
talking to you, it's me." Short of turning to prose fiction, he was thus
confronted by natural limits to the range of work that he could undertake on such a scale. This is not to say that Pagnol's extant prose
work exhausted his reserves of memory and imagination; his fund of
anecdotes, his gift for humorous characterization, and the ability to
compose a sharp, whip-lash line would have made him an excellent
essayist or short-story writer. One can only regret that no *Lettres de
La Treille* were ever written.

Conclusion

STANDING astride the two very different worlds of cinema and classical culture, Pagnol maintained a remarkable consistency in the setting and theme of his work. In differing media and in differing literary forms, he returns to that small, county-sized area east of Marseilles which is bounded by the Huveaune River and the Massif de l'Étoile; he seems to feel freer to create within this fortress but, as with Giono at Manosque or Faulkner in Yoknapatawpha, the interest of his work extends far beyond these confines. Alert to the possibilities of new mass media but also a classical scholar, he was doubly sensitive to the universal humanity of the most simple, familiar aspects of Provençal life. With an original, intuitive vision which spanned the poetry of Mistral and Virgil on the one hand and the mechanics of the modern film studio on the other, Pagnol could have played a valuable rôle in the *Félibrige*, which is shrinking from its original popular *élan* into esoteric self-analysis. As if afraid of losing his freedom, he remained a great independent.

Deriving much strength from the intimacy of his world, Pagnol was a fundamentally happy extrovert who believed in happy endings. His moral stamina was constantly an inspiration to his colleagues in the corporate efforts, *Fortunio, Les Moins de Trente Ans*, and his many film sets, which he enjoyed so much. His lonely début in sound cinema required not only considerable reserves of self-confidence and energy but also a shrewd, hard-headed approach to business matters. These masterful qualities make it virtually impossible to isolate the man from his work; he was ready to accept the world as it is, confident in his capacity to create the conditions necessary to his enjoyment of life. Earthly happiness lay in reform only for as long as success eluded the young, satirical playwright who, after *Topaze*, turned to a form of pastoral hedonism. Decidedly unpretentious on the moral plane, Pagnol's work has the sovereign virtue of communicating his own appetite for life and human intercourse. The verve and intuitive flair with which he wrote serve as a further expression of his zest and energy.

The impression of facility is, however, deceptive. In sociological terms, Pagnol's enormous popularity can be partially attributed to the unfailing public interest in a rags-to-riches story. The *boursier* from the *école communale* who became a member of the *Académie Française* was a reassuring demonstration of the efficacy of republican traditions. Yet that success which engenders even greater success must first be achieved. The independent, innovative creator of masterpieces in several different media and literary forms, Pagnol was possessed by a compulsive energy to write and he joined a lively interest in science to his rigorous classical education. His correspondence with Professor Rimattei of the science faculty at the University of Marseilles shows a natural, if untutored, grasp of scientific and mechanical concepts. Above all, Pagnol is able to convey with unfailing warmth and humor the enduring satisfaction to be derived from certain virtues which have the simplicity and strength of truth: filial respect, loyalty to friends, and freedom enjoyed among his roots. Always a man of action, he transposed the code by which he lived into his creative work with such consistency that his tombstone epitaph is a summary of his art:

"Fontes, amicos, uxorem dilexit"
(*He loved the fresh-water springs, his friends, and his wife*).

Notes and References

All references to Pagnol's works are in the Livre de Poche edition, unless otherwise stated.

Preface

1. Louis Combaluzier, *Le Jardin de Pagnol* (Paris: Oeuvres Françaises, 1937). Françoise Giroud, *Nouveaux Portraits* (Paris: Gallimard, 1954). Charles Blavette, *Ma Provence en Cuisine* (Paris: Editions France Empire, 1961). Odette Lutgen, *En Dépit de leur Gloire* (Paris: Editions Mondiales, 1961). Yvan Audouard, *Audouard Raconte Pagnol* (Paris: Stock, 1973). Raymond Castans, *Marcel Pagnol m'a Raconté* (Paris: Editions de la Table Ronde, 1975).

2. The only book yet to be written exclusively about any aspect of Pagnol's art, as distinct from his life, is by Claude Beylie, *Marcel Pagnol*, Coll. Cinéma d'Aujourd'hui, N⁰ 80 (Paris: Seghers, 1974).

3. Marcel Achard, *Rions avec Eux — Grands Auteurs Comiques* (Paris: Fayard, 1957).

4. Charles Rostaing, "Le Français de Marseille dans la Trilogie de Marcel Pagnol," *Le Français Moderne* (January, 1942), pp. 29 - 44, (April, 1942), pp. 118 - 131.

5. Paul Surer, *Cinquante Ans de Théâtre 1919 - 1969* (Paris: S.E.D.E.S., 1973). Dorothy Knowles, *French Drama of the Inter-War Years* (London: Harrap, 1967). Quéant et Towarnicki, *Encyclopédie du Théâtre Contemporain*, Vol. 2 (Paris: Perrin, 1959).

6. *Pour Vous*, N⁰ 451 (1937) and see below.

7. Renoir, Clair, Feyder, de Baroncelli, Raymond Bernard, and Marcel l'Herbier all signed a letter dated Paris, October 11, 1939, inviting Pagnol to join their recently formed group in these terms: "Nous t'avons demandé dès le premier jour. On ne t'a pas trouvé, mais nous avons toujours pensé que ta place était au milieu de nous . . ." Catalogue of Pagnol Exhibition, Bibliothèque Municipale, Marseilles, 1975, Item N⁰ 190.

8. *Ecran Français*, N⁰ 114. In 1947, Welles and Pagnol planned to work together in a consortium.

9. Article by Fieschi, Guégan, and Rivette, *Cahiers du Cinéma* (December, 1965), p. 27.

10. André Bazin, *Qu'est-ce que le Cinéma?*, Vol. 2, Coll. 7e Art (Paris: Editions du Cerf, 1959).

11. Pauline Kael, *Kiss Kiss Bang Bang* (London: Calder and Boyars, 1970).

12. *Cahiers du Cinéma*, N⁰ Spécial (December, 1965) and Delahaye, "La Saga Pagnol," Ibid. (June, 1969).

13. Claude Gauteur, "Marcel Pagnol Aujourd'hui," *L'Avant - Scène du Cinéma* (July - September, 1970).

14. Op. cit., see note 2.

15. In *Les Cahiers de la Cinémathèque*, N⁰ 13 - 15 (1973).

16. With the exception of Maurice Rat, "La Succulence des Romans de Pagnol," *Vie et Langage* (March, 1964); Yvonne Georges, *Les Provençalismes dans l'Eau des Collines*, La Pensée Universitaire, N⁰ XL11 (Annales de la Faculté d'Aix, 1966).

17. Henri Peyre, *The Contemporary French Novel* (New York: Oxford University Press, 1955).

18. Maxwell Smith, *Jean Giono* (New York: Twayne, 1966).

19. All re-edited by Pierre Rollet, Edicioun Ramoun Berenguiè, Aix-en-Provence, 1970.

20. Quoted in introduction to *Jean des Figues* (Aix: ed. Rollet, 1970).

21. Ibid.

22. A sensitive article about the cultural consciousness of Mediterranean man by Raymond Jean, "Le Jeune Homme et la Mer," *Cahiers du Sud*, No 373 - 4 (1963), is well worth reading in this context.

23. Statistics announced in TV presentation by Christiane Collange entitled *Best-Seller*, a French O.R.T.F. production which included Gaston Deferre (mayor of Marseilles), Yvan Audouard, and Raymond Castans in a discussion of Pagnol's work, January, 1975.

24. *Marius* and *Fanny*, the first two plays of the "trilogy," had already been filmed in the U.S.A. in 1938 under the title *Port of the Seven Seas* starring Wallace Beery and Maureen O'Sullivan, directed by James Whale.

Chapter One

1. Beylie, op. cit., p. 10.

2. *Livres de France*, 15e année No 3 (March, 1964), 14.

3. (Paris: Grasset, 1958).

4. "A propos des origines coutançaises de Pagnol," *Revue du Département de la Manche*, 2 (1960).

5. Chronology drafted by author and checked by Pagnol on May 23, 1964. Details confirmed by chronology published in catalogue of Pagnol exhibition in Marseilles. op. cit., drafted in cooperation with members of Pagnol's family.

6. *Massilia,* N⁰ 53 (June 1, 1910); N⁰ 57 (August 1, 1910); N⁰ 58 (August 15, 1910); N⁰ 61 (October 1, 1910); N⁰ 76 (May 15, 1911); N⁰ 77 (June 1, 1911).

7. *Massilia,* No. 57 (August 1, 1910).

8. Catalogue, Pagnol Exhibition, Item 40.

9. Ibid. See also *La Gloire de Pagnol,* Album Souvenir (Paris: Editions Paris Match, 1974) and the copiously illustrated editions of *La Gloire de Mon Père,* ed. Yves Brunsvick, Paul Ginestier & Claude Jacquet, Coll. Les Classiques de la Civilisation Française (Paris: Marcel Didier, 1964), and *Le Château de Ma Mère,* same editors and series (Paris: Marcel Didier, 1967).

10. *Le Château de Ma Mère* (Paris: Livre de Poche, 1974), p. 281.

11. *La Gloire de Mon Père,* p. 23.

12. *Les Sermons de Marcel Pagnol,* ed. Norbert Calmels (Forcalquier: Robert Morel, 1967).

13. "La Saga Pagnol," *Cahiers du Cinéma,* N⁰ 213 (June, 1969), pp. 45 - 57.

14. Archives of *Cahiers du Sud,* Cours d'Estienne d'Orves, Marseilles, made accessible by kind permission of Monsieur and Madame Jean Ballard. See also Catalogue, Pagnol Exhibition, Item 53. *Fortunio,* No 2 (February 25, 1914).

15. Records of Lycée Thiers, made accessible by kind permission of *proviseur,* 1964.

16. Lucien Grimaud, *Histoires d'Aubagne* (Roquevaire: La Lithotyp, 1973), p. 163.

17. Preface to verse translation of Virgil's *Bucoliques* (Paris: Bernard Grasset, 1958), p. 19.

18. Ibid.

19. *Pirouettes* (Paris: Fasquelle, 1932), p. 10.

20. Preface to *Bucoliques,* p. 20.

21. Catalogue, Pagnol Exhibition, Item 50.

22. *Fortunio* (February, 1920), pp. 1 - 5

23. Paul Arène, *Jean des Figues* in *La Gueuse Parfumée*(Paris: Fasquelle, 1929), p. 19.

24. *Cahiers du Sud,* N⁰ 349 (1958), p. 459.

25. *De la littérature considérée comme une tauromachie* in *L'Age d'homme* (Paris: Gallimard Folio, 1973).

26. *La Gloire de Mon Père,* p. 11.

27. Moral *en épigraphe, Topaze,* p. 10.

28. Conversation with Pagnol, May 23, 1964.

29. Ch. Koella, "The Teacher's Gallery in Pagnol," *Modern Languages Journal,* N⁰ 32 (October, 1960), pp. 404 - 408.

30. Charles Maurras, *Mistral* (Paris: Aubier-Montaigne, n.d.), Cap. 3, "La Filiation Helleno-Romaine," p. 126.

31. Preface to *Pirouettes,* loc. cit., p. 6. Pagnol explains in this reference how all his early work, from *Topaze* onwards, came to be edited by Fasquelle.

32. Introduction to *Jean des Figues*, ed. Pierre Rollet (Aix: Rollet, 1970).

33. Conversation between Pagnol and Brauquier in *Café du Glacier*, Marseilles, circa 1930, according to Brauquier in conversation with author, April, 1964.

34. According to Jean Ballard, Pagnol's colleague in *Fortunio* and latterly director of *Cahiers du Sud;* much of the information relating to *Fortunio* derives from the dialogue maintained throughout 1963 - 64 between the author and Jean Ballard during research sessions in the congenial *grenier* of *Cahiers du Sud*, Marseilles.

35. *Le Feu*, Nº 1 (January 1, 1917), p. 16.

36. *Marseille et les Marseillais* (Paris: Bourdillat, 1860), p. 51.

37. Ibid. p. 75.

38. Ibid. p. 94.

39. See note 34 above.

40. *Fortunio* (March 15, 1923), p. 185.

41. Ibid. (January 1, 1924), pp. 27 - 31.

42. Ibid. (February 15, 1923), p. 119.

43. Ibid. (March 15, 1923), p. 184.

44. *Catulle*, Act 1 Sc. 3.

45. Ibid., Act 4 Sc. 1.

46. Ibid., Act 2 Sc. 5.

Chapter Two

1. Pagnol's memoirs of his theatrical and movie career have been published in five weekly episodes August 10 - September 7, 1963, in *Le Figaro Littéraire*, repeated in one installment for *Lectures pour Tous*, November, 1963; a further series of four weekly episodes August 6 - 27, 1964, in *Le Figaro Littéraire*, repeated in one installment for *Lectures pour Tous*, March, 1965; a third series of weekly articles contributed October 21 - November 4, 1965 to *Le Figaro Littéraire*. All these articles have been collated and republished as prefaces to the appropriate works in the definitive edition of Pagnol's *Oeuvres Complètes*, Editions de Provence, 1964 to the present.

2. "Quand Pagnol Créait *Topaze*," *Historia*, No 137 (April, 1958), 382.

3. Ibid.

4. *Critique des Critiques*, (Paris: Nagel, 1949), p. 140.

5. Achard, *Rions avec eux*, op, cit., Cap. 1X reproduced in *Historia*, op. cit.; André Antoine, *Antoine Père et Fils* (Paris: Julliard, 1962), of which extracts were published as "Pagnol, Achard, Jeanson," *Revue des Deux Mondes* (May - June, 1962), pp. 522 - 533; Pagnol *passim*.

6. Antoine, *Revue des Deux Mondes*, op. cit., p. 522.

7. Ibid., p. 523.

8. Achard, *Rions avec Eux*, op. cit., p. 311.

9. Commentary on *Je t'attendais* by Jacques Natanson published by *La Petite Illustration* (December 28, 1929).

10. Dorothy Knowles, *French Drama of the Inter-War Years* (London: Harrap, 1967), p. 34.

11. Quéant & Towarnicki, *Encyclopédie*, op. cit., Vol. 2, p. 18.

12. Paul Surer, *Le Théâtre Français Contemporain*, op. cit., p. 117.

13. *La Petite Illustration*, Nº 274 — Théâtre No 157 (1926).

14. Editions de Provence.

15. *Le Figaro Littéraire* (August 10, 1963), p. 16.

16. Ibid.

17. 1926 edition.

18. Ibid., Act 1, Scene 4, p. 10.

19. Ibid., Act 2, Scene 4, p. 17.

20. In 1926 edition.

21. All the press citations are included in above edition.

22. "Après la générale des *Marchands de Gloire*," May, 1925.

23. *Comoedia* (March 12th, 1926).

24. *Antoine Père et Fils*, p. 231.

25. "Il y a deux mille ans à Sparte . . . il y avait plus d'intelligence et de poésie dans la cheville d'une vierge que dans le crâne enflé de Sully Prud'homme." *Jazz* (Paris: Livre de Poche, 1975), Act 2, Scene 8, pp. 86 - 87. The same passage can be found in *Pirouettes*, op. cit., pp. 42 - 44; "Le Mariage de Peluque," *Fortunio* (November 1, 1923), pp. 167 - 168; "Les Mémoires de Jacques Panier," *Fortunio* (April, 1920), pp. 75 - 76. Sully Prud'homme thus provided the Romantic Pagnol with his favorite line. The *Livre de Poche* (1975) edition of *Jazz* differs in a number of respects from the original (*La Petite Illustration*, 1927, and Fasquelle, 1954) but Pagnol has not changed this particular passage.

26. p. 60 (Fasquelle); p. 63 (Livre de Poche).

27. p. 120 (Fasquelle); cut from 1975 edition.

28. p. 143 (Fasquelle and Livre de Poche).

29. See Note 1.

30. See Note 2 above.

31. *Antoine Père et Fils*, p. 232.

32. Achard, *Rions Avec Eux*, op. cit., p. 313.

33. Ibid.

34. Act 2, Scene XI, p. 202.

35. Act 1, Scene XIII, p. 92.

36. Act III, Scene XI, p. 273.

37. "Ainsi Naquit *Topaze*," *Lectures Pour Tous* (1965), op, cit. p. 42.

38. Quoted in Quéant & Towarnicki, op. cit., p. 41.

39. *Lectures Pour Tous*, op. cit., p. 46.

40. *Le Monde*, Nº 6599, April 1, 1966.

41. Pagnol's and Antoine's versions of the story differ.

42. *Lectures Pour Tous*, p. 43.

43. See also Roger Régent, *Raimu*, coll. *Cinéma en Marche* (Paris: Chavane, 1951) and Paul Olivier, *Raimu ou la Vie de César* (Paris: Fournier Valdès, 1947).

44. Quoted in *La Gloire de Pagnol,* Album Souvenir (Paris: Editions Paris Match, 1974), p. 42.

45. "Mes Premières," *Lectures Pour Tous* (November, 1963), p. 19.

46. Loc. cit.

47. Op. cit., p. 20.

48. Act 4, Scene 5, p. 280.

49. Act 1, Scene 5, p. 59.

50. Conversation between author and Brauquier January 31, 1964; see also *Samedi Soir,* June 17, 1950.

51. His latest anthology *Eau douce pour Navires* won the *Grand Prix Littéraire de Provence* in 1962. See also Gabriel Audisio, *Louis Brauquier,* coll. *Poètes d'Aujourd'hui* (Paris: Seghers, 1966).

52. *Fanny:* "Oui, j'ai habité à Oran." Act 1 Scene 2, p. 23; also "Je vais me la faire tapisser [her bedroom] en bleu parce que ça va très bien avec mes cheveux." Act 3, Second Tableau, Scene 1, p. 219.

53. Dedication of *Fanny* by René Fauchois.

54. Charles Rostaing, "Le Français de Marseille dans la Trilogie de Marcel Pagnol," *Le Français Moderne* (January, 1942), pp. 29 - 44 and ibid. (April, 1942), pp. 118 - 131.

55. Act 1, Scene 3, pp. 34 - 35.

56. Ibid., p. 38.

57. "My little one sleeping with a man, that brigand Marius!" Act 4, Scene 4, p. 266.

58. "I am *maître* Panisse and you are not smart enough to fool me!" Act 3, Scene 1, p. 188.

59. Act 2, Scene 4, p. 153.

60. *Antoine Père et Fils,* p. 248.

61. "Marcel Pagnol Raconte ses Débuts au Cinéma," *Le Figaro Littéraire* (October 21, 1965), p. 9; *Cinématurgie de Paris, Oeuvres Complètes,* Vol. 3 (Paris: Editions de Provence, 1967), p. 20.

62. Preface to the definitive edition of *Judas,* Vol. 4 *Oeuvres Complètes* (Paris: Editions de Provence, 1968), pp. 14 - 15.

63. See Arnold Ages, "Pagnol's New Look at Judas," *Revue de l'Université d'Ottawa* (July - September, 1965), pp. 314 - 322.

64. Petain, hero of Verdun in 1916, signed the surrender to Germany in 1940 and became leader of the Vichy government until the liberation of France when he was tried and sentenced to death, a sentence later commuted to life imprisonment.

65. Preface to definitive edition of *Fabien,* Vol.4 *O.C.* (Paris: Ed. de Provence, 1968), p. 163.

Chapter Three

1. Much of the information in this section is derived from the remarkable triple number of *Les Cahiers de la Cinémathèque* (N° 13 - 15), edited at Perpignan by Marcel Oms.

2. Reassembled extracts of articles previously published by *Le Figaro*

Littéraire (October 21 - November 4, 1965) included in Vol. 3 of *Oeuvres Complètes,* loc. cit., under title of *Cinématurgie de Paris.*

3. See esp. Charles Blavette, *Ma Provence en Cuisine* (Paris: Editions France Empire, 1961), *passim.*

4. "Mes Débuts au Cinéma," art. cit. and Vol. 3 of *Oeuvres Complètes,* op. cit., p. 41.

5. Ibid.

6. Vol. 3 *O.C.,* op. cit., p. 47.

7. The most complete in existence, including details of Pagnol's unrealized film projects and films directed by others in his studios.

8. *Le Courrier Cinématographique* No 41 (October 10, 1931).

9. Géo Saacke in *Ciné-Journal,* No 1160 (November 27, 1931).

10. René Clair, *Réflexion Faite* (Paris: Gallimard, 1951).

11. Ibid., p. 197.

12. *Comoedia,* Nos 6363 - 6366 (June 19 - 22, 1930).

13. *Pour Vous,* No 47 (October 10, 1929).

14. "Réflexions sur l'Art Cinématographique," *Revue Politique et Parlementaire,* No 742 (February, 1964), p. 22.

15. "La Cinématurgie de Paris," Chapter 2, *Les Cahiers du Film,* No 2 (January 15, 1934).

16. "La Cinématurgie de Paris," Chapter 3, *Les Cahiers du Film,* No 3 (March 1, 1934).

17. Quoted by Pierre Leprohon in *Jean Renoir,* Coll. Cinéma d'Aujourd'hui (Paris: Seghers, 1967), p. 54.

18. "Principaux Faits de la Semaine," *L'Actualité Cinématographique,* August 24, 1933.

19. Details of the case are contained in the minutes of the *Greffe de la Troisième Chambre du Tribunal Civil,* Marseilles, Tuesday, October 14, 1941.

20. An analysis of the case is contained in Caldicott, "Notice Bibliographique et Judiciaire sur la Collaboration de Jean Giono avec Marcel Pagnol," *Revue de l'Université d'Ottawa,* (December, 1971), pp. 563 - 566.

21. Foreword to *Les Sermons de Marcel Pagnol,* op. cit., p. 22.

22. *Présences Contemporaines — Cinéma* (Paris: Nlles Editions Debresse, 1956), pp. 217 - 218.

23. In *Solitude de la Pitié* (Paris: Gallimard, 1932), pp. 123 - 143.

24. "Le Cas Pagnol," *France Observateur,* November 19, 1954, pp. 29 - 30.

25. See minutes of the *Greffe,* note 20.

26. *Un de Baumugnes,* Livre de Poche, p. 188.

27. Beylie, *Marcel Pagnol,* p. 63.

28. See also interesting comparison of Mamèche with Baptistine of *Manon des Sources* in Fernand Vial, "Provence and Provençals in the Works of Marcel Pagnol," *American Society of Legion of Honor Magazine,* Vol. XXXV (1964), pp. 29 - 47.

29. Interview in special number of *Cahiers du Cinéma* (December, 1965).

30. *Les Cahiers du Film*, Série 2 N⁰ 2 (January 15, 1941).

31. *Nouvelle Revue Française*, N⁰ 227 (August, 1932), pp. 194 - 206.

32. Interview with Claude Beylie in *Cinéma 69* (March, 1969).

33. Reported in minutes of *Greffe*.

34. Jean Giono, *Théâtre. Le Bout de la Route, Lanceurs de Graines, La Femme du Boulanger* (Paris: Gallimard, 1943).

35. *Les Cahiers du Film*, N⁰ 33 (July, 1942).

36. The above number also contains a generous section on the couple's connubial bliss without specifying details of any marriage ceremony.

37. *La Fille du Puisatier*, p. 271.

38. Ibid., p. 270.

39. The I.D.H.E.C. is the national cinema school of France. It also has a library which is open to researchers at 92, avenue des Champs-Elysées, Paris; there are also film files there.

40. *Les Cahiers du Film*, N⁰ 31 (June, 1942).

41. Jeanne & Ford, *Histoire Encyclopédique du Cinéma*, Vol. 4, cap. "Le Cinéma et la Guerre," (Paris: S.E.D.E., 1962), pp. 371 - 376.

42. *Les Cahiers du Film*, N⁰ 16 (October, 1941).

43. Beylie, op. cit., p. 98.

44. In conversation with author, May 26, 1964.

45. *Présences Contemporaines — Cinéma*, op. cit., p. 218.

46. Bazin, *Qu'est-ce que le Cinéma?*, Vol. 2, op. cit., p. 124.

47. *Ma Provence en Cuisine*, op cit., pp. 71 - 74.

48. Preface to *César*, Vol. 3, *Oeuvres Complètes*, ed. cit., p. 161.

49. *Le Schpountz*, Coll. les Films Qu'On peut Lire, No 6 (Paris: Fasquelle-Marcel Pagnol, 1938), pp. 115 - 120.

50. Ibid.

51. *L'Avant-Scène du Cinéma* (July - September, 1970).

52. *Revue Politique et Parlementaire*, op. cit., 1964.

53. Op. cit., p. 26.

54. *Cahiers du Cinéma* (December, 1965).

Chapter Four

1. *Discours de Réception* (Paris: Firmin Didot, 1947).

2. *Discours de Réception* (Paris: Fasquelle, 1947), p. 8.

3. Catalogue, Pagnol Exhibition, Item 240.

4. "A French Hamlet," *The Observer* (London), July 4, 1954.

5. Confirmed in letter from Sylvie Chevalley, *Archiviste-Bibliothécaire* at the Comédie-Française, March 7, 1975.

6. "Autour du Masque de Fer," *Revue des Deux Mondes* (October 1, 1965), pp. 421 - 427.

7. *Discours sous la Coupole* (Paris: Nagel, 1960), p. 45.

8. Ibid., pp. 46 - 47.

9. In conversation with the author, May 26, 1964.

10. *Histoire d'une Vie*, Vol. 13 (Paris: Plon, 1973).

Chapter Five

1. p. 211.
2. p. 16.
3. p. 132.
4. p. 93.
5. *Le Livre de Mon Ami* (Paris: Calmann-Levy, 1886), p. 159.
6. *Jean des Figues* (Paris: Fasquelle, 1929), p. 37.
7. *La Gloire de Mon Père*, p. 77.
8. *Le Château de Ma Mère*, p. 149.
9. Ibid., p. 95.
10. For further information about plants see: Harant and Jarry, *Guide du Naturaliste dans le Midi de la France*, Vol. 2. *La garrigue. Le maquis. Les cultures* (Delachaux and Niestlé). For birds see: Paul Géroudet, *Guide des Oiseaux d'Europe* (Delachaux and Niestlé).
11. *La Gloire de Mon Père*, p. 26.
12. Ibid., p. 65
13. Ibid., p. 61.
14. Ibid., p. 89.
15. *Le Temps des Secrets*, p. 153.
16. *La Gloire de Mon Père*, p. 19.
17. *Le Château de Ma Mère*, p. 10.
18. *La Gloire de Mon Père*, p. 163.
19. Ibid., p. 115.
20. Ibid., p. 70.
21. Ibid., p. 145.
22. *La Gloire de Mon Père*, p. 37.
23. *Si le Grain ne Meurt* (London: Oxford University Press, 1946).
24. *Le Château de Ma Mère*, p. 29.
25. Ibid., p. 39.
26. Ibid., p. 35.
27. Ibid., p. 36.
28. Loc. cit.
29. *Le Château de Ma Mère*, p. 139.
30. Ibid., p. 85.
31. Ibid., p. 175.
32. Ibid., p. 223.
33. *Jean des Figues*, op. cit., p. 42.
34. *Le Château de Ma Mère*, p. 146.
35. *Le Temps des Secrets*, p. 192.
36. Ibid., p. 309.
37. Ibid., p. 321.
38. *Pirouettes* (Paris: Fasquelle, 1932), p. 12.
39. Ibid., p. 15.
40. *Le Château de Ma Mère*, p. 23.

41. *Manon des Sources*, p. 22.

42. Ibid., p. 66.

43. *Nouvelles Beautés de Provence* (Paris: Grasset, 1928), p. 163.

44. Canteperdrix was the name Arène gave to his native town of Sisteron; Anglade mentions his property there in *Manon des Sources*, p. 238.

45. *Jean de Florette*, p. 253.

46. *Jean des Figues*, op. cit., cap. 2.

47. *Jean de Florette*, p. 215.

48. Loc. cit.

49. Ibid., p. 216.

50. Ibid., p. 224.

Selected Bibliography

PRIMARY SOURCES

The following list includes only the first editions, English translations, and the readily available *Livre de Poche* editions of Pagnol's work; unless otherwise stated, the place of publication is Paris. Of the many prefaces and articles written by Pagnol, as of the many other editions of his work, those which represent a particular interest are alluded to at appropriate points elsewhere. In addition, all Pagnol's work is currently available, either separately or in collection as *Oeuvres Complètes*, from the Editions de Provence, Paris. The editions of this publisher have the added advantage of including recent prefaces by Pagnol and, on occasion, final alterations to the text itself.

1922 *Catulle*, a verse play in 4 acts. Marseilles: Editions *Fortunio*.
1924 *Les Marchands de Gloire*, a play in 4 acts with a Prologue. *La Petite Illustration*, No 274. Théâtre, No 157.
1927 *Jazz*, a play in 4 acts. *La Petite Illustration*, No 511. Théâtre, No 180. Livre de Poche, 1975.
1931 *Topaze*, a play in 4 acts. Fasquelle and *La Petite Illustration*, No 511. Théâtre, No 271. Translated by A. Rossi, London: Heinemann Educational Books, 1962. Livre de Poche, 1973.
       Marius, a play in 4 acts and 6 tableaux. Fasquelle and *La Petite Illustration*, No 528. Théâtre, No 277. Livre de Poche, 1973.
1932 *Fanny*, a play in 3 acts and 4 tableaux. Fasquelle. Livre de Poche, 1973.
       Pirouettes, a novel. Fasquelle. Bibliothèque Charpentier.
1933 *Cinématurgie de Paris*, a treatise. *Cahiers du Film* (December, 1933, January & March, 1934).
1935 *Merlusse*, scenario. *La Petite Illustration*, No 725. Théâtre, No 371.
1936 *Cigalon*, scenario. Fasquelle, published with *Merlusse*.
1937 *César*, scenario. Fasquelle. Livre de Poche, 1974.
       Regain, scenario. Marcel Pagnol, Coll. Films qu'on peut lire, No 5.

1938 *Le Schpountz*, scenario. Pagnol, Coll. Films qu'on peut lire, Nᵒ 6. *La
      Femme du Boulanger*, scenario. Pagnol, Coll. Films qu'on peut Lire,
      Nᵒ 7. Livre de Poche, 1974.
1941 *La Fille du Puisatier*, scenario. Fasquelle and Pagnol, Coll. Films
      qu'on peut lire, Nᵒ 8. Livre de Poche, 1975.
1946 *Le Premier Amour*, scenario. Editions de la Renaissance, illustrated by
      Pierre Lafaux.
1947 *Notes sur le Rire*, an essay. Nagel.
      Hamlet, a translation. Nagel.
      Discours de Réception à l'Académie Française, speech. Fasquelle.
1948 *La Belle Meunière*, scenario. Editions Self.
1949 *Critique des Critiques*, an essay. Nagel.
1953 *Angèle*, scenario. Fasquelle. Livre de Poche, 1973.
      Manon des Sources, scenario. Monte Carlo: Productions de Monte
      Carlo.
1954 *Oeuvres Dramatiques*, collected screen and stage plays. Gallimard.
      Trois Lettres de Mon Moulin, scenario. Flammarion.
1955 *Judas*, a play in 5 acts. Monte Carlo: Pastorelly.
1956 *Fabien*, a play in 4 acts, *Paris-Théâtre*, Nᵒ 115.
      Rapport sur les Prix de Vertu, speech. Firmin Didot.
1957 *Souvenirs d'Enfance*, a cycle of memoirs.
      Vol. 1. La Gloire de Mon Père, Monte Carlo: Pastorelly. Translated
      with Vol. 2 as *The Days were too Short* by Rita Barisse, London:
      Hamish Hamilton, 1960. Livre de Poche, 1974.
      Vol. 2. Le Château de Ma Mère, Monte Carlo: Pastorelly. Translated
      with Vol 1, see above. Livre de Poche, 1974.
1958 *Bucoliques*, translation of Virgil. Grasset.
1959 *Discours*, speech of welcome to Marcel Achard at the Académie Fran-
      çaise. Firmin Didot.
1960 *Souvenirs d'Enfance* Vol. 3. *Le Temps des Secrets*, Monte Carlo:
      Pastorelly. Translated by Rita Barisse as *The Time of Secrets*, New
      York: Doubleday, 1962. Livre de Poche, 1974.
1962 *Discours*, speech to open Lycée Marcel Pagnol, Marseilles. *Paris-
      Match*, Nᵒ 706, Oct. 20th, 1962.
1963 *L'Eau des Collines*, a novel in two volumes.
      Vol. 1. Jean de Florette, Editions de Provence. Livre de Poche, 1974.
      Vol. 2. Manon des Sources, Editions de Provence. Livre de Poche,
      1974.
1965 *Le Masque de Fer*, an historical investigation. Editions de Provence.
1967 *Cinématurgie de Paris*, collection of memoirs of movie career, in-
      cludes extracts from 1933 treatise of the same title. Editions de
      Provence, *Oeuvres Complètes*, Vol. 3.
      Les Sermons de Marcel Pagnol, presented by Norbert Calmels, Abbé-
      Général des Prémontrés, Forcalquier: Robert Morel.
1974 *Naïs*, scenario. Editions de Provence.

SECONDARY SOURCES

Pagnol's Literary Work

It goes without saying that only the criticism considered most useful to an understanding of Pagnol the writer has been included; the many books and articles of popular journalism that relate to the private life of Pagnol have been systematically excluded. Attention is drawn to the following special issues devoted to Pagnol: *Biblio*, Bibliographie Littéraire, Nº 2, Vol. 21, Feb., 1953. *Livres de France*, Revue Littéraire Mensuelle, Nº 3, Vol. 15, March, 1964. *La Gloire de Pagnol*, Album Souvenir, Editions Paris - March, 1974.

ACHARD, MARCEL. *Rions avec Eux—Grands Auteurs Comiques* (Paris: Arthème Fayard, 1957), Cap. IX, "Marcel Pagnol — Mon Ami." In spite of the threats of subjectivity Achard adds a rare technical appraisal to the all-too-common biographical detail.

ANTOINE, ANDRÉ. "Pagnol, Achard, Jeanson," *Revue des Deux Mondes* (May - June, 1962), pp. 522 - 533. Valuable assessment by a contemporary of the goals of the little-known movement of the *Moins de Trente Ans*.

BABIN, J. "A Propos d'une Partie de Cartes," *Revue de Linguistique Romane*, Nº XIX 1955. An entertaining comparison of two of the most famous card games in French literature — *manille* in *Marius* and *piquet* in Molière's *Les Fâcheux*.

BALLARD, Jean. "Coup d'Oeil sur notre Demi-Siècle," *Cahiers du Sud*, 50th anniversary number, Nºs 373 - 4, 1963. A summary of Pagnol's contribution to the journal which was once *Fortunio* by the director and co-founder with Pagnol.

BERNI, GEORGES. *Marcel Pagnol, Enfant d'Aubagne et de la Treille* (Aubagne: Lartigot, 1975). A *plaquette* produced on the first anniversary of Pagnol's death; contains much valuable information on Pagnol's film sets and other activity in the area.

BRAUQUIER, LOUIS. As for Jean Ballard; memories of a contemporary.

GAUTIER, JEAN-JACQUES. *Livres de France*, March, 1964. An engaging portrait of Pagnol by a self-confessed admirer, literary critic of *Le Figaro*.

MITHOIS, MARCEL. *Livres de France*, March, 1964. An interview which elicits some interesting comments from Pagnol.

RAT, MAURICE. "La Succulence des Romans de Pagnol," *Vie et Langage*, March, 1964, pp. 147 - 150. A limited but useful etymological survey of Pagnol's novels; argues that Pagnol's natural use of local idiom is evidence of authentic knowledge of Provence.

ROSTAING, CHARLES. "Le Français de Marseille dans la Trilogie de Marcel Pagnol," *Le Français Moderne*, Vol. X, 1942, pp. 29 - 44 and 117 - 131. An excellent, exhaustive study of the language of the trilogy;

himself an eminent Provençal, Rostaing demonstrates Pagnol's skillful use of dialogue within a dramatic context.

Surer, Paul. *Le Théâtre Français Contemporain* (Paris: S.E.D.E.S., 1964). Compares Topaze with the cynics of Le Sage and Becque and prefers him; makes a welcome stand for popular theater.

Vial, Fernand. "Provence and Provençals in the Works of Marcel Pagnol," *American Society of Legion of Honor Magazine*, No 1, 1964, pp. 29 - 47. A study of Pagnol's main characters which includes an interesting comparison between Mamèche of *Regain* and Baptistine of *L'Eau des Collines*. *(They could also be compared with the 'mandres' and Domnine of Arène's novel*, author's note).

Cinematic Work

Attention is drawn to two special numbers on Pagnol's movies: *'L'Avant-Scène du Cinéma*, July-September, 1970, and *Cahiers du Cinéma*, No 173, December, 1965.

Aubriant, Michel. "Marcel Pagnol et les Historiens du Cinéma," *Paris-Théâtre*, No 115, 1956. In praise of the unpretentious directness of Pagnol's movies in contrast to contemporary productions.

Bazin, André. *Qu'est-ce que le Cinéma?* Vol. 2, *Le Cinéma et les autres Arts* (Paris: Editions du Cerf, 1959). The outstanding critic of Neorealist cinema, Bazin admires Pagnol's work and attributes a special place to him in the history of French cinema although regretting a lack of finish.

Beylie, Charles. *Marcel Pagnol*, No 80, Coll. Cinéma d'Aujourd'hui, (Paris: Seghers, 1974). Contains an exhaustive filmography and a valuable reappraisal of many of Pagnol's films. Sometimes makes a case too strongly, which is perhaps understandable in the first book ever to be devoted exclusively to any form of Pagnol's work.

Blavette, Charles. *Ma Provence en Cuisine* (Paris: Editions France Empire, 1961). An original testimony to Pagnol's conviviality and powers of leadership on set.

Clair, René. *Réflexion Faite* (Paris: N.R.F., 1951). An essential book in the study of Pagnol's stormy entry into movies. Fair and humorous, presents the original texts from his famous controversy with Pagnol who afterwards became a firm friend.

Delahaye, Michel. "La Saga Pagnol," *Cahiers du Cinéma*, June, 1969. A most perceptive analysis of the main themes of Pagnol's movies.

Gauteur, Claude. "Marcel Pagnol Aujourd'hui," *L'Avant-Scène du Cinéma*, July-Sept., 1970. Presents one of the best-documented surveys of Pagnol's work to date.

Lapierre, Marcel. *Anthologie du Cinéma* (Paris: La Nouvelle Edition, 1946). Considerably more fair and thorough in his assessment of Pagnol's achievement than most other histories of cinema.

LEPROHON, PIERRE. *Présences Contemporaines* (Paris: Nouvelles Editions Debresse, 1956). A good account of Pagnol's collaboration with Giono and of the contribution of each.

VATTIER, ROBERT. *Les Souvenirs de Monsieur Brun* (Paris: Laffont, 1961).

Filmography

Reasons of space prohibit the reproduction of as much detail as the filmography of Claude Beylie, the most complete yet published, which can be obtained through any bookstore specializing in movie literature. The following list was checked by Marcel Pagnol at his Paris home on May 26,1964; the films are listed in chronological order and the following British Film Institute abbreviations are used: *p.c.*-production company (or producer; the post of production manager, delegated to Pagnol's brother René on numerous occasions, has been suppressed here since it always remained under the close control of Marcel Pagnol himself); *d.*- director; *sc.*- scriptwriter; *ph.*- photography; *ed.*- editor (montage); *m.*- music; *s.*- sound (the technician's name always follows that of the subcontracting company); *l.p.*- leading players. When available, running time is given in brackets after each film.

1931   *Marius p.* Paramount Studios. *d.* Alexander Korda in consultation with Marcel Pagnol. *sc.* Marcel Pagnol. *ph.* Ted Pahle. *ed.* R. Mercanton. *m.* Francis Gramon. *l.p.* Raimu, Orane Demazis, Fernand Charpin, Pierre Fresnay, Alida Rouffe, Robert Vattier, Dullac, Mihalesco, Delmont, Maupi, Giovanni, Milly Mathis. (130 min.)

1932   *Fanny p.* Films Marcel Pagnol et Braunberger-Richebé. *d.* Marc Allégret. *sc.* Marcel Pagnol. *ph.* Toporkoff. *ed.* Gourdji. *m.* Vincent Scotto. *s.* Bell. *l.p.* as above but with Mouriès replacing Dullac as Escartefigue. (142 min.)
     Un Direct au Coeur p. Pagnol & R. Boulay. *d.* Roger Lion. *sc.* Pagnol. *ph.* Riccioni & Coutelin. *ed.* Roger Saurin. *s.* R.C.A. & Bardis-banian. *l.p.* Arnaudy, Jacques Maury, Gustave Libeau, Nicole Ray, Suzanne Rissler, Maxudian. (73 min.)

1933   *L'Agonie des Aigles p.* Pagnol & Roger Richebé. *d.* R. Richebé. *sc.* Pagnol from a novel by Esparbès. *ph.* Riccioni. *m.* Vincent Scotto. *l.p.* Pierre Renoir, Jean Debucourt, Annie Ducaux, Constant Rémy, Philippe Rolla, Berthe Fusier, Paul Azaïs etc.
     Léopold le Bien Aimé p. Les Auteurs Associés. *d.* Ch. Arno-Brun. *sc.* Jean Sarment. *m.* Vincent Scotto. *l.p.* Marguerite Valmont, Jean Sarment, Pierre Feuillère, Arielle, Michel Simon.

1934 *Le Gendre de Monsieur Poirier p.* Les Auteurs Associés. *d.* Marcel Pagnol. *sc.* Marcel Pagnol from the play by Augier & Sandeau. *ph.* Willy Faktorovitch. *ed.* Suzanne de Troye. *m.* Scotto. *l.p.* Annie Ducaux, Léon Bernard, Jean Debucourt, Maurice Escande, Fernand Charpin. (100 min.)

Jofroi p. Les Auteurs Associés. *d.* Marcel Pagnol. *sc.* Marcel Pagnol from a story by Giono in *Solitude de la Pitié. ph.* Willy. *ed.* Suzanne de Troye. *m.* Scotto. *s.* Philips & Pierre Calvet. *l.p.* Vincent Scotto, Henri Poupon, Annie Toinon, Charles Blavette, André Robert, José Tyrand etc. (52 min.)

L'Article 330 p. Les Auteurs Associés. *d.* Marcel Pagnol. *sc.* Pagnol, from play by Courteline. *ph.* Willy. *ed.* André Robert. *l.p.* le Vigan, Jean d'Yd. (40 min.)

Marseille p. Marcel Pagnol. *d.* Jean Monti & Jean Marguerite. *ed.* Arno-Brun. *m.* Vincent Scotto.

Toni p. Marcel Pagnol. *d.* Jean Renoir. *ph.* Renoir, Visconti & Assouad. *ed.* Suzanne de Troye & Marguerite Renoir. *l.p.* Blavette, Andrex, Delmont & Jenny Hélia. (90 min.)

Tartarin de Tarascon p. Pathé-Natan. *d.* Raymond Bernard. *sc.* Pagnol from Daudet's novel. *ph.* Kruger & Lefèbvre. *m.* Darius Milhaud. *s.* Antoine Archimbaud. *l.p.* Raimu, Charpin, Saint-Granier, Jean d'Yd, Milly Mathis, Auguste Mouriès, Jenny Hélia, Blanche Poupon. (95 min.)

Angèle p. Films Marcel Pagnol. *d.* Pagnol. *sc.* Pagnol from *Un de Baumugnes* by Giono. *ph.* Willy & Ledru. *ed.* Suzanne de Troye. *m.* Scotto. *s.* R.C.A. & Lecocq. *l.p.* Henri Poupon, Annie Toinon, Orane Demazis, Jean Servais, Fernandel, Delmont, Andrex. (150 min.)

1935 *Merlusse p.* Films Marcel Pagnol *d.* Pagnol. *sc.* Pagnol. *ph.* Assouad & Ledru. *ed.* de Troye. *m.* Scotto. *s.* Philips & Lecocq. *l.p.* Poupon, Pollack, Thommeray, André Robert, Jean Castan, le Petit Jacques, Le Van Kim (*later chief-of-staff in Vietnamese army under President Diem* author's note). (72 min.)

Cigalon p. Films Marcel Pagnol. *d.* Pagnol. *sc.* Pagnol. *ph.* Assouad. *ed.* de Troye. *m.* Scotto. *s.* Philips & Lecocq. *l.p.* Arnaudy, Poupon, Léon Brouzet, Fernand Bruno, Jean Castan, Ch. Blavette, Chabert, Alida Rouffe. (70 min.)

1936 *Topaze p.* Films Marcel Pagnol. *d.* Pagnol. *sc.* Pagnol. *ph.* Assouad. *m.* Scotto. *s.* Philips. *l.p.* Arnaudy, Sylvie Bataille, Brouzet, Alida Rouffe, Léon Belières, Poupon, Jean Castan. (*This film was Pagnol's first version but it remained less well known than the previous version made for Paramount by Louis Gasnier with Jouvet in the lead*). (110 min.)

César p. Films Marcel Pagnol *d.* Pagnol. *sc.* Pagnol. *ph.* Willy & Ledru. *ed.* Suzanne de Troye. *m.* Scotto. *s.* Julien Coutellier. *l.p.* Raimu, Pierre Fresnay, Orane Demazis, André Fouché, Charpin,

Delmont, Milly Mathis, Robert Vattier, Alida Rouffe, Doumel, Rellys, Dullac, Maupi. (160 min.)

1937 *Regain p.* Films Marcel Pagnol. *d.* Pagnol. *sc.* Pagnol from Giono's novel. *ph.* Willy & Ledru. *ed.* S. de Troye. *m.* Honegger. *s.* Lecocq, Lavoignat et. al. *l.p.* Fernandel, Orane Demazis, Gabriel Gabrio, Marguerite Moreno, le Vigan, Poupon, Milly Mathis, Blavette, Delmont, Dullac, Castan. *(The original credits include many more names, omitting none of the plasterers, painters, carpenters etc., who worked on the set).* (150 min.)

1938 *Le Schpountz p.* Films Marcel Pagnol. *d.* Pagnol. *sc.* Pagnol. *ph.* Willy & Ledru. *ed.* S. de Troye et al. *m.* Oberfeld & Manse. *s.* Philips, Lecocq & Lavoignat. *l.p.* Fernandel, Orane Demazis, Belières, Vattier, Maupi, Poupon, Bessac, Charpin, Blavette, Jean Castan, Pollack, Alida Rouffe, Odette Roger et al. (160 min.)

La Femme du Boulanger p. Films Marcel Pagnol. *d.* Pagnol. *sc.* Pagnol from Giono's *Jean le Bleu. ph.* G. Benoit. *ed.* S. de Troye et al. *m.* Scotto. *l.p.* Raimu, Ginette Leclerc, Charpin, Vattier, Bassac, Ch. Moulin, Delmont, Alida Rouffe, Maupi, Dullac, Blavette, Odette Roger, Castan. (130 min.)

1939 *Monsieur Brotonneau p.* Films Marcel Pagnol. *d.* Alex. Esway. *sc.* Pagnol from play by Flers & Caiillavet. *ph.* Benoit & Ledru. *m.* Scotto. *s.* Philips & Lavoignat. *l.p.* Raimu, Josette Day, Marguerite Pierry, Vattier, Belières, Bassac. (100 min.).

Le Président Haudecoeur p. Films Marcel Pagnol. *d.* Jean Dréville. *sc.* Roger Ferdinand. *l.p.* Harry Baur, Betty Stockfield, Jeanne Provost.

La Fille du Puisatier p. Films Marcel Pagnol. *d.* Pagnol. *sc.* Pagnol. *ph.* Willy. *ed.* Jennette Ginestet & Mme Gastyne. *m.* Scotto. *s.* Philips & Lavoignat. *l.p.* Raimu, Josette Day, Fernandel, Charpin, Line Noro, Georges Grey, Milly Mathis, Maupi, Blavette, Clairette. (170 min.)

1945 *Naïs p.* Soc. Nouvelle des Films Marcel Pagnol. *d.* Raymond Leboursier. *sc.* Pagnol from Zola's short story. *ph.* Suin & Wottitz. *m.* Scotto & Thomasi. *s.* Privat & Legras. *l.p.* Fernandel, Poupon, Jacqueline Bouvier, Arius, Raymond Pellegrin, Blavette. (127 min.)

1948 *La Belle Meunière p.* Pagnol. *d.* Pagnol & de Rieux. *sc.* Pagnol. *ph.* Willy (in RouxColor in 16mm.). *ed.* Jeannette Rougier. *m.* Franz Schubert & Tony Aubin. *l.p.* Tino Rossi, Jacqueline Pagnol, Raoul Marco, Lilia Vetti, Raphaël Patorni, Emma Lyonnel, Suzanne Després, Pierrette Rossi. (120 min.)

1950 *Le Rosier de Madame Husson p.* Agiman-Eminente Films. *d.* Jean Boyer. *sc.* Pagnol from Maupassant's short story. *ph.* Ch. Suin. *ed.* Fanchette Mazin. *m.* Misraki. *s.* Tony Leenhardt. *l.p.* Bourvil, Pauline Carton, Germaine Reuver, Jean Dunot, Yvette Etiévant, Jacqueline Pagnol et al. (100 min.).

Topaze p. Films Marcel Pagnol. *d.* Pagnol. *sc.* Pagnol. *ph.* Ph. Agostini. *ed.* Monique Lacombe. *m.* Raymond Legrand. *s.* Western Electric & Marcel Royné. *l.p.* Fernandel, Hélène Perdrière, Jacqueline Pagnol, Pierre Larquey, Jacques Morel, Milly Mathis, Yvette Etiévant. *(Pagnol's second version.)*

1952　*Manon des Sources p.* Les Films Marcel Pagnol. *d.* Pagnol. *sc.* Pagnol. *ph.* Willy. *ed.* Raymonde et Jacques Bianchi. *m.* Raymond Legrand. *l.p.* Jacqueline Pagnol, Raymond Pellegrin, Annie Roudier, Rellys, Henri Poupon, Robert Vattier, Ardisson, Arius, Blavette, Milly Mathis, Fernand Sardou, Henri Vilbert et al. (190 min.)

1953　*Carnaval p.* Soc. Nouvelle des Films Marcel Pagnol. *d.* Henri Verneuil. *sc.* from the play *Dardamelle* by Emile Mazaud. *ph.* André Germain. *ed.* Raymonde Bianchi. *m.* Raymond Legrand. *s.* R.C.A. & Marcel Royné. *l.p.* Fernandel, Jacqueline Pagnol, Mireille Perrey, Pauline Carton, Géo. Dorlys, Saturnin Fabre, Berval, Arius, Blavette et al. (90 min.)

1954　*Les Lettres de Mon Moulin p.* C.M.F. & Eminente Films. *d.* Pagnol. *sc.* Pagnol from *Les Trois Messes Basses, L'Elixir du Père Gaucher,* & *Le Secret de Maitre Cornille* by Daudet. *ph.* Willy. *ed.* Monique Lacombe. *m.* Tomasi. *s.* R.C.A. & Marcel Royné. *l.p.* Roger Crouzet, Pierrette Bruno, Delmont, Bervil, Rellys, Robert Vattier, Christian Lude, Sardou, Henri Vilbert, Daxely et al. (120 min.)

The sound - tracks of the better-known films are available on 33 r.p.m. records made by C.M.F. (Compagnie Méditerranéenne de Films). Extracts of the trilogy are available from Columbia Records.

Index